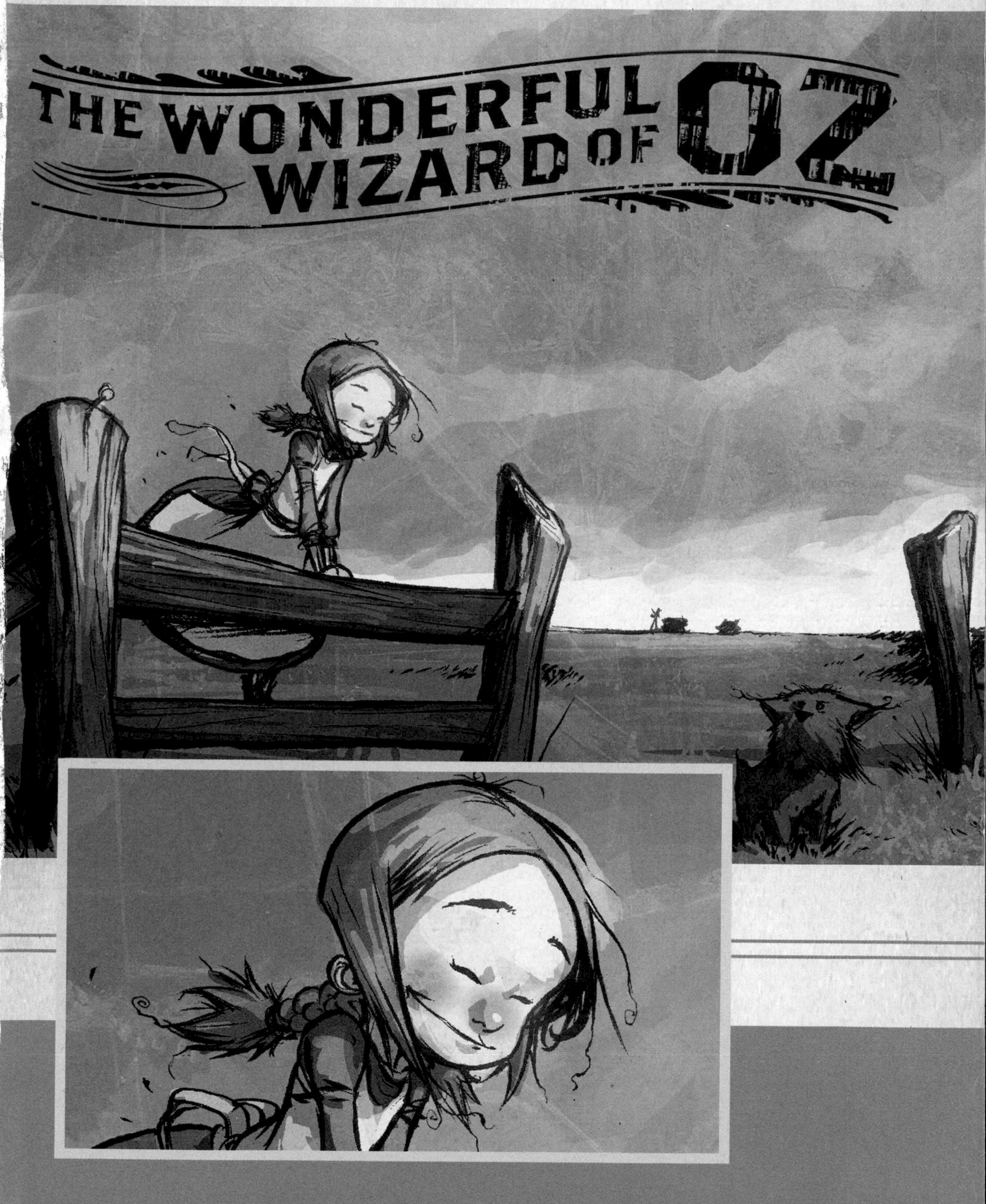
THE WONDERFUL WIZARD OF OZ

Z: THE WONDERFUL WIZARD OF OZ. Contains material originally published in magazine form as THE WONDERFUL WIZARD OF OZ #1-8. First printing 2011. ISBN# 978-0-7851-2922-6. Published by MARVEL VORLDWIDE, INC., a subsidiary of MARVEL ENTERTAINMENT, LLC. OFFICE OF PUBLICATION: 135 West 50th Street, New York, NY 10020. 24.99 per copy in the U.S. and $27.99 in Canada (GST #R127032852); Canadian Agreement #40668537. **Printed in the U.S.A.** ALAN FINE, EVP - Office of the President, Marvel Worldwide, Inc. and EVP & CMO Marvel Characters B.V.; DAN BUCKLEY, Publisher & President - Print, nimation & Digital Divisions; JOE QUESADA, Chief Creative Officer; JIM SOKOLOWSKI, Chief Operating Officer; DAVID BOGART, SVP of Business Affairs & Talent Management; TOM BREVOORT, SVP of Publishing; C.B. EBULSKI, SVP of Creator & Content Development; DAVID GABRIEL, SVP of Publishing Sales & Circulation; MICHAEL PASCIULLO, SVP of Brand Planning & Communications; JIM O'KEEFE, VP of Operations & Logistics; DAN ARR, Executive Director of Publishing Technology; SUSAN CRESPI, Editorial Operations Manager; ALEX MORALES, Publishing Operations Manager; STAN LEE, Chairman Emeritus. For information regarding advertising Marvel Comics or on Marvel.com, please contact John Dokes, SVP Integrated Sales and Marketing, at jdokes@marvel.com. For Marvel subscription inquiries, please call 800-217-9158. **Manufactured between /6/2011 and 10/25/2011 by QUAD/GRAPHICS, DUBUQUE, IA, USA.**

987654321

THE WONDERFUL WIZARD OF OZ

ADAPTED FROM THE NOVEL BY L. FRANK BAUM

Writer: ERIC SHANOWER

Artist: SKOTTIE YOUNG

Colorist: JEAN-FRANCOIS BEAULIEU

Letterer: JEFF ECKLEBERRY

Assistant Editors: LAUREN SANKOVITCH & LAUREN HENRY

Associate Editor: NATE COSBY

Senior Editor: RALPH MACCHIO

Special Thanks to Chris Allo, Rich Ginter, Jeff Suter & Jim Nausedas

Collection Editor: MARK D. BEAZLEY

Editorial Assistants: JAMES EMMETT & JOE HOCHSTEIN

Assistant Editors: NELSON RIBEIRO & ALEX STARBUCK

Editor, Special Projects: JENNIFER GRÜNWALD

Senior Editor, Special Projects: JEFF YOUNGQUIST

Senior Vice President of Sales: DAVID GABRIEL

SVP of Brand Planning & Communications: MICHAEL PASCIULLO

Production: JERRY KALINOWSKI

Book Design: SPRING HOTELING

Sketchbook Design: ROMMEL ALAMA & SPRING HOTELING

Editor in Chief: AXEL ALONSO

Chief Creative Officer: JOE QUESADA

Publisher: DAN BUCKLEY

Executive Producer: ALAN FINE

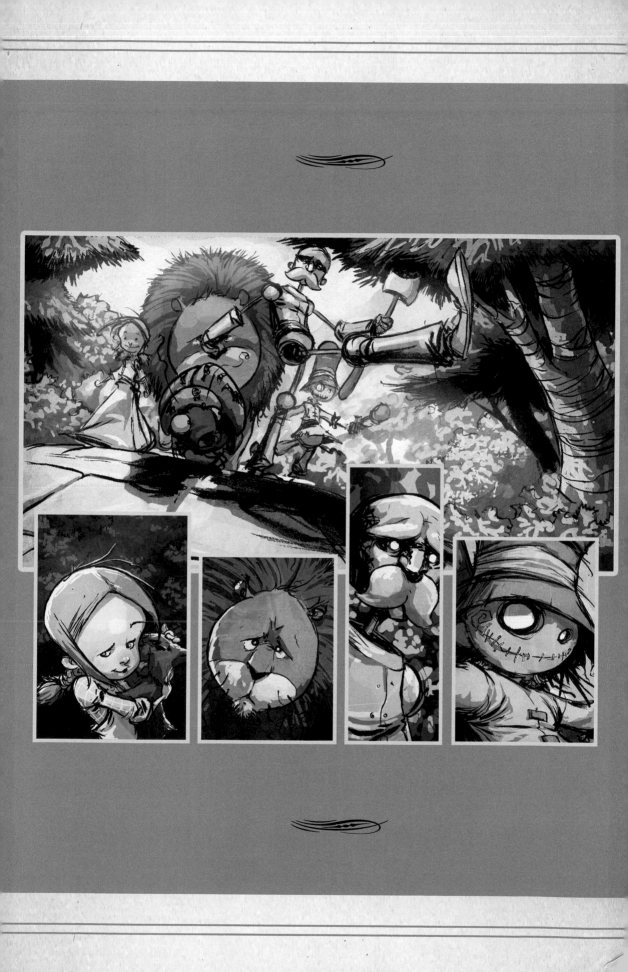

BLAME IT ON TOTO

If Dorothy Gale's dog hadn't scrambled under the bed to escape a cyclone, then Dorothy would have found safety in the cyclone cellar. Her adventures in the Land of Oz would never have occurred. Dorothy would have emerged from the cellar and life would have gone on much as before, as she lived through gray days on the Kansas prairies. Dorothy would never know how huge a gap had been left in her life.

If Toto hadn't scrambled under the bed, Dorothy's life isn't the only one that would have been left with a huge gap. Consider the author of *The Wonderful Wizard of Oz*, L. Frank Baum.

He was born Lyman Frank Baum in Chittenango, New York, in 1856. He didn't like the name Lyman, so settled for being called Frank, shortening his first name to its initial. Baum tried many professions before he became primarily a writer of children's books. Biographers seem fond of reducing his life story to a string of professional failures before he hit it big with *The Wonderful Wizard of Oz*. But that version is oversimplified. He didn't fail at everything. Before Oz he was a breeder of fancy chickens (successful), an oil salesman (unsuccessful), a playwright (successful), an actor (successful), a theater director (successful), a manager of a dry goods store (unsuccessful), a newspaper editor (unsuccessful), a journalist (successful), a crockery salesman (he missed his wife and children, so he gave it up), and an author (successful).

Baum's personal life before Oz had as many successes as his professional life. He was born on a large estate to rich parents who educated their children well and even indulged young Frank with a small printing press on which he published a family newspaper. In 1882, Baum married Maud Gage. Their marriage was a happy partnership, and they eventually had four sons. Maud was the daughter of Matilda Joslyn Gage, a prominent figure in the movement to obtain women the right to vote. Matilda encouraged her son-in-law to write down and publish the stories he invented for his sons and their friends.

The publication in 1900 of *The Wonderful Wizard of Oz* was a turning point for Baum. The book's popularity propelled the already best-selling writer into the top rank of children's authors. Baum, ever with an eye on theater, began a stage adaptation of the book. The result reached Broadway in 1903, running and touring for years, making stars of its lead actors, and prompting Baum to write more Oz books and more Oz theatricals (both on stage and on film). Oz's success led Baum to write books of many types, to travel, and to live the life of a wealthy man. The Oz books became so popular that when Baum tried to quit the series, he couldn't afford to. Oz had entered not only Baum's life and the lives of his family, but the lives of publishers, illustrators, actors, producers, and the lives of every child who read an Oz book and every adult who went to the theater to see the antics of the Scarecrow and Tin Woodman.

L. Frank Baum died in 1919, but Oz lived on. Other writers continued the Oz books through 1963 and forty volumes in the "official" series. Oz theatrical adaptations reached a peak in 1939 when MGM studios filmed the story with Judy Garland in the role of Dorothy. For many people, that film's version of Oz, ingrained into the American consciousness through annual television airings, eclipses all other versions, including Baum's original book. But Oz books and Oz movies have never stopped.

My own exposure to Oz probably began with a television broadcast of the MGM movie. Then one day in a bookstore, I found, next to a copy of *The Wizard of Oz*, three more Oz books by L. Frank Baum.

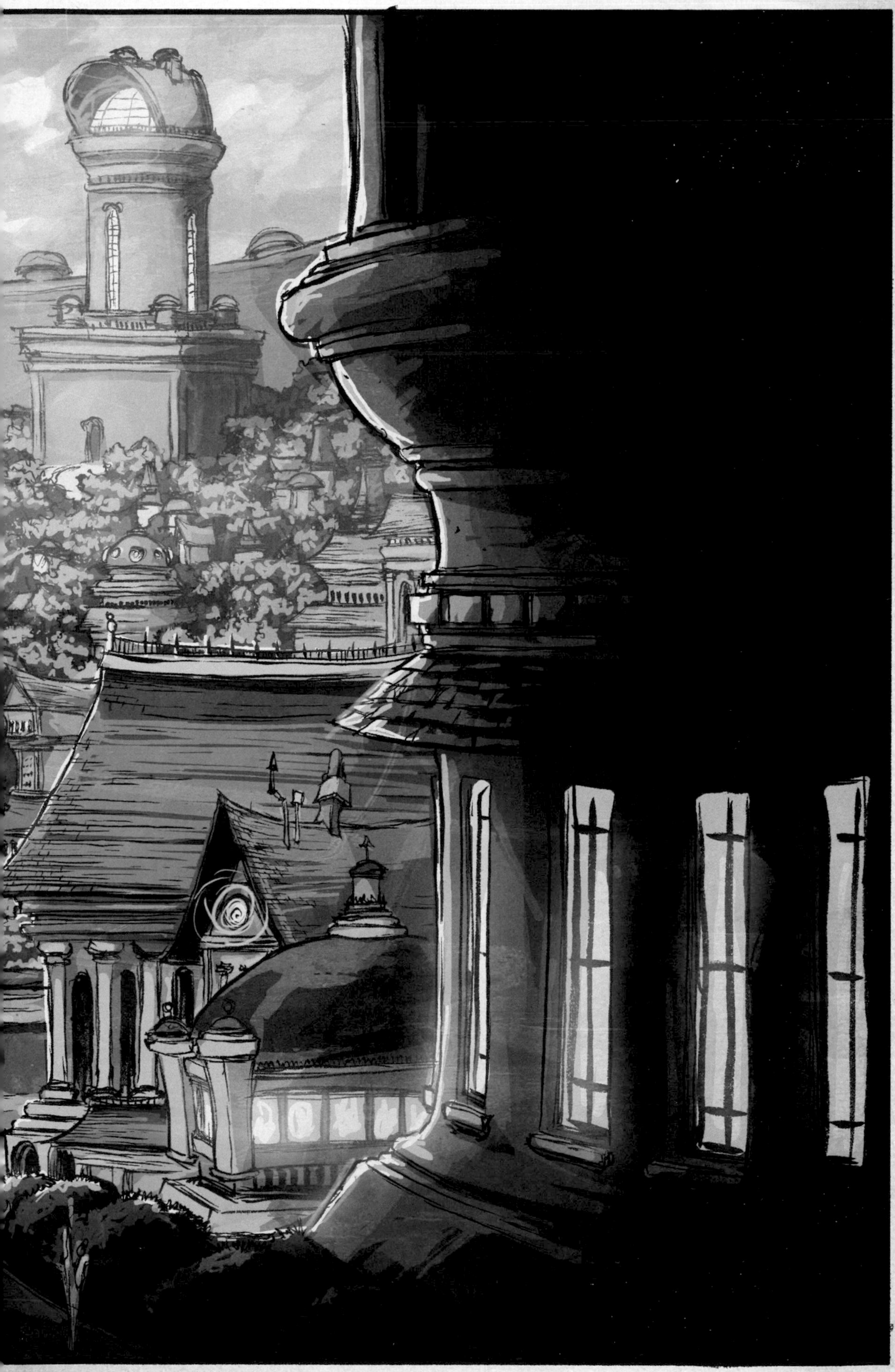

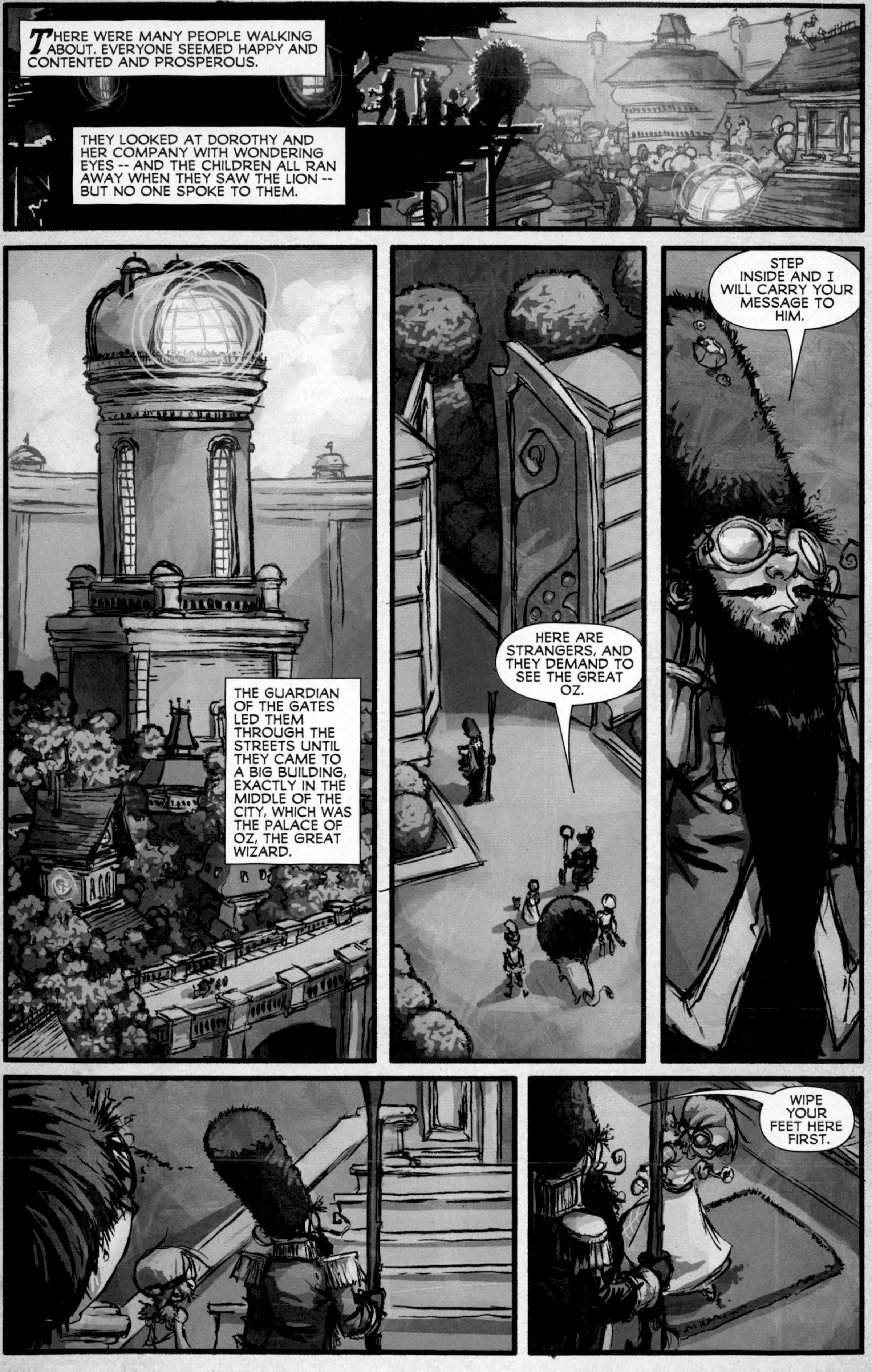
THERE WERE MANY PEOPLE WALKING ABOUT. EVERYONE SEEMED HAPPY AND CONTENTED AND PROSPEROUS.
THEY LOOKED AT DOROTHY AND HER COMPANY WITH WONDERING EYES -- AND THE CHILDREN ALL RAN AWAY WHEN THEY SAW THE LION -- BUT NO ONE SPOKE TO THEM.
THE GUARDIAN OF THE GATES LED THEM THROUGH THE STREETS UNTIL THEY CAME TO A BIG BUILDING, EXACTLY IN THE MIDDLE OF THE CITY, WHICH WAS THE PALACE OF OZ, THE GREAT WIZARD.
HERE ARE STRANGERS, AND THEY DEMAND TO SEE THE GREAT OZ.
STEP INSIDE AND I WILL CARRY YOUR MESSAGE TO HIM.
WIPE YOUR FEET HERE FIRST.

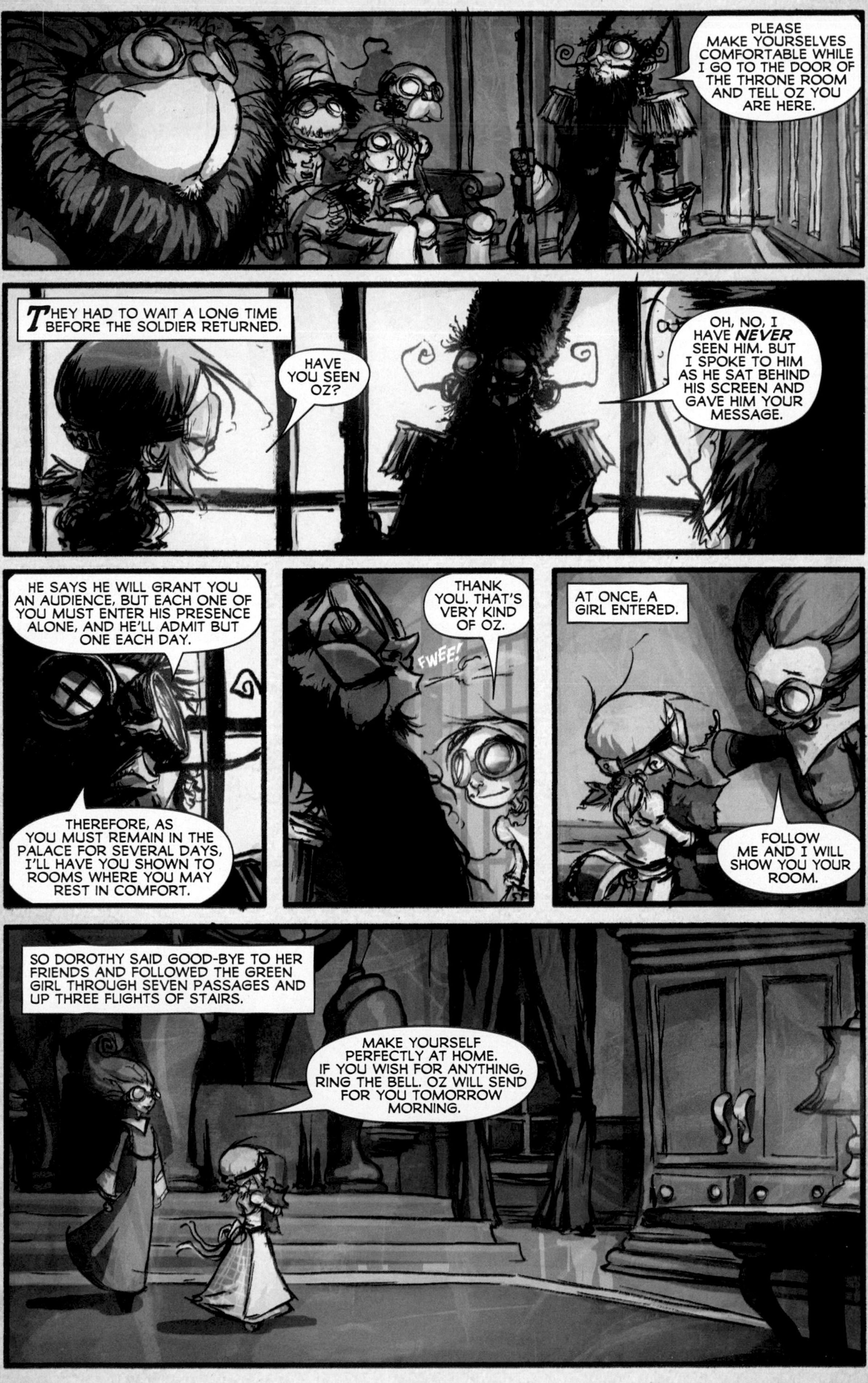
PLEASE MAKE YOURSELVES COMFORTABLE WHILE I GO TO THE DOOR OF THE THRONE ROOM AND TELL OZ YOU ARE HERE.
THEY HAD TO WAIT A LONG TIME BEFORE THE SOLDIER RETURNED.
HAVE YOU SEEN OZ?
OH, NO, I HAVE NEVER SEEN HIM. BUT I SPOKE TO HIM AS HE SAT BEHIND HIS SCREEN AND GAVE HIM YOUR MESSAGE.
HE SAYS HE WILL GRANT YOU AN AUDIENCE, BUT EACH ONE OF YOU MUST ENTER HIS PRESENCE ALONE, AND HE'LL ADMIT BUT ONE EACH DAY.
THEREFORE, AS YOU MUST REMAIN IN THE PALACE FOR SEVERAL DAYS, I'LL HAVE YOU SHOWN TO ROOMS WHERE YOU MAY REST IN COMFORT.
THANK YOU. THAT'S VERY KIND OF OZ.
FWEE!
AT ONCE, A GIRL ENTERED.
FOLLOW ME AND I WILL SHOW YOU YOUR ROOM.
SO DOROTHY SAID GOOD-BYE TO HER FRIENDS AND FOLLOWED THE GREEN GIRL THROUGH SEVEN PASSAGES AND UP THREE FLIGHTS OF STAIRS.
MAKE YOURSELF PERFECTLY AT HOME. IF YOU WISH FOR ANYTHING, RING THE BELL. OZ WILL SEND FOR YOU TOMORROW MORNING.

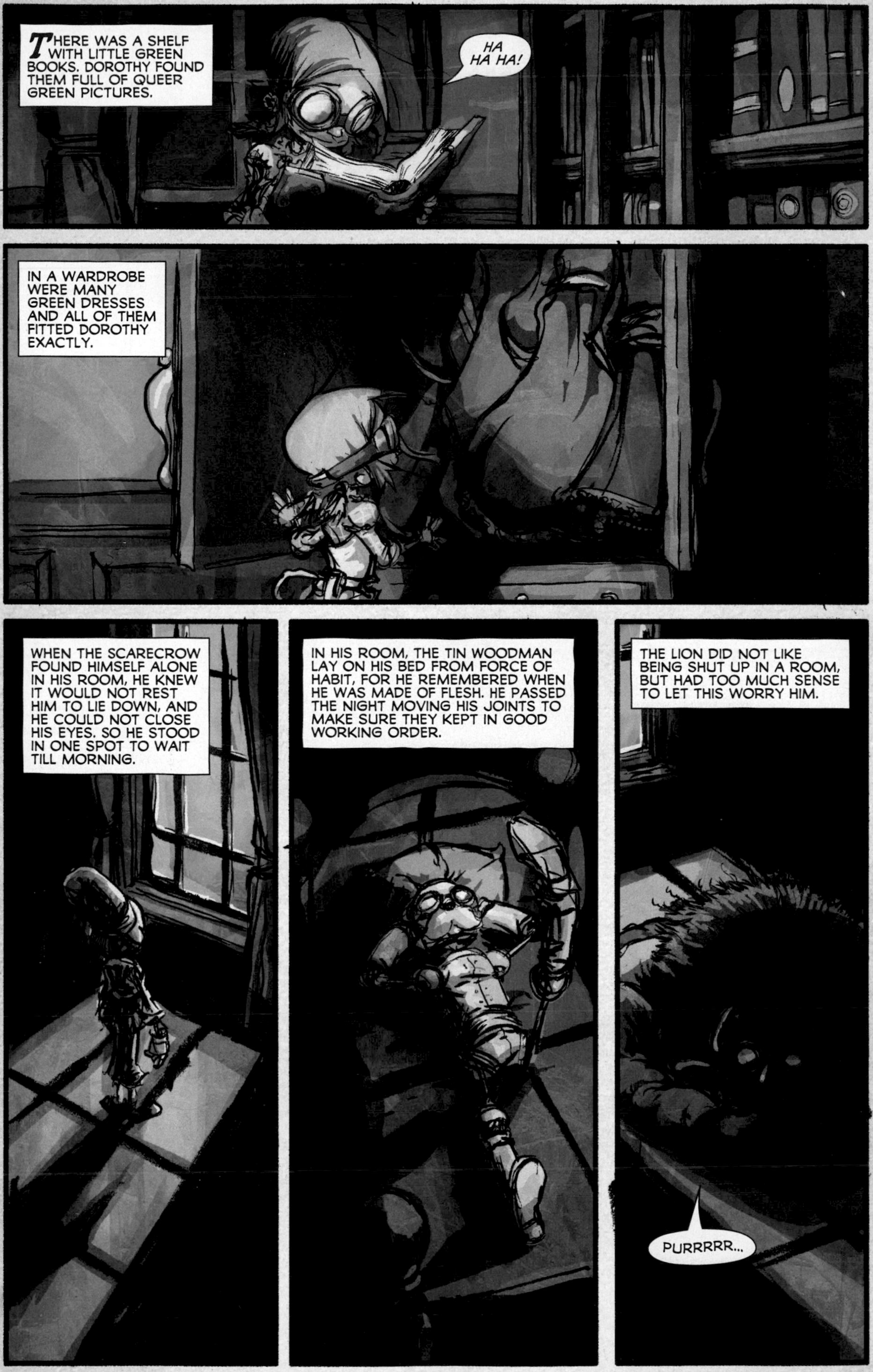
THERE WAS A SHELF WITH LITTLE GREEN BOOKS. DOROTHY FOUND THEM FULL OF QUEER GREEN PICTURES.
HA HA HA!
IN A WARDROBE WERE MANY GREEN DRESSES AND ALL OF THEM FITTED DOROTHY EXACTLY.
WHEN THE SCARECROW FOUND HIMSELF ALONE IN HIS ROOM, HE KNEW IT WOULD NOT REST HIM TO LIE DOWN, AND HE COULD NOT CLOSE HIS EYES. SO HE STOOD IN ONE SPOT TO WAIT TILL MORNING.
IN HIS ROOM, THE TIN WOODMAN LAY ON HIS BED FROM FORCE OF HABIT, FOR HE REMEMBERED WHEN HE WAS MADE OF FLESH. HE PASSED THE NIGHT MOVING HIS JOINTS TO MAKE SURE THEY KEPT IN GOOD WORKING ORDER.
THE LION DID NOT LIKE BEING SHUT UP IN A ROOM, BUT HAD TOO MUCH SENSE TO LET THIS WORRY HIM.
PURRRRR...

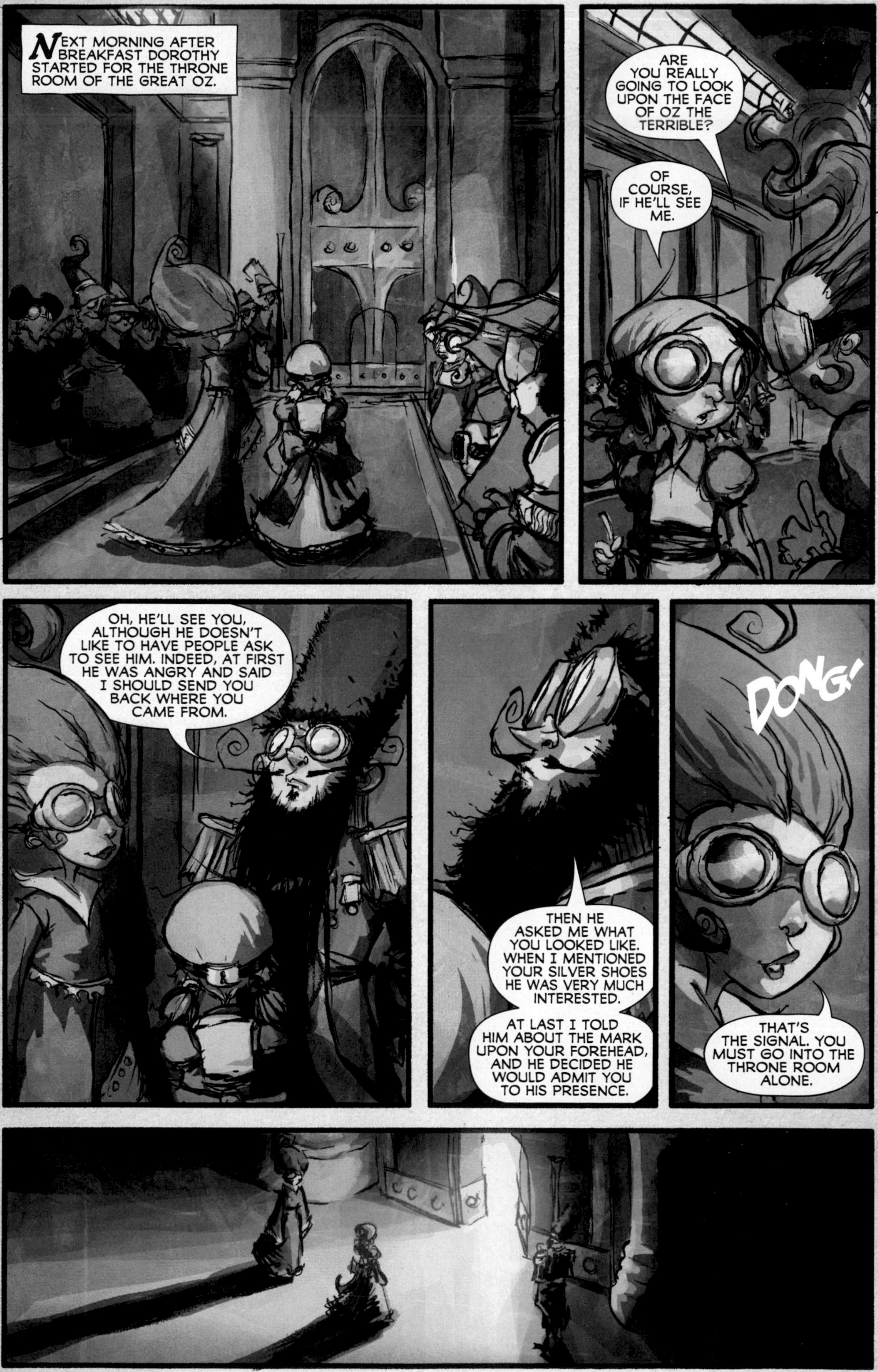
NEXT MORNING AFTER BREAKFAST DOROTHY STARTED FOR THE THRONE ROOM OF THE GREAT OZ.
ARE YOU REALLY GOING TO LOOK UPON THE FACE OF OZ THE TERRIBLE?
OF COURSE, IF HE'LL SEE ME.
OH, HE'LL SEE YOU, ALTHOUGH HE DOESN'T LIKE TO HAVE PEOPLE ASK TO SEE HIM. INDEED, AT FIRST HE WAS ANGRY AND SAID I SHOULD SEND YOU BACK WHERE YOU CAME FROM.
THEN HE ASKED ME WHAT YOU LOOKED LIKE. WHEN I MENTIONED YOUR SILVER SHOES HE WAS VERY MUCH INTERESTED.
AT LAST I TOLD HIM ABOUT THE MARK UPON YOUR FOREHEAD, AND HE DECIDED HE WOULD ADMIT YOU TO HIS PRESENCE.
DONG!
THAT'S THE SIGNAL. YOU MUST GO INTO THE THRONE ROOM ALONE.

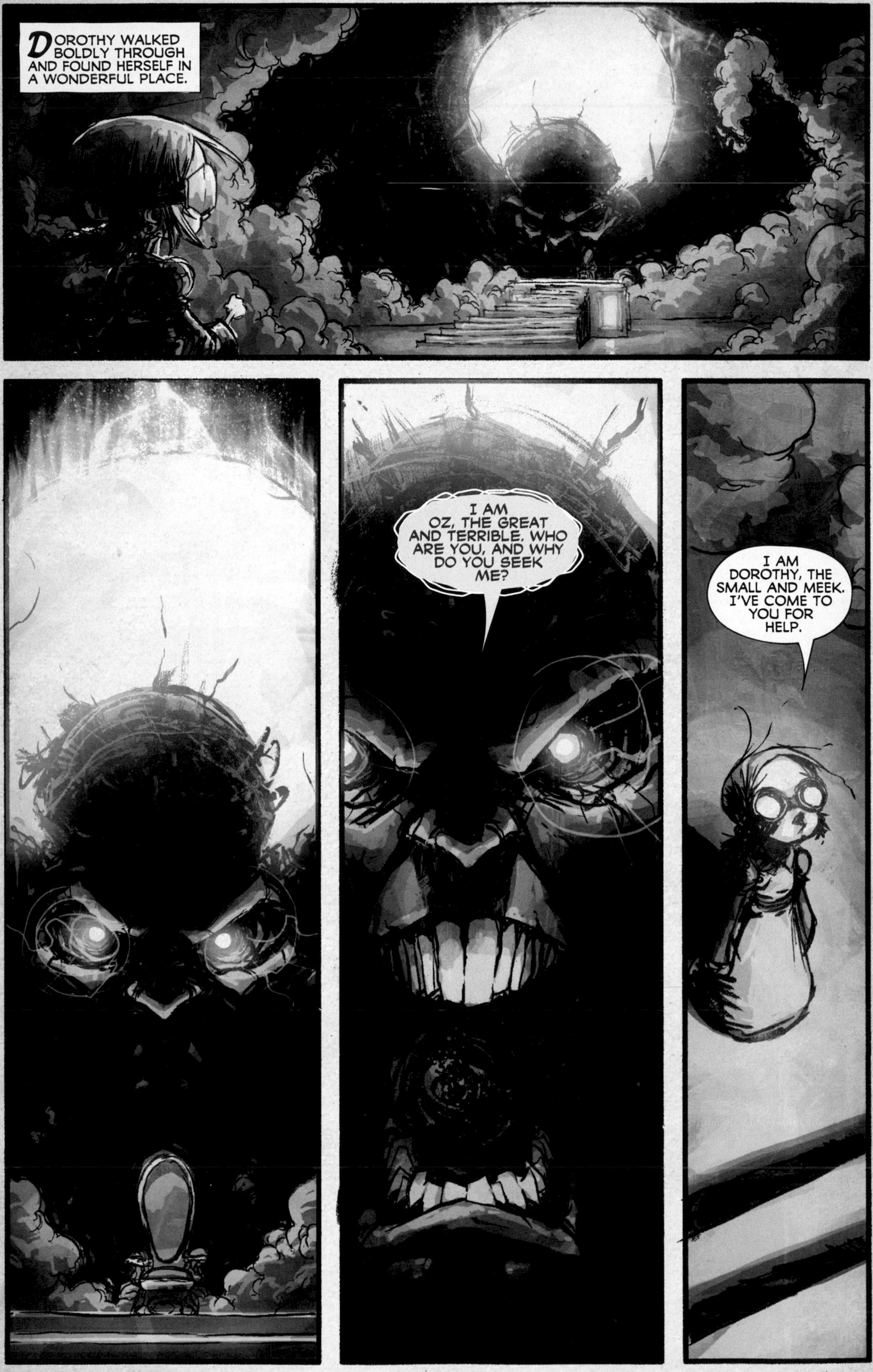
DOROTHY WALKED BOLDLY THROUGH AND FOUND HERSELF IN A WONDERFUL PLACE.
I AM OZ, THE GREAT AND TERRIBLE. WHO ARE YOU, AND WHY DO YOU SEEK ME?
I AM DOROTHY, THE SMALL AND MEEK. I'VE COME TO YOU FOR HELP.

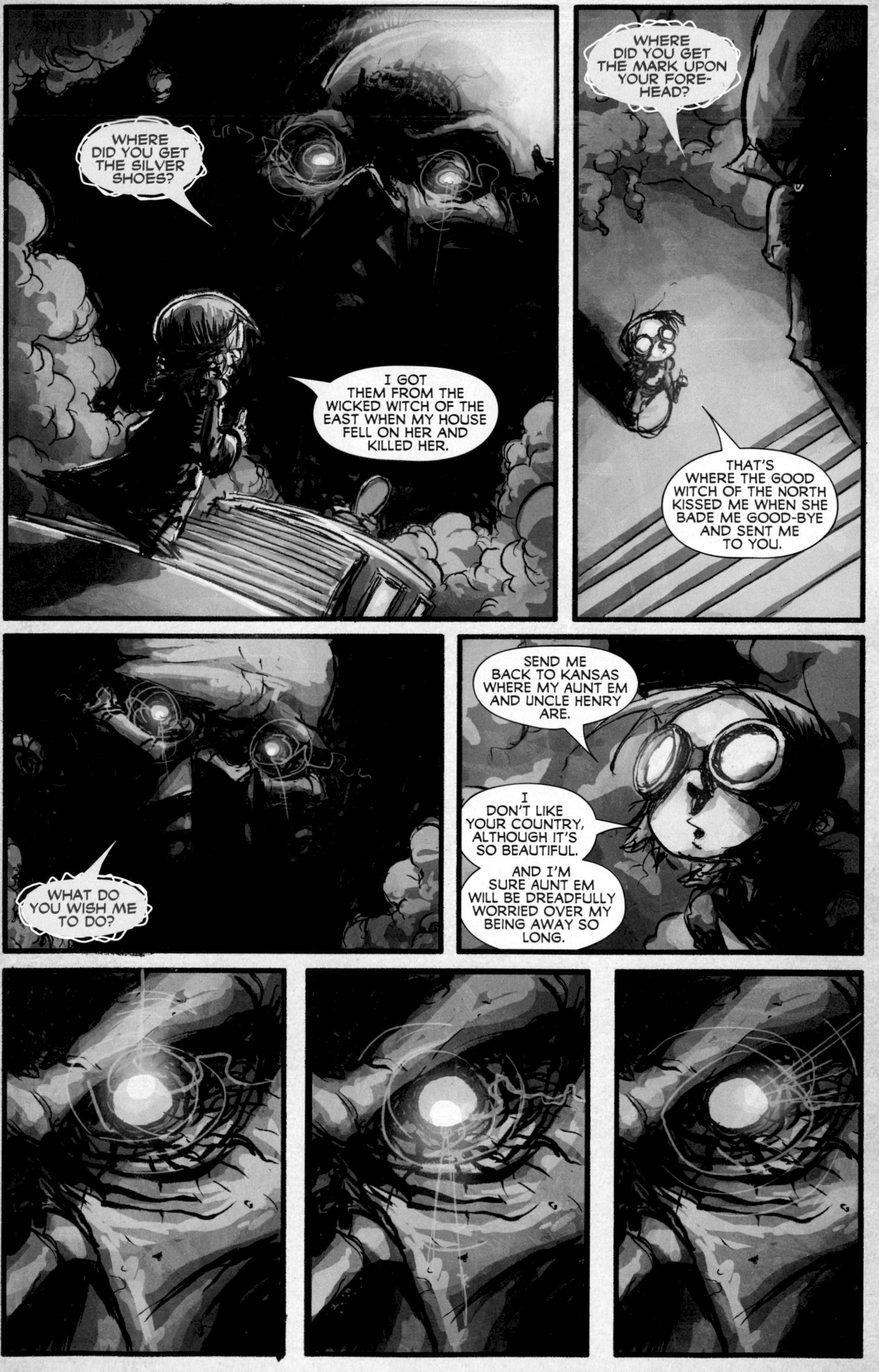
WHERE DID YOU GET THE SILVER SHOES?
I GOT THEM FROM THE WICKED WITCH OF THE EAST WHEN MY HOUSE FELL ON HER AND KILLED HER.
WHERE DID YOU GET THE MARK UPON YOUR FORE-HEAD?
THAT'S WHERE THE GOOD WITCH OF THE NORTH KISSED ME WHEN SHE BADE ME GOOD-BYE AND SENT ME TO YOU.
WHAT DO YOU WISH ME TO DO?
SEND ME BACK TO KANSAS WHERE MY AUNT EM AND UNCLE HENRY ARE.
I DON'T LIKE YOUR COUNTRY, ALTHOUGH IT'S SO BEAUTIFUL.
AND I'M SURE AUNT EM WILL BE DREADFULLY WORRIED OVER MY BEING AWAY SO LONG.

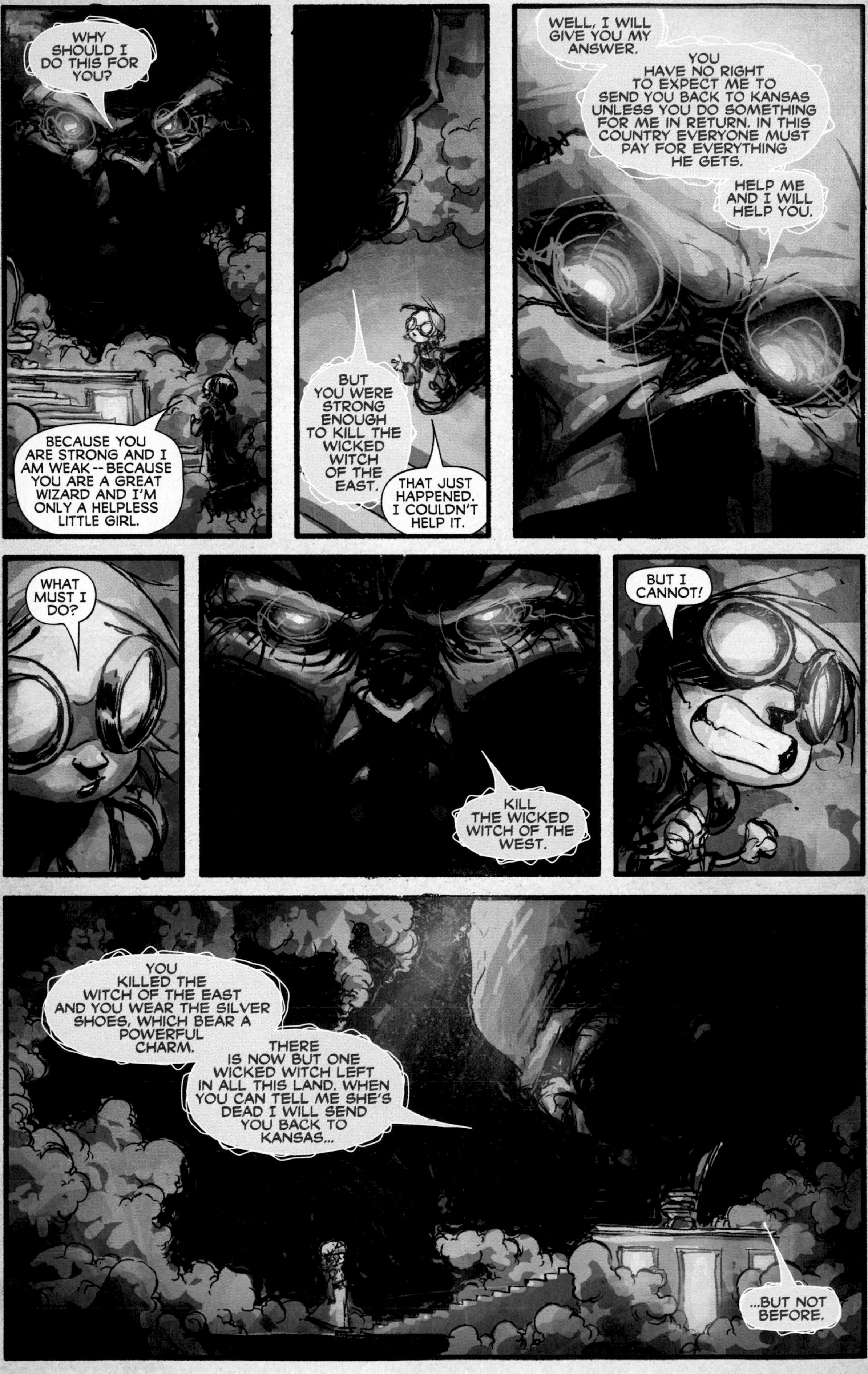
WHY SHOULD I DO THIS FOR YOU?
BECAUSE YOU ARE STRONG AND I AM WEAK--BECAUSE YOU ARE A GREAT WIZARD AND I'M ONLY A HELPLESS LITTLE GIRL.
BUT YOU WERE STRONG ENOUGH TO KILL THE WICKED WITCH OF THE EAST.
THAT JUST HAPPENED. I COULDN'T HELP IT.
WELL, I WILL GIVE YOU MY ANSWER.
YOU HAVE NO RIGHT TO EXPECT ME TO SEND YOU BACK TO KANSAS UNLESS YOU DO SOMETHING FOR ME IN RETURN. IN THIS COUNTRY EVERYONE MUST PAY FOR EVERYTHING HE GETS.
HELP ME AND I WILL HELP YOU.
WHAT MUST I DO?
KILL THE WICKED WITCH OF THE WEST.
BUT I CANNOT!
YOU KILLED THE WITCH OF THE EAST AND YOU WEAR THE SILVER SHOES, WHICH BEAR A POWERFUL CHARM.
THERE IS NOW BUT ONE WICKED WITCH LEFT IN ALL THIS LAND. WHEN YOU CAN TELL ME SHE'S DEAD I WILL SEND YOU BACK TO KANSAS...
...BUT NOT BEFORE.

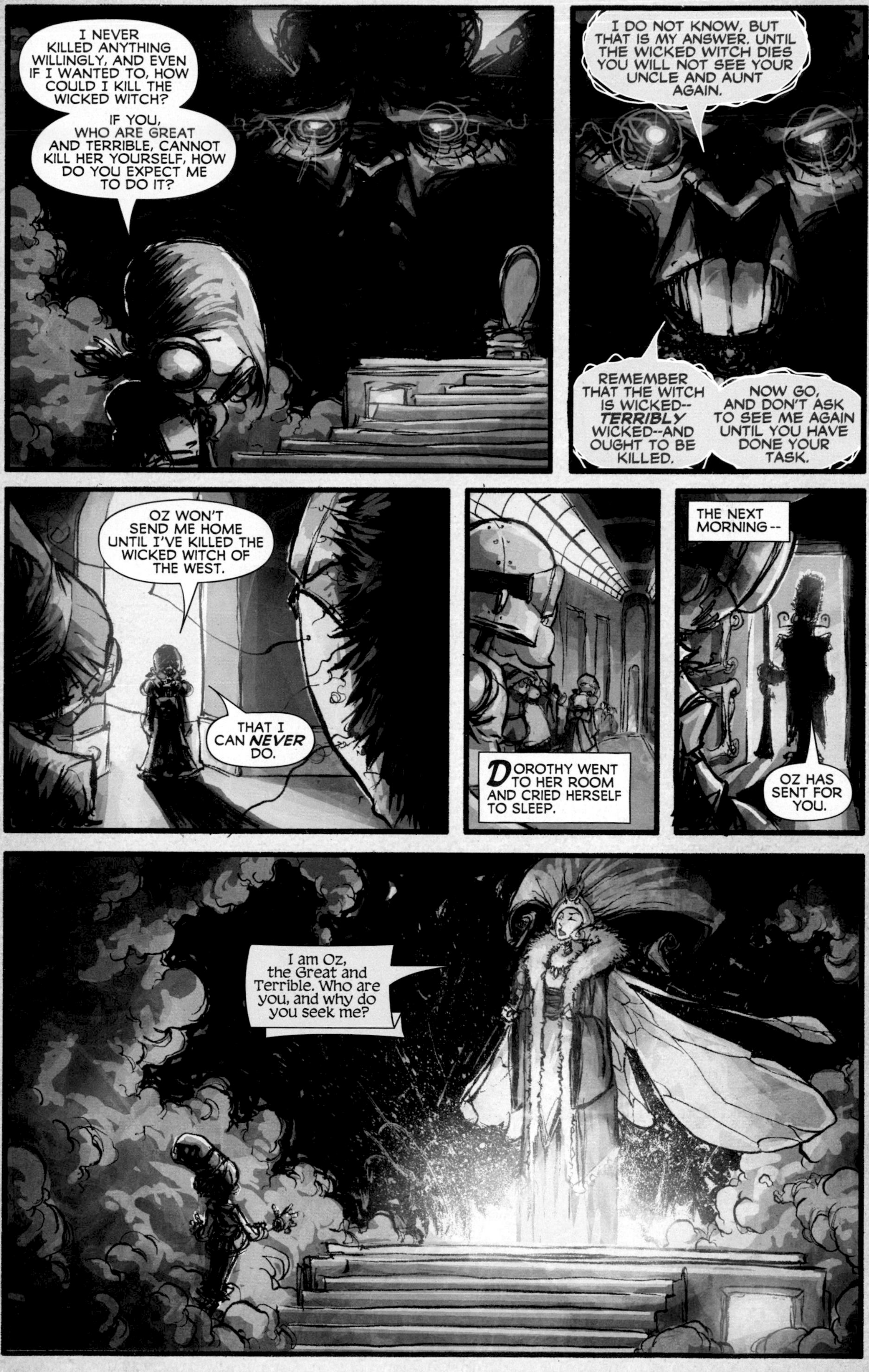
I NEVER KILLED ANYTHING WILLINGLY, AND EVEN IF I WANTED TO, HOW COULD I KILL THE WICKED WITCH?
IF YOU, WHO ARE GREAT AND TERRIBLE, CANNOT KILL HER YOURSELF, HOW DO YOU EXPECT ME TO DO IT?
I DO NOT KNOW, BUT THAT IS MY ANSWER. UNTIL THE WICKED WITCH DIES YOU WILL NOT SEE YOUR UNCLE AND AUNT AGAIN.
REMEMBER THAT THE WITCH IS WICKED-- ***TERRIBLY*** WICKED--AND OUGHT TO BE KILLED.
NOW GO, AND DON'T ASK TO SEE ME AGAIN UNTIL YOU HAVE DONE YOUR TASK.
OZ WON'T SEND ME HOME UNTIL I'VE KILLED THE WICKED WITCH OF THE WEST.
THAT I CAN ***NEVER*** DO.
DOROTHY WENT TO HER ROOM AND CRIED HERSELF TO SLEEP.
THE NEXT MORNING --
OZ HAS SENT FOR YOU.
I am Oz, the Great and Terrible. Who are you, and why do you seek me?

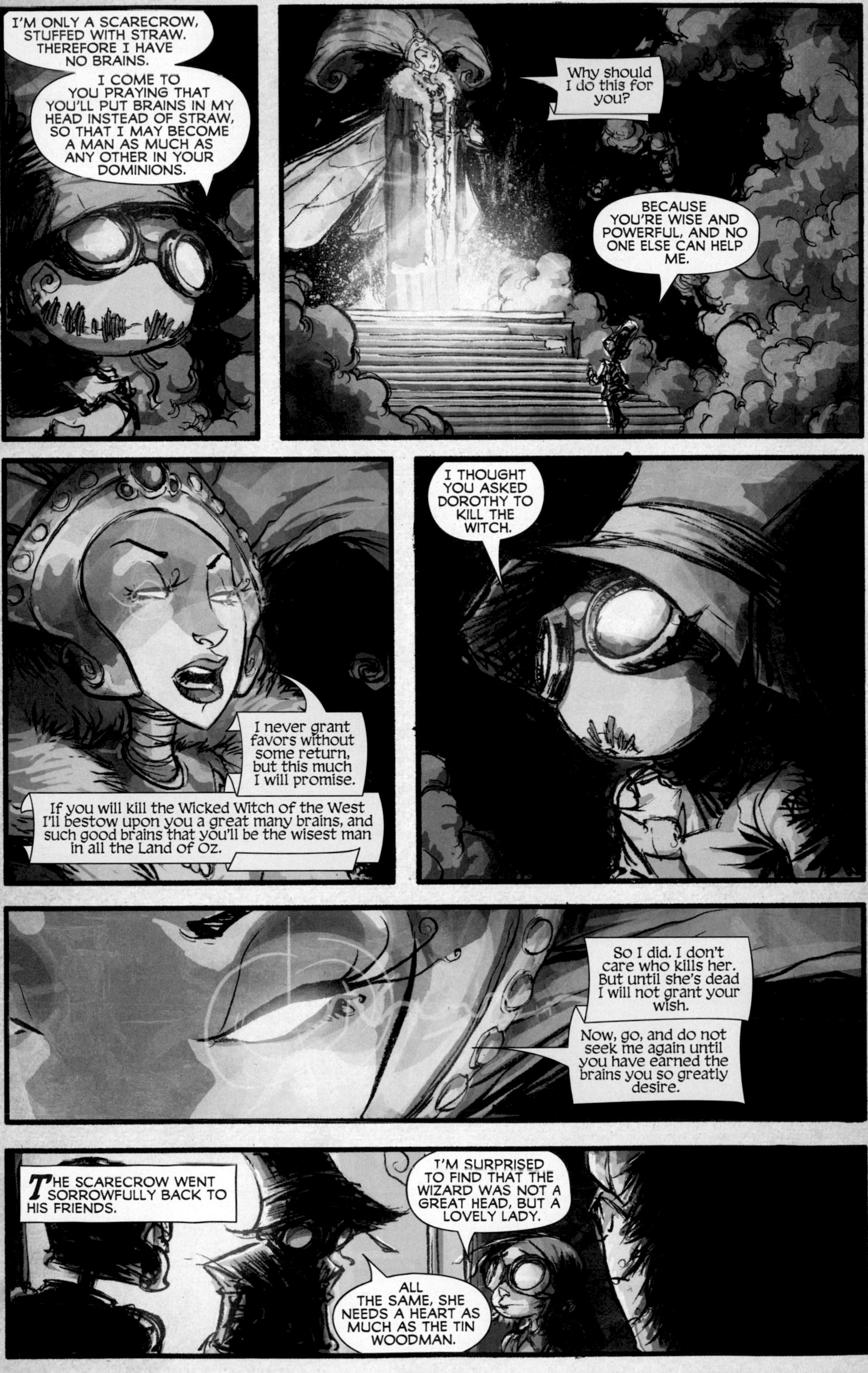
I'M ONLY A SCARECROW, STUFFED WITH STRAW. THEREFORE I HAVE NO BRAINS.
I COME TO YOU PRAYING THAT YOU'LL PUT BRAINS IN MY HEAD INSTEAD OF STRAW, SO THAT I MAY BECOME A MAN AS MUCH AS ANY OTHER IN YOUR DOMINIONS.
Why should I do this for you?
BECAUSE YOU'RE WISE AND POWERFUL, AND NO ONE ELSE CAN HELP ME.
I never grant favors without some return, but this much I will promise.
If you will kill the Wicked Witch of the West I'll bestow upon you a great many brains, and such good brains that you'll be the wisest man in all the Land of Oz.
I THOUGHT YOU ASKED DOROTHY TO KILL THE WITCH.
So I did. I don't care who kills her. But until she's dead I will not grant your wish.
Now, go, and do not seek me again until you have earned the brains you so greatly desire.
THE SCARECROW WENT SORROWFULLY BACK TO HIS FRIENDS.
I'M SURPRISED TO FIND THAT THE WIZARD WAS NOT A GREAT HEAD, BUT A LOVELY LADY.
ALL THE SAME, SHE NEEDS A HEART AS MUCH AS THE TIN WOODMAN.

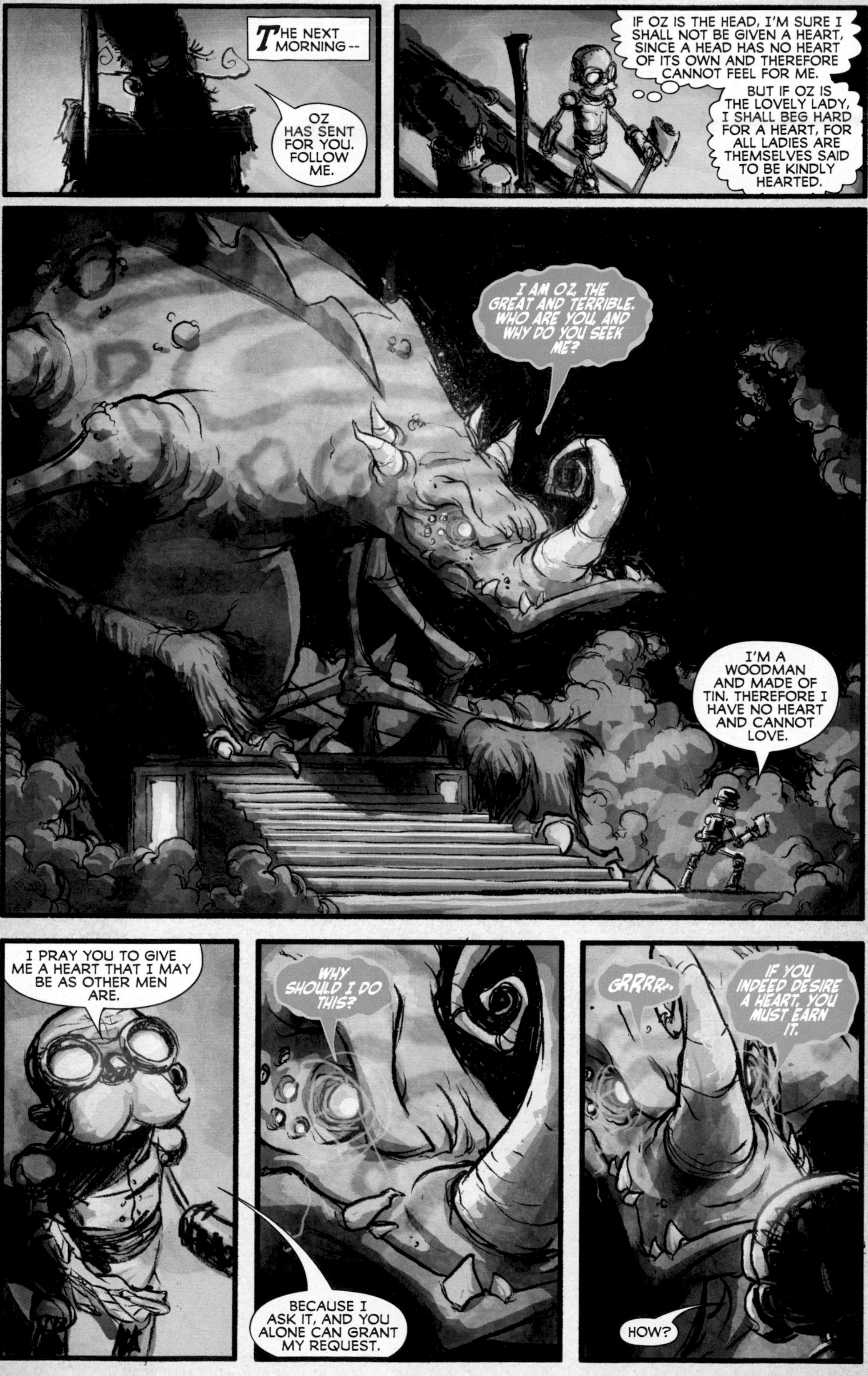
THE NEXT MORNING --
OZ HAS SENT FOR YOU. FOLLOW ME.
IF OZ IS THE HEAD, I'M SURE I SHALL NOT BE GIVEN A HEART, SINCE A HEAD HAS NO HEART OF ITS OWN AND THEREFORE CANNOT FEEL FOR ME.
BUT IF OZ IS THE LOVELY LADY, I SHALL BEG HARD FOR A HEART, FOR ALL LADIES ARE THEMSELVES SAID TO BE KINDLY HEARTED.
I AM OZ, THE GREAT AND TERRIBLE. WHO ARE YOU, AND WHY DO YOU SEEK ME?
I'M A WOODMAN AND MADE OF TIN. THEREFORE I HAVE NO HEART AND CANNOT LOVE.
I PRAY YOU TO GIVE ME A HEART THAT I MAY BE AS OTHER MEN ARE.
WHY SHOULD I DO THIS?
BECAUSE I ASK IT, AND YOU ALONE CAN GRANT MY REQUEST.
GRRRR...
IF YOU INDEED DESIRE A HEART, YOU MUST EARN IT.
HOW?

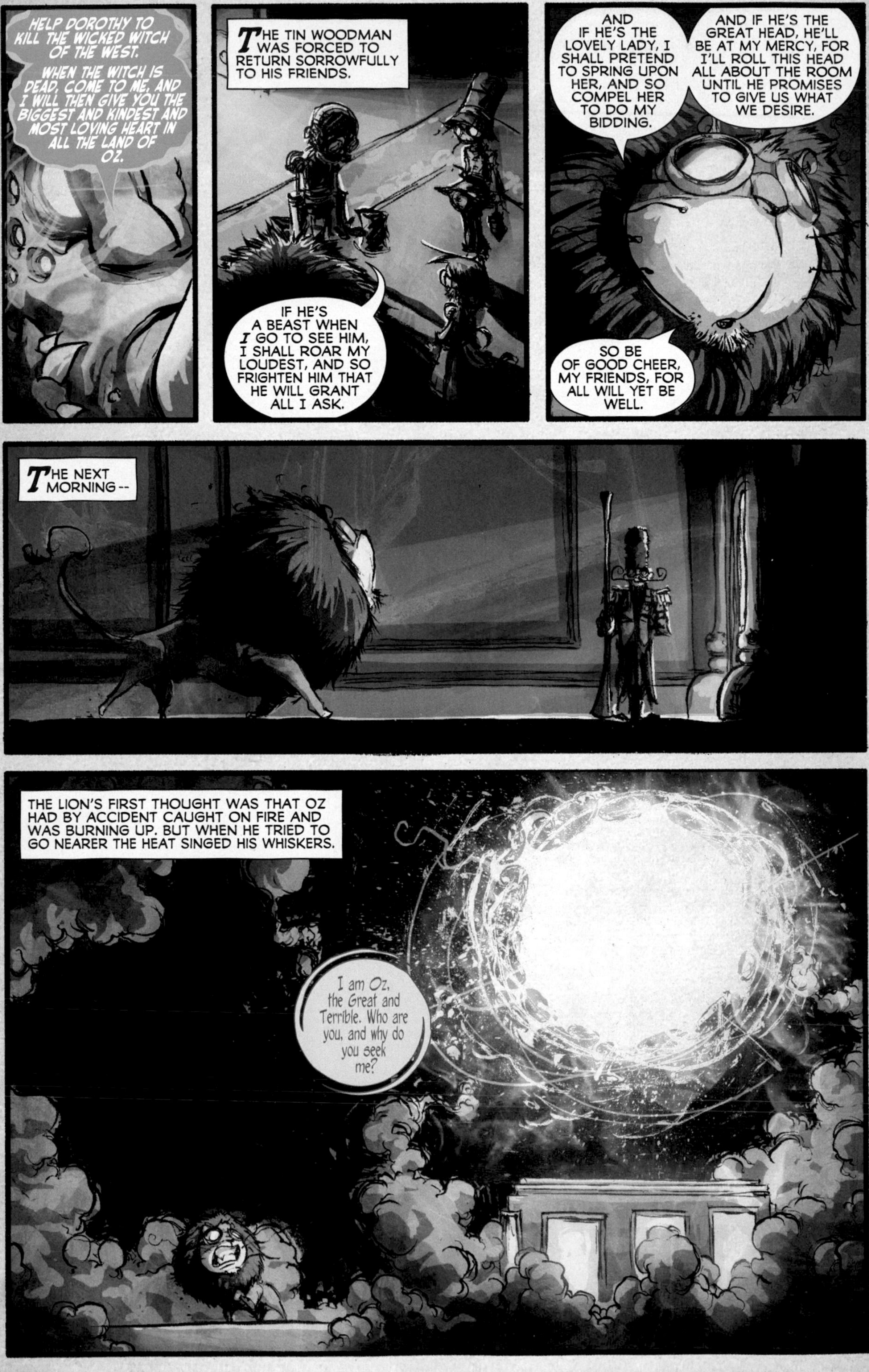
HELP DOROTHY TO KILL THE WICKED WITCH OF THE WEST.
WHEN THE WITCH IS DEAD, COME TO ME, AND I WILL THEN GIVE YOU THE BIGGEST AND KINDEST AND MOST LOVING HEART IN ALL THE LAND OF OZ.
THE TIN WOODMAN WAS FORCED TO RETURN SORROWFULLY TO HIS FRIENDS.
IF HE'S A BEAST WHEN I GO TO SEE HIM, I SHALL ROAR MY LOUDEST, AND SO FRIGHTEN HIM THAT HE WILL GRANT ALL I ASK.
AND IF HE'S THE LOVELY LADY, I SHALL PRETEND TO SPRING UPON HER, AND SO COMPEL HER TO DO MY BIDDING.
AND IF HE'S THE GREAT HEAD, HE'LL BE AT MY MERCY, FOR I'LL ROLL THIS HEAD ALL ABOUT THE ROOM UNTIL HE PROMISES TO GIVE US WHAT WE DESIRE.
SO BE OF GOOD CHEER, MY FRIENDS, FOR ALL WILL YET BE WELL.
THE NEXT MORNING--
THE LION'S FIRST THOUGHT WAS THAT OZ HAD BY ACCIDENT CAUGHT ON FIRE AND WAS BURNING UP. BUT WHEN HE TRIED TO GO NEARER THE HEAT SINGED HIS WHISKERS.
I am Oz, the Great and Terrible. Who are you, and why do you seek me?

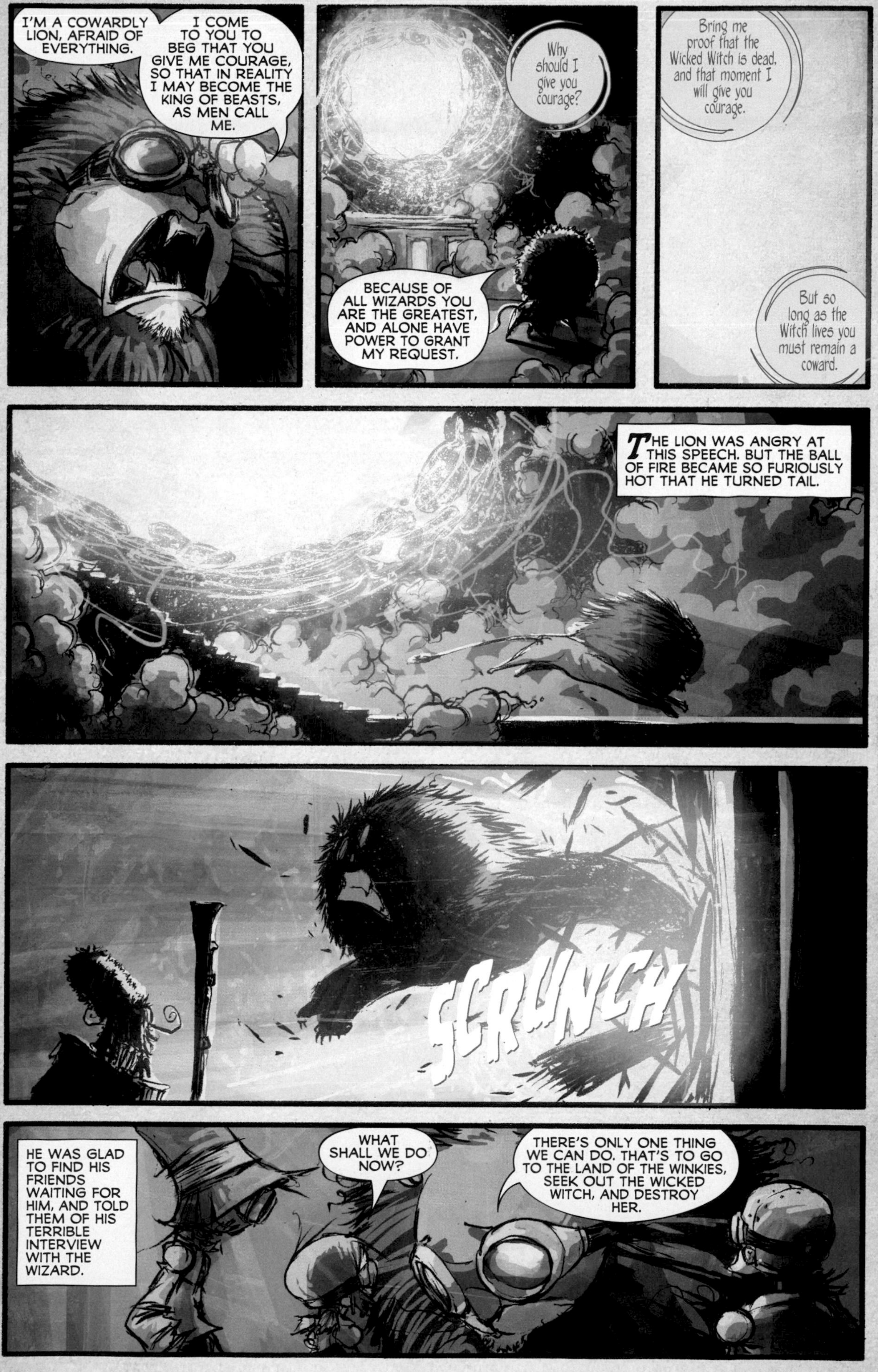
I'M A COWARDLY LION, AFRAID OF EVERYTHING.
I COME TO YOU TO BEG THAT YOU GIVE ME COURAGE, SO THAT IN REALITY I MAY BECOME THE KING OF BEASTS, AS MEN CALL ME.
Why should I give you courage?
BECAUSE OF ALL WIZARDS YOU ARE THE GREATEST, AND ALONE HAVE POWER TO GRANT MY REQUEST.
Bring me proof that the Wicked Witch is dead, and that moment I will give you courage.
But so long as the Witch lives you must remain a coward.
THE LION WAS ANGRY AT THIS SPEECH. BUT THE BALL OF FIRE BECAME SO FURIOUSLY HOT THAT HE TURNED TAIL.
SCRUNCH
HE WAS GLAD TO FIND HIS FRIENDS WAITING FOR HIM, AND TOLD THEM OF HIS TERRIBLE INTERVIEW WITH THE WIZARD.
WHAT SHALL WE DO NOW?
THERE'S ONLY ONE THING WE CAN DO. THAT'S TO GO TO THE LAND OF THE WINKIES, SEEK OUT THE WICKED WITCH, AND DESTROY HER.

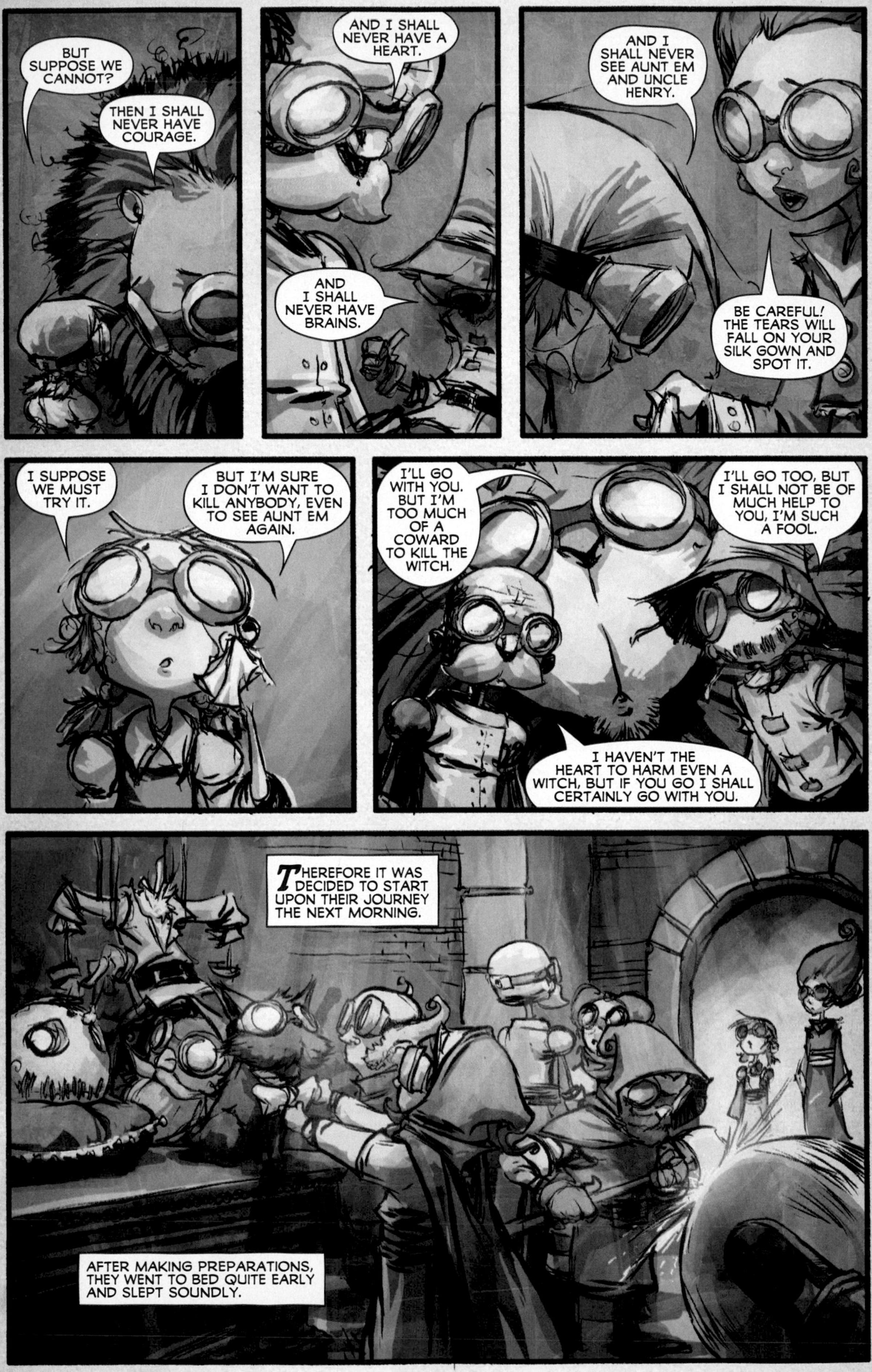
BUT SUPPOSE WE CANNOT?
THEN I SHALL NEVER HAVE COURAGE.
AND I SHALL NEVER HAVE A HEART.
AND I SHALL NEVER HAVE BRAINS.
AND I SHALL NEVER SEE AUNT EM AND UNCLE HENRY.
BE CAREFUL! THE TEARS WILL FALL ON YOUR SILK GOWN AND SPOT IT.
I SUPPOSE WE MUST TRY IT.
BUT I'M SURE I DON'T WANT TO KILL ANYBODY, EVEN TO SEE AUNT EM AGAIN.
I'LL GO WITH YOU. BUT I'M TOO MUCH OF A COWARD TO KILL THE WITCH.
I'LL GO TOO, BUT I SHALL NOT BE OF MUCH HELP TO YOU, I'M SUCH A FOOL.
I HAVEN'T THE HEART TO HARM EVEN A WITCH, BUT IF YOU GO I SHALL CERTAINLY GO WITH YOU.
THEREFORE IT WAS DECIDED TO START UPON THEIR JOURNEY THE NEXT MORNING.
AFTER MAKING PREPARATIONS, THEY WENT TO BED QUITE EARLY AND SLEPT SOUNDLY.

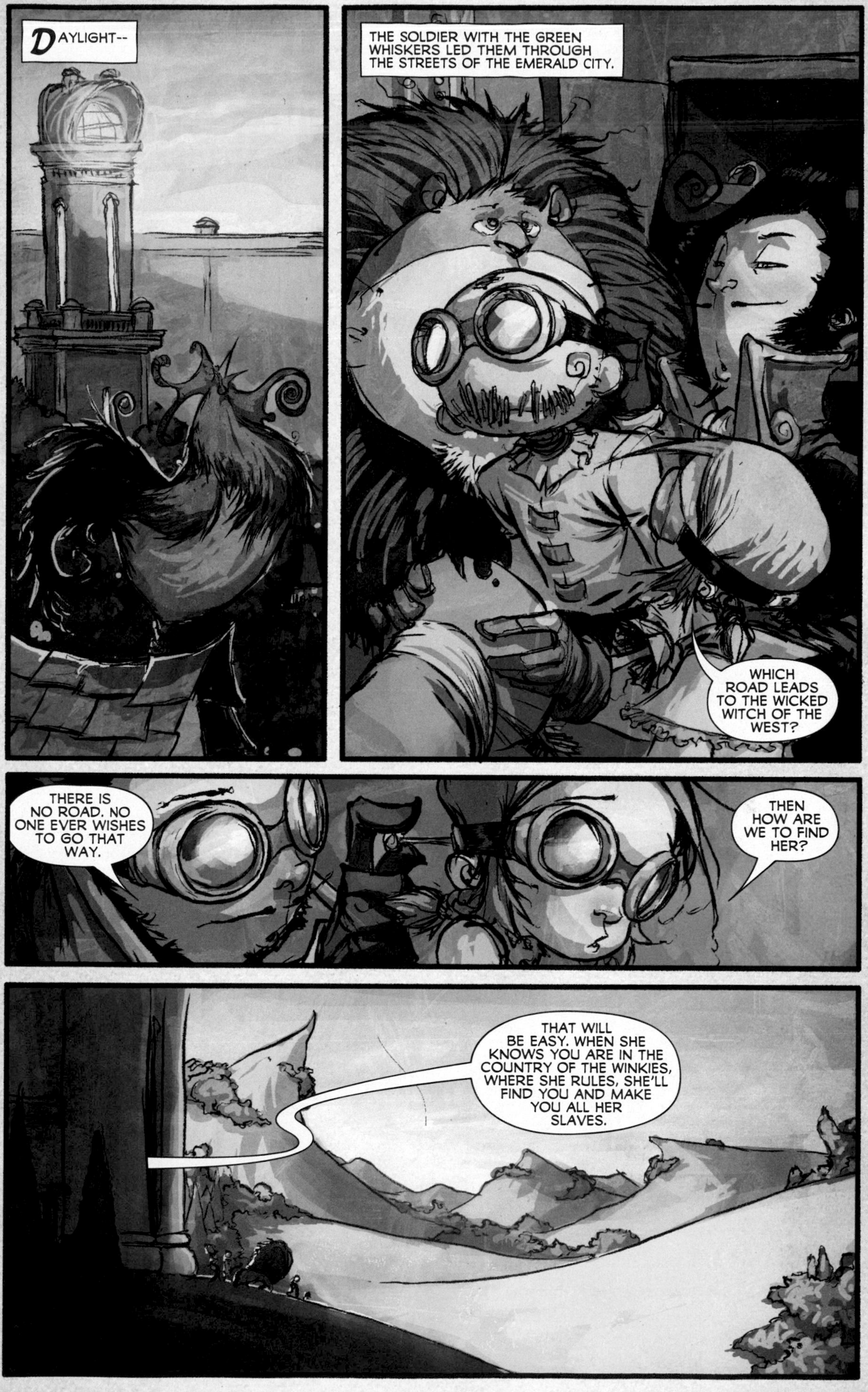
DAYLIGHT--
THE SOLDIER WITH THE GREEN WHISKERS LED THEM THROUGH THE STREETS OF THE EMERALD CITY.
WHICH ROAD LEADS TO THE WICKED WITCH OF THE WEST?
THERE IS NO ROAD. NO ONE EVER WISHES TO GO THAT WAY.
THEN HOW ARE WE TO FIND HER?
THAT WILL BE EASY. WHEN SHE KNOWS YOU ARE IN THE COUNTRY OF THE WINKIES, WHERE SHE RULES, SHE'LL FIND YOU AND MAKE YOU ALL HER SLAVES.

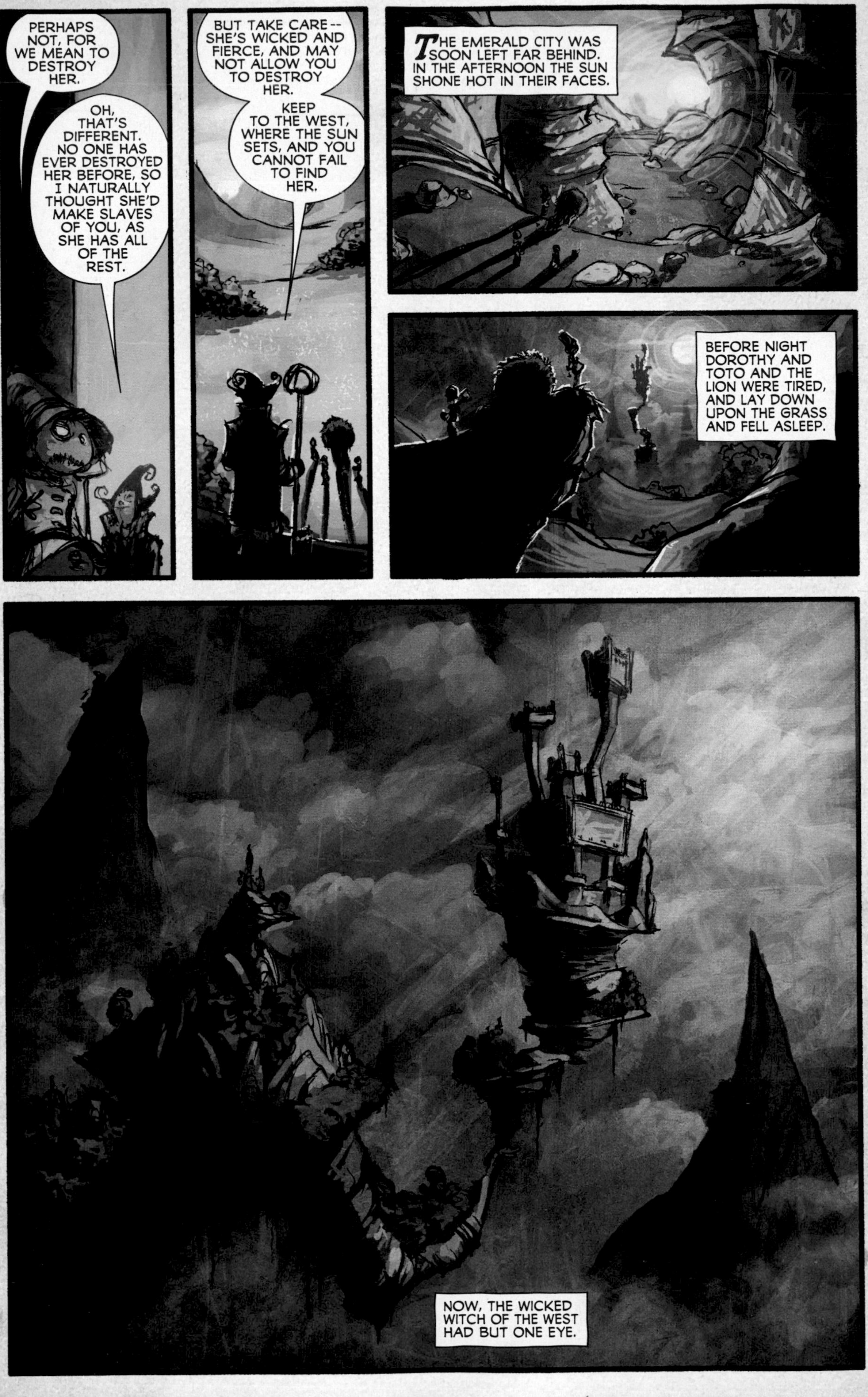
PERHAPS NOT, FOR WE MEAN TO DESTROY HER.
OH, THAT'S DIFFERENT. NO ONE HAS EVER DESTROYED HER BEFORE, SO I NATURALLY THOUGHT SHE'D MAKE SLAVES OF YOU, AS SHE HAS ALL OF THE REST.
BUT TAKE CARE-- SHE'S WICKED AND FIERCE, AND MAY NOT ALLOW YOU TO DESTROY HER.
KEEP TO THE WEST, WHERE THE SUN SETS, AND YOU CANNOT FAIL TO FIND HER.
THE EMERALD CITY WAS SOON LEFT FAR BEHIND. IN THE AFTERNOON THE SUN SHONE HOT IN THEIR FACES.
BEFORE NIGHT DOROTHY AND TOTO AND THE LION WERE TIRED, AND LAY DOWN UPON THE GRASS AND FELL ASLEEP.
NOW, THE WICKED WITCH OF THE WEST HAD BUT ONE EYE.

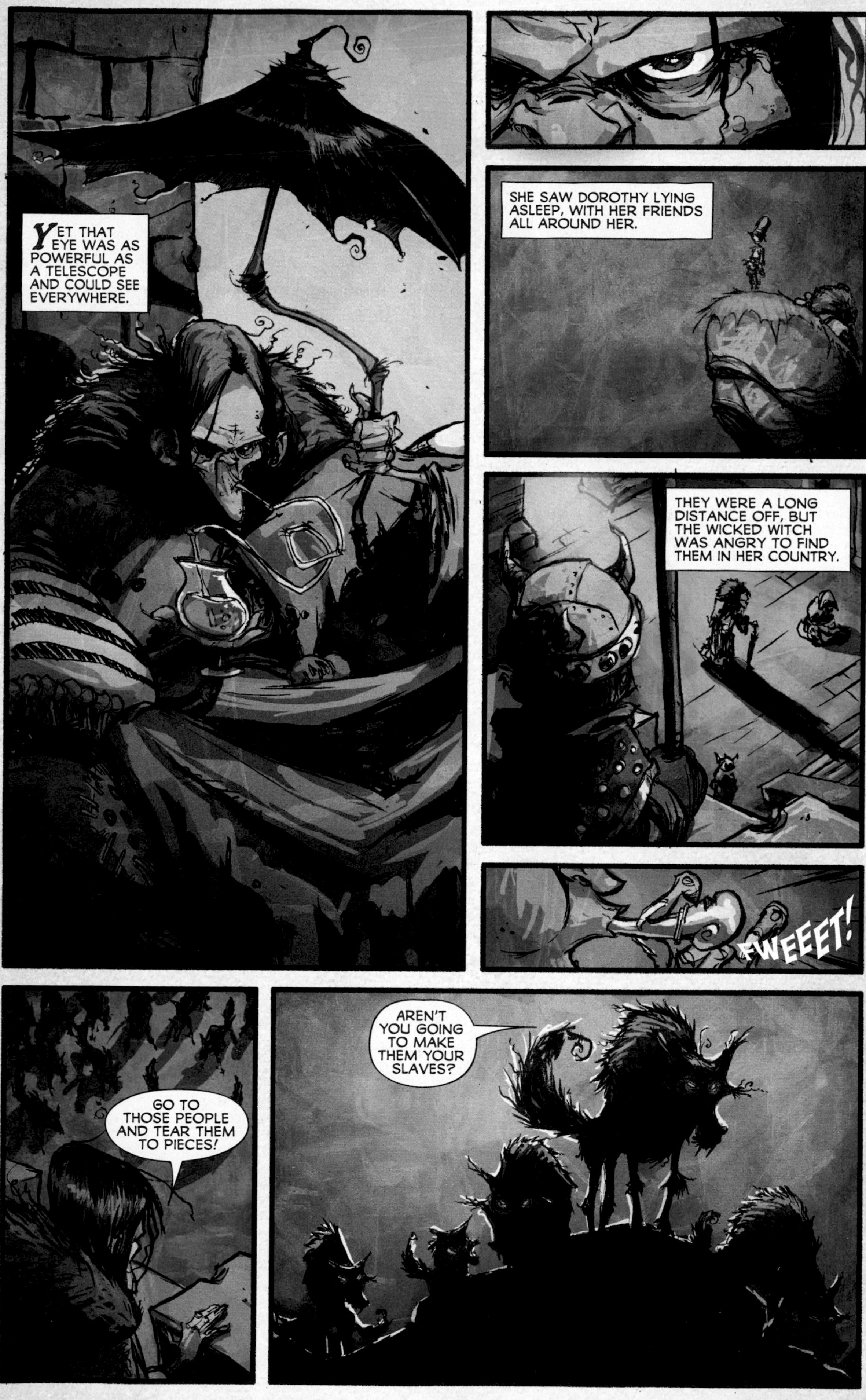
YET THAT EYE WAS AS POWERFUL AS A TELESCOPE AND COULD SEE EVERYWHERE.
SHE SAW DOROTHY LYING ASLEEP, WITH HER FRIENDS ALL AROUND HER.
THEY WERE A LONG DISTANCE OFF, BUT THE WICKED WITCH WAS ANGRY TO FIND THEM IN HER COUNTRY.
FWEEET!
GO TO THOSE PEOPLE AND TEAR THEM TO PIECES!
AREN'T YOU GOING TO MAKE THEM YOUR SLAVES?

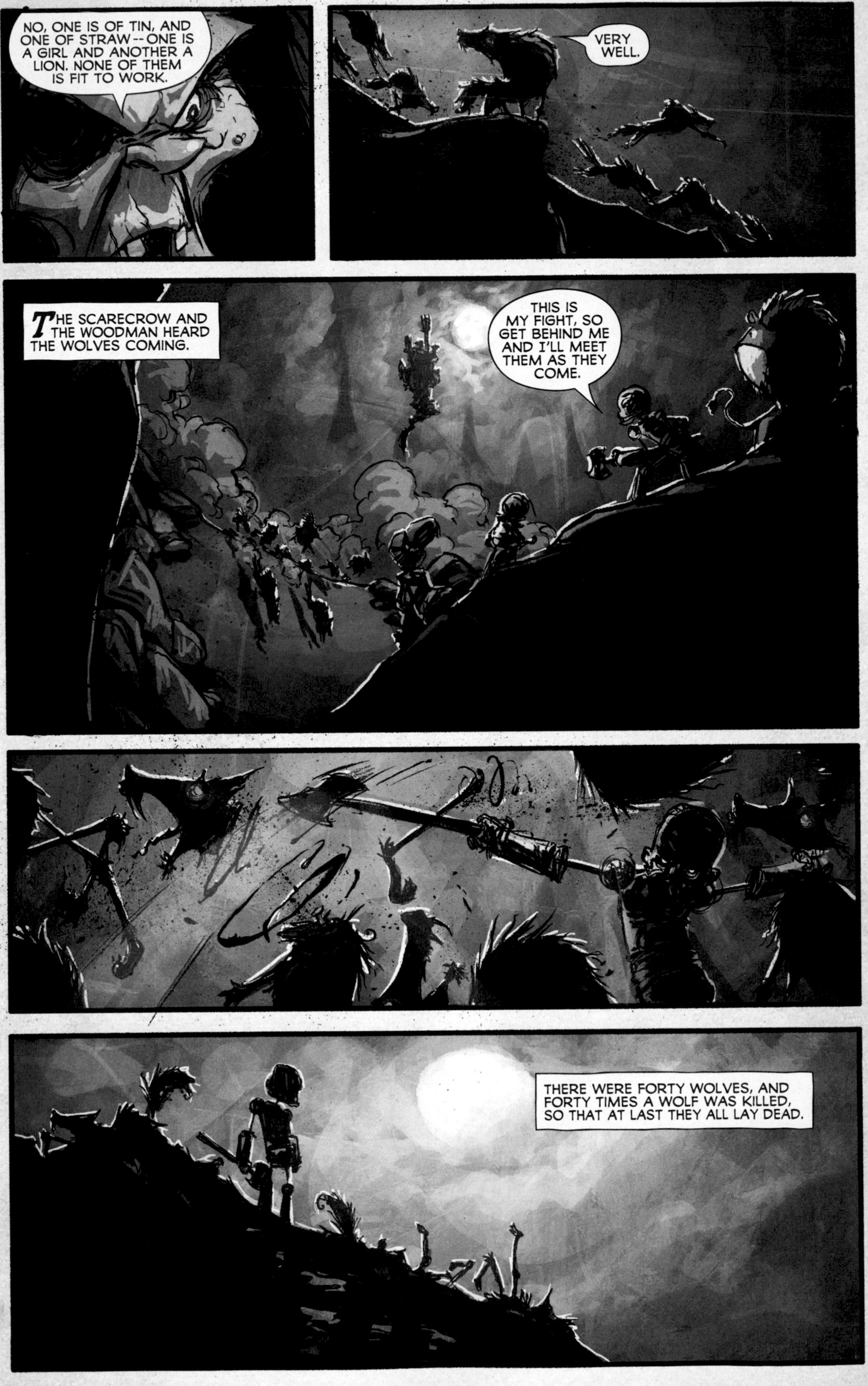
NO, ONE IS OF TIN, AND ONE OF STRAW--ONE IS A GIRL AND ANOTHER A LION. NONE OF THEM IS FIT TO WORK.
VERY WELL.
THE SCARECROW AND THE WOODMAN HEARD THE WOLVES COMING.
THIS IS MY FIGHT, SO GET BEHIND ME AND I'LL MEET THEM AS THEY COME.
THERE WERE FORTY WOLVES, AND FORTY TIMES A WOLF WAS KILLED, SO THAT AT LAST THEY ALL LAY DEAD.

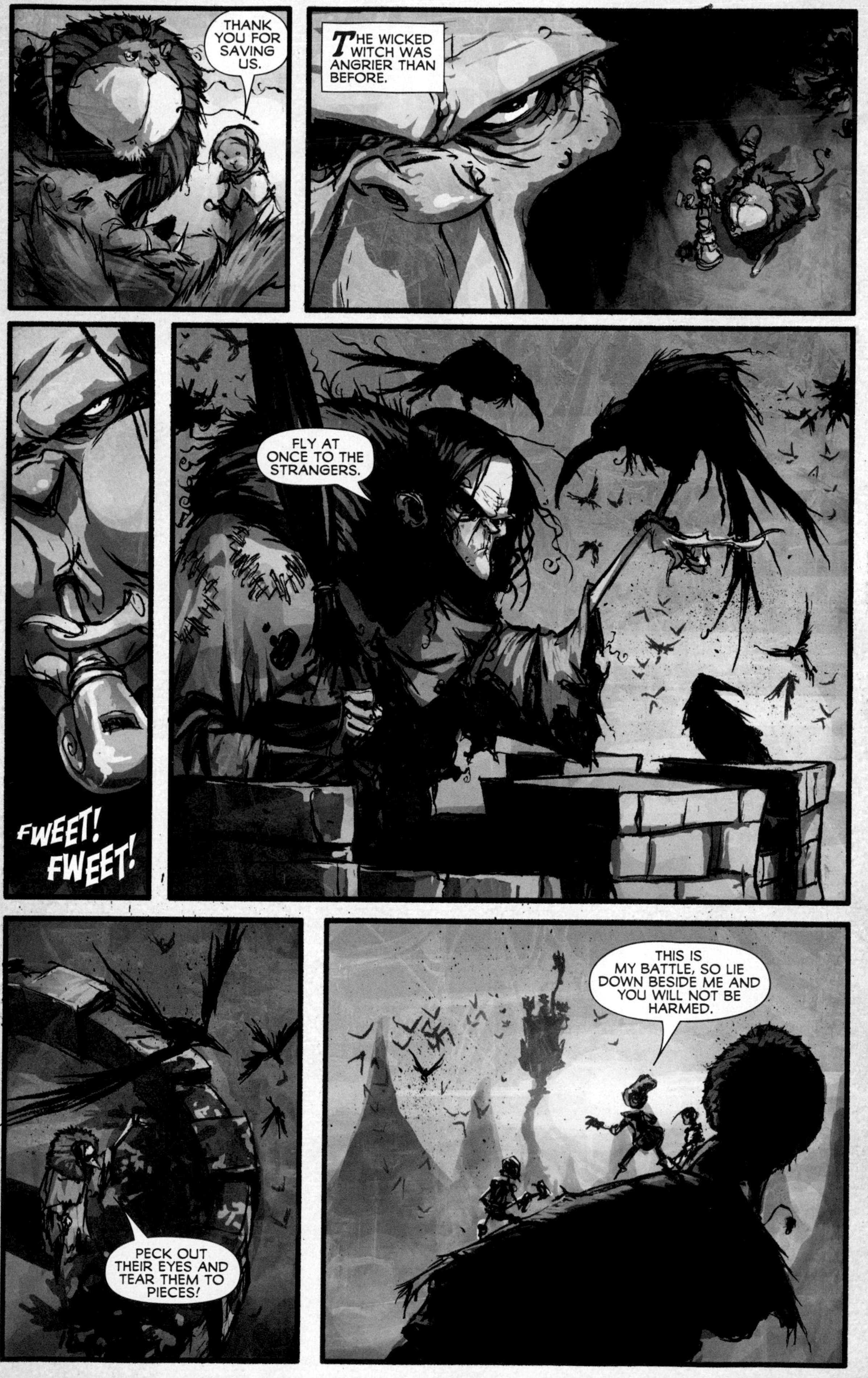
THANK YOU FOR SAVING US.
THE WICKED WITCH WAS ANGRIER THAN BEFORE.
FWEET! FWEET!
FLY AT ONCE TO THE STRANGERS.
PECK OUT THEIR EYES AND TEAR THEM TO PIECES!
THIS IS MY BATTLE, SO LIE DOWN BESIDE ME AND YOU WILL NOT BE HARMED.

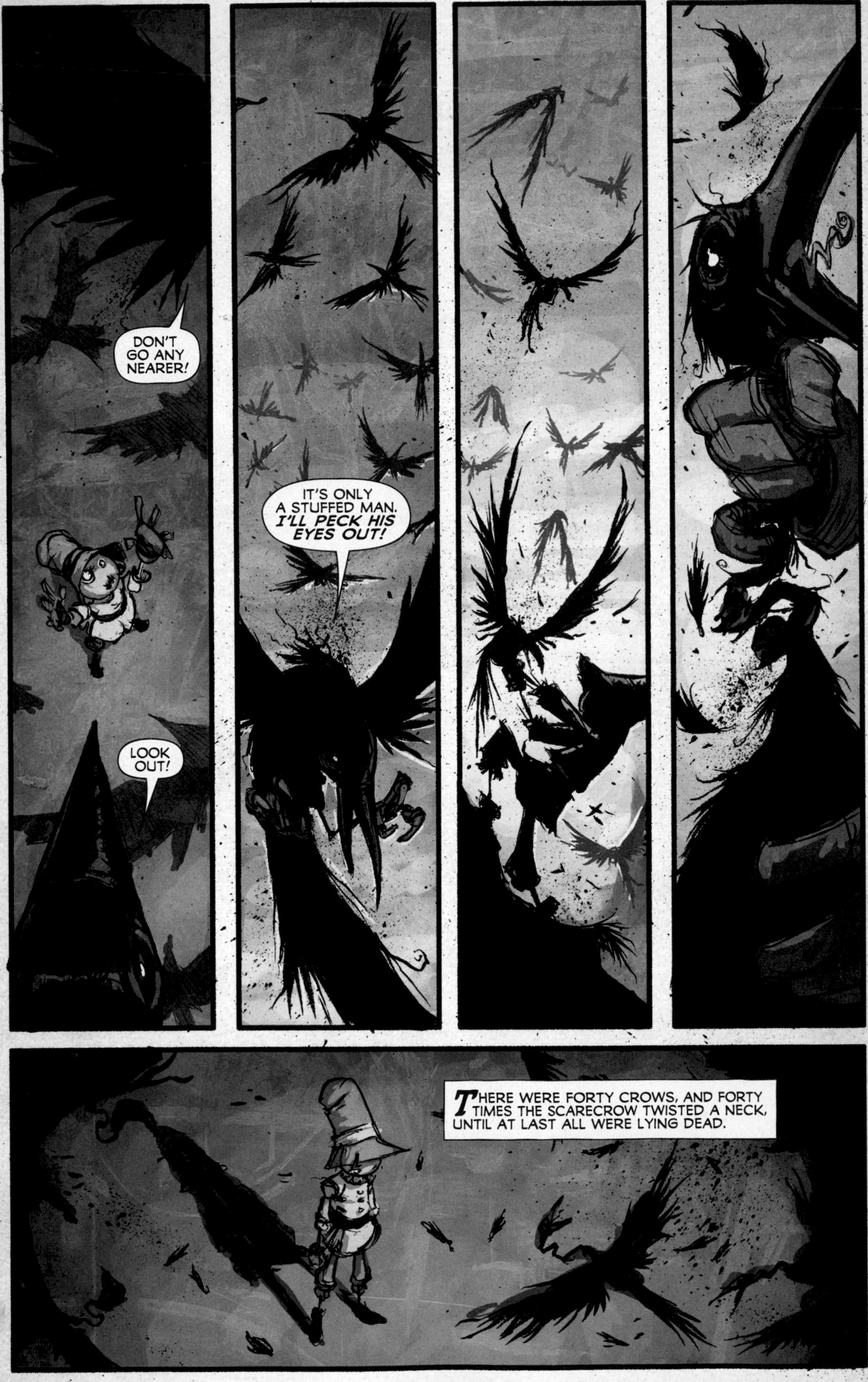
DON'T GO ANY NEARER!
LOOK OUT!
IT'S ONLY A STUFFED MAN. *I'LL PECK HIS EYES OUT!*
THERE WERE FORTY CROWS, AND FORTY TIMES THE SCARECROW TWISTED A NECK, UNTIL AT LAST ALL WERE LYING DEAD.

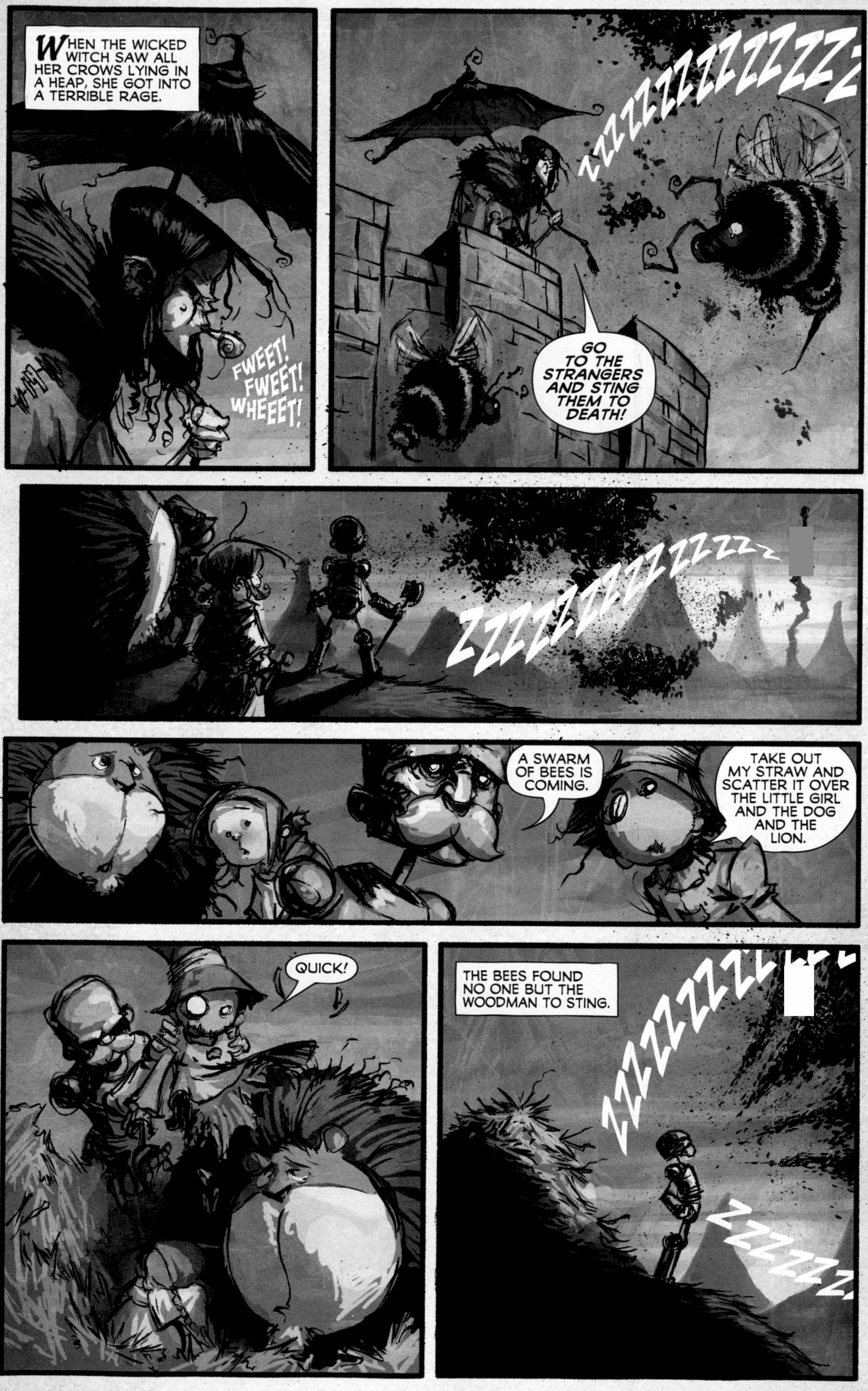

WHEN THE WICKED WITCH SAW ALL HER CROWS LYING IN A HEAP, SHE GOT INTO A TERRIBLE RAGE.
FWEET! FWEET! WHEEET!
ZZZZZZZZZZZZZZZ
GO TO THE STRANGERS AND STING THEM TO DEATH!
ZZZZZZZZZZZZZZZ
A SWARM OF BEES IS COMING.
TAKE OUT MY STRAW AND SCATTER IT OVER THE LITTLE GIRL AND THE DOG AND THE LION.
QUICK!
THE BEES FOUND NO ONE BUT THE WOODMAN TO STING.
ZZZZZZZZZZZ
ZZZZZ

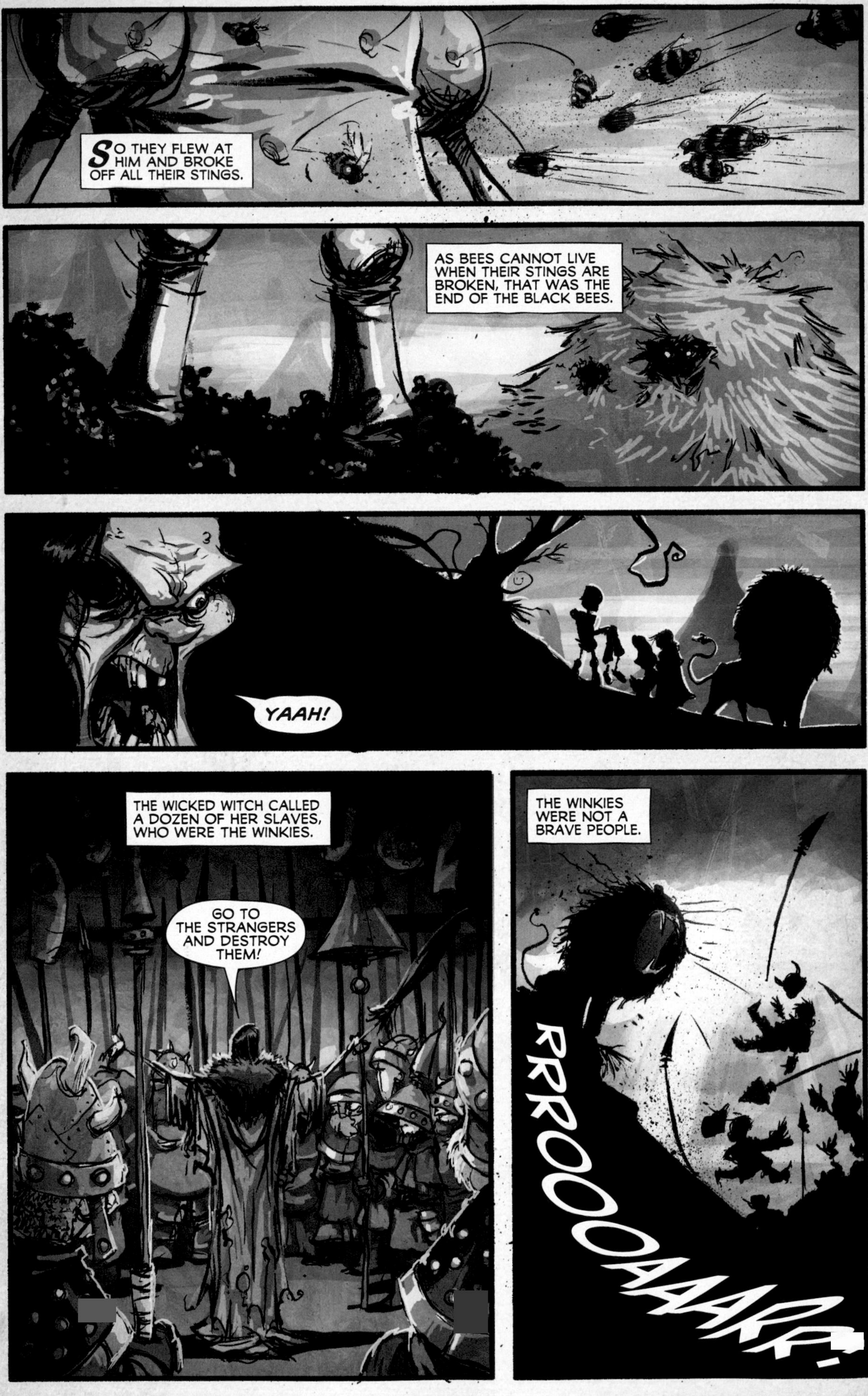
SO THEY FLEW AT HIM AND BROKE OFF ALL THEIR STINGS.
AS BEES CANNOT LIVE WHEN THEIR STINGS ARE BROKEN, THAT WAS THE END OF THE BLACK BEES.
YAAH!
THE WICKED WITCH CALLED A DOZEN OF HER SLAVES, WHO WERE THE WINKIES.
GO TO THE STRANGERS AND DESTROY THEM!
THE WINKIES WERE NOT A BRAVE PEOPLE.
RRROOOAAARR!

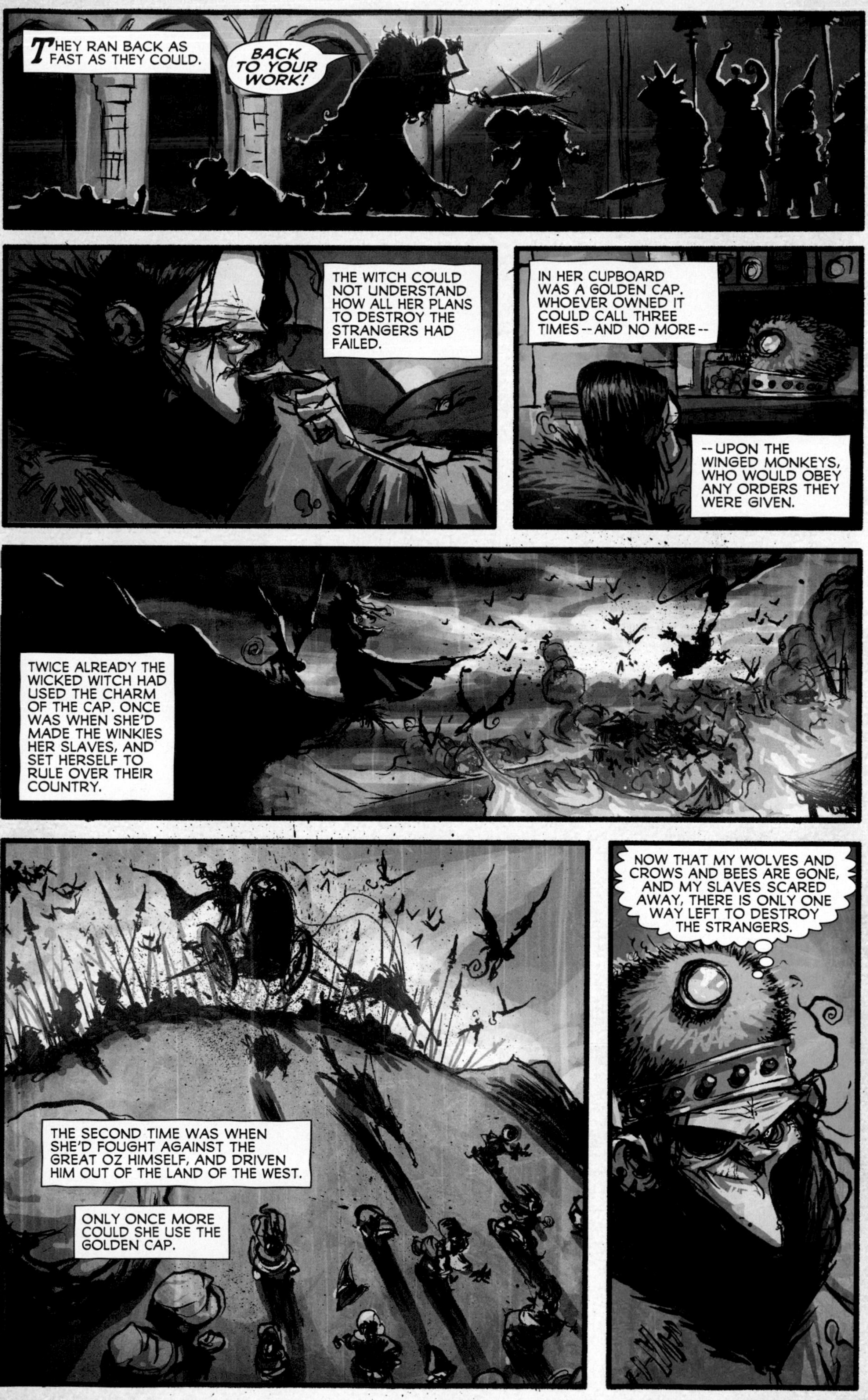
THEY RAN BACK AS FAST AS THEY COULD.
BACK TO YOUR WORK!
THE WITCH COULD NOT UNDERSTAND HOW ALL HER PLANS TO DESTROY THE STRANGERS HAD FAILED.
IN HER CUPBOARD WAS A GOLDEN CAP. WHOEVER OWNED IT COULD CALL THREE TIMES -- AND NO MORE --
-- UPON THE WINGED MONKEYS, WHO WOULD OBEY ANY ORDERS THEY WERE GIVEN.
TWICE ALREADY THE WICKED WITCH HAD USED THE CHARM OF THE CAP. ONCE WAS WHEN SHE'D MADE THE WINKIES HER SLAVES, AND SET HERSELF TO RULE OVER THEIR COUNTRY.
THE SECOND TIME WAS WHEN SHE'D FOUGHT AGAINST THE GREAT OZ HIMSELF, AND DRIVEN HIM OUT OF THE LAND OF THE WEST.
ONLY ONCE MORE COULD SHE USE THE GOLDEN CAP.
NOW THAT MY WOLVES AND CROWS AND BEES ARE GONE, AND MY SLAVES SCARED AWAY, THERE IS ONLY ONE WAY LEFT TO DESTROY THE STRANGERS.

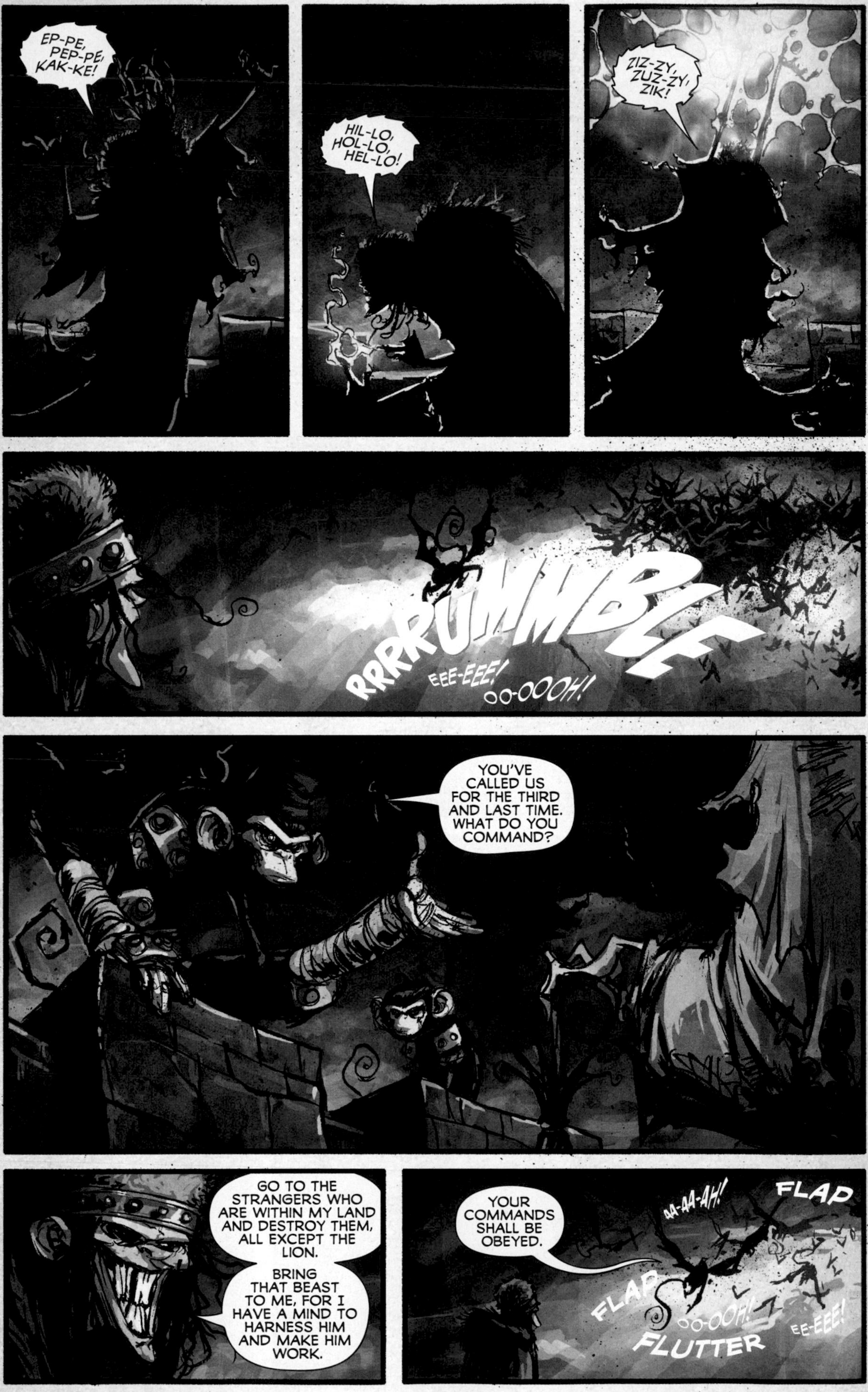
EP-PE, PEP-PE, KAK-KE!
HIL-LO, HOL-LO, HEL-LO!
ZIZ-ZY, ZUZ-ZY, ZIK!
RRRRUMMBLE
EEE-EEE!
OO-OOOH!
YOU'VE CALLED US FOR THE THIRD AND LAST TIME. WHAT DO YOU COMMAND?
GO TO THE STRANGERS WHO ARE WITHIN MY LAND AND DESTROY THEM, ALL EXCEPT THE LION.
BRING THAT BEAST TO ME, FOR I HAVE A MIND TO HARNESS HIM AND MAKE HIM WORK.
YOUR COMMANDS SHALL BE OBEYED.
AA-AA-AH!
FLAP
FLAP
OO-OOH!
EE-EEE!
FLUTTER

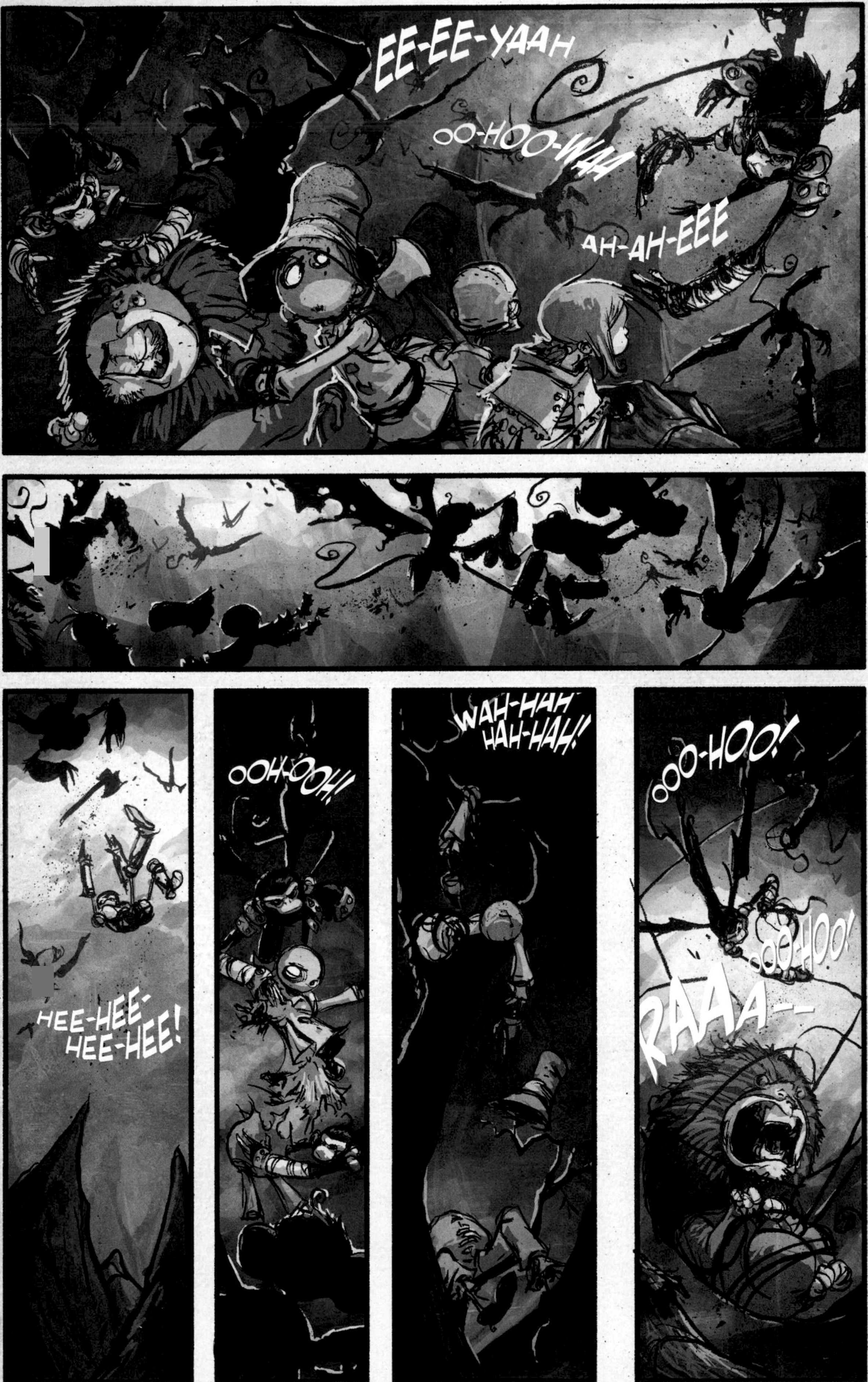
EE-EE-YAAH
OO-HOO-WAA
AH-AH-EEE
HEE-HEE-
HEE-HEE!
OOH-OOH!
WAH-HAH-
HAH-HAH!
OOO-HOO!
OO-HOO!
RAAA--

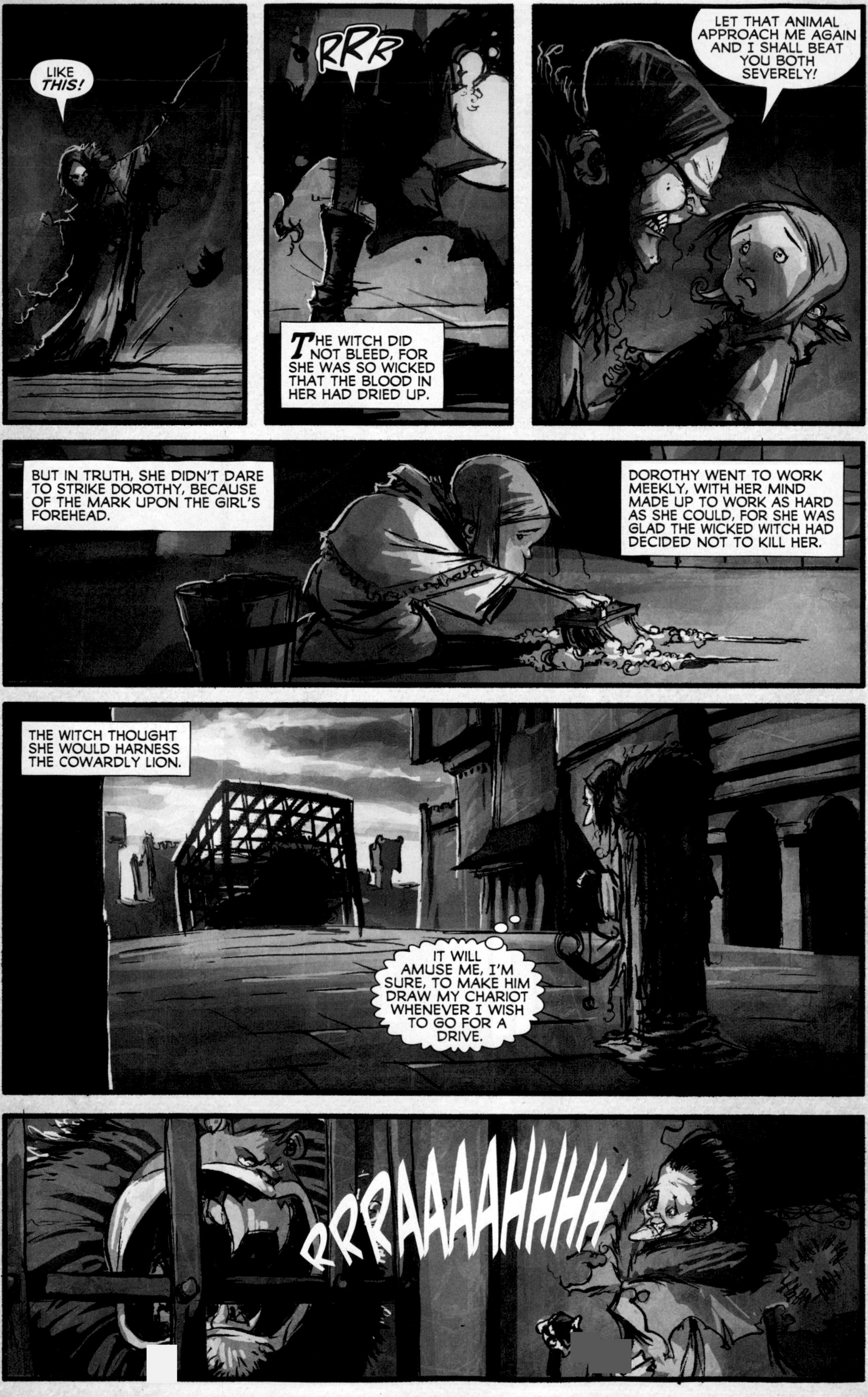
LIKE THIS!
RRR
THE WITCH DID NOT BLEED, FOR SHE WAS SO WICKED THAT THE BLOOD IN HER HAD DRIED UP.
LET THAT ANIMAL APPROACH ME AGAIN AND I SHALL BEAT YOU BOTH SEVERELY!
BUT IN TRUTH, SHE DIDN'T DARE TO STRIKE DOROTHY, BECAUSE OF THE MARK UPON THE GIRL'S FOREHEAD.
DOROTHY WENT TO WORK MEEKLY, WITH HER MIND MADE UP TO WORK AS HARD AS SHE COULD, FOR SHE WAS GLAD THE WICKED WITCH HAD DECIDED NOT TO KILL HER.
THE WITCH THOUGHT SHE WOULD HARNESS THE COWARDLY LION.
IT WILL AMUSE ME, I'M SURE, TO MAKE HIM DRAW MY CHARIOT WHENEVER I WISH TO GO FOR A DRIVE.
RRRAAAAHHHH

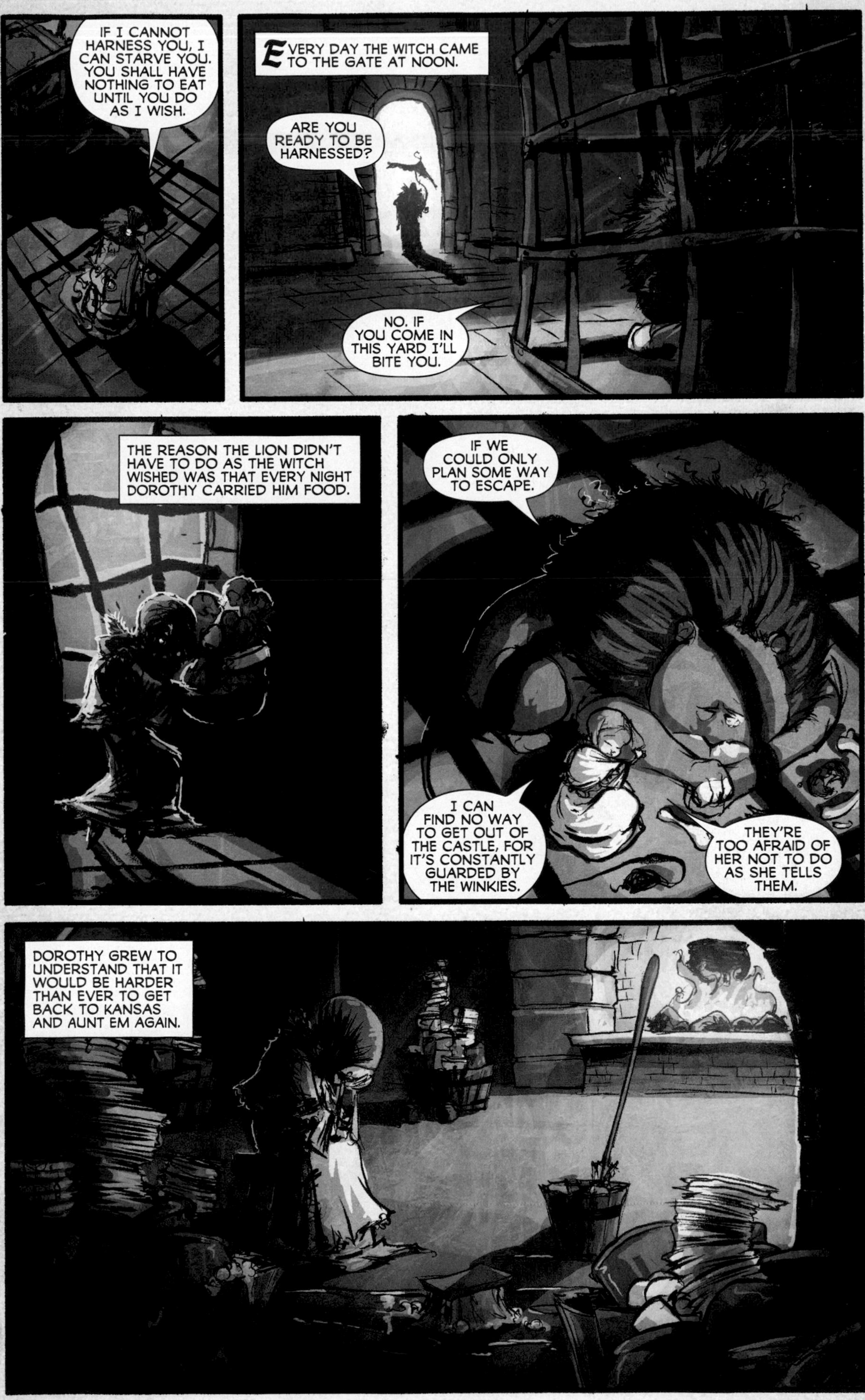
IF I CANNOT HARNESS YOU, I CAN STARVE YOU. YOU SHALL HAVE NOTHING TO EAT UNTIL YOU DO AS I WISH.
EVERY DAY THE WITCH CAME TO THE GATE AT NOON.
ARE YOU READY TO BE HARNESSED?
NO. IF YOU COME IN THIS YARD I'LL BITE YOU.
THE REASON THE LION DIDN'T HAVE TO DO AS THE WITCH WISHED WAS THAT EVERY NIGHT DOROTHY CARRIED HIM FOOD.
IF WE COULD ONLY PLAN SOME WAY TO ESCAPE.
I CAN FIND NO WAY TO GET OUT OF THE CASTLE, FOR IT'S CONSTANTLY GUARDED BY THE WINKIES.
THEY'RE TOO AFRAID OF HER NOT TO DO AS SHE TELLS THEM.
DOROTHY GREW TO UNDERSTAND THAT IT WOULD BE HARDER THAN EVER TO GET BACK TO KANSAS AND AUNT EM AGAIN.

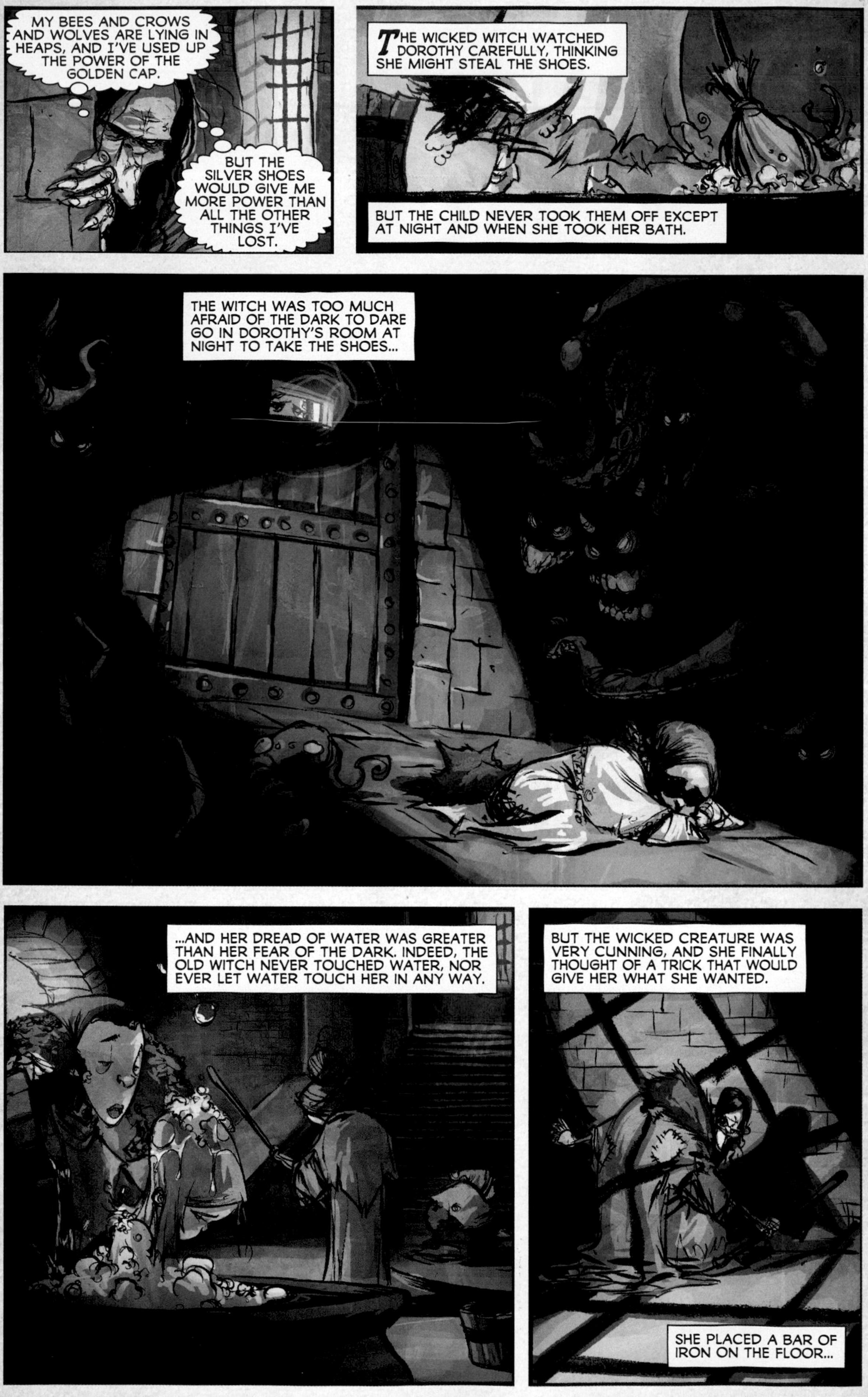
MY BEES AND CROWS AND WOLVES ARE LYING IN HEAPS, AND I'VE USED UP THE POWER OF THE GOLDEN CAP.
BUT THE SILVER SHOES WOULD GIVE ME MORE POWER THAN ALL THE OTHER THINGS I'VE LOST.
THE WICKED WITCH WATCHED DOROTHY CAREFULLY, THINKING SHE MIGHT STEAL THE SHOES.
BUT THE CHILD NEVER TOOK THEM OFF EXCEPT AT NIGHT AND WHEN SHE TOOK HER BATH.
THE WITCH WAS TOO MUCH AFRAID OF THE DARK TO DARE GO IN DOROTHY'S ROOM AT NIGHT TO TAKE THE SHOES...
...AND HER DREAD OF WATER WAS GREATER THAN HER FEAR OF THE DARK. INDEED, THE OLD WITCH NEVER TOUCHED WATER, NOR EVER LET WATER TOUCH HER IN ANY WAY.
BUT THE WICKED CREATURE WAS VERY CUNNING, AND SHE FINALLY THOUGHT OF A TRICK THAT WOULD GIVE HER WHAT SHE WANTED.
SHE PLACED A BAR OF IRON ON THE FLOOR...

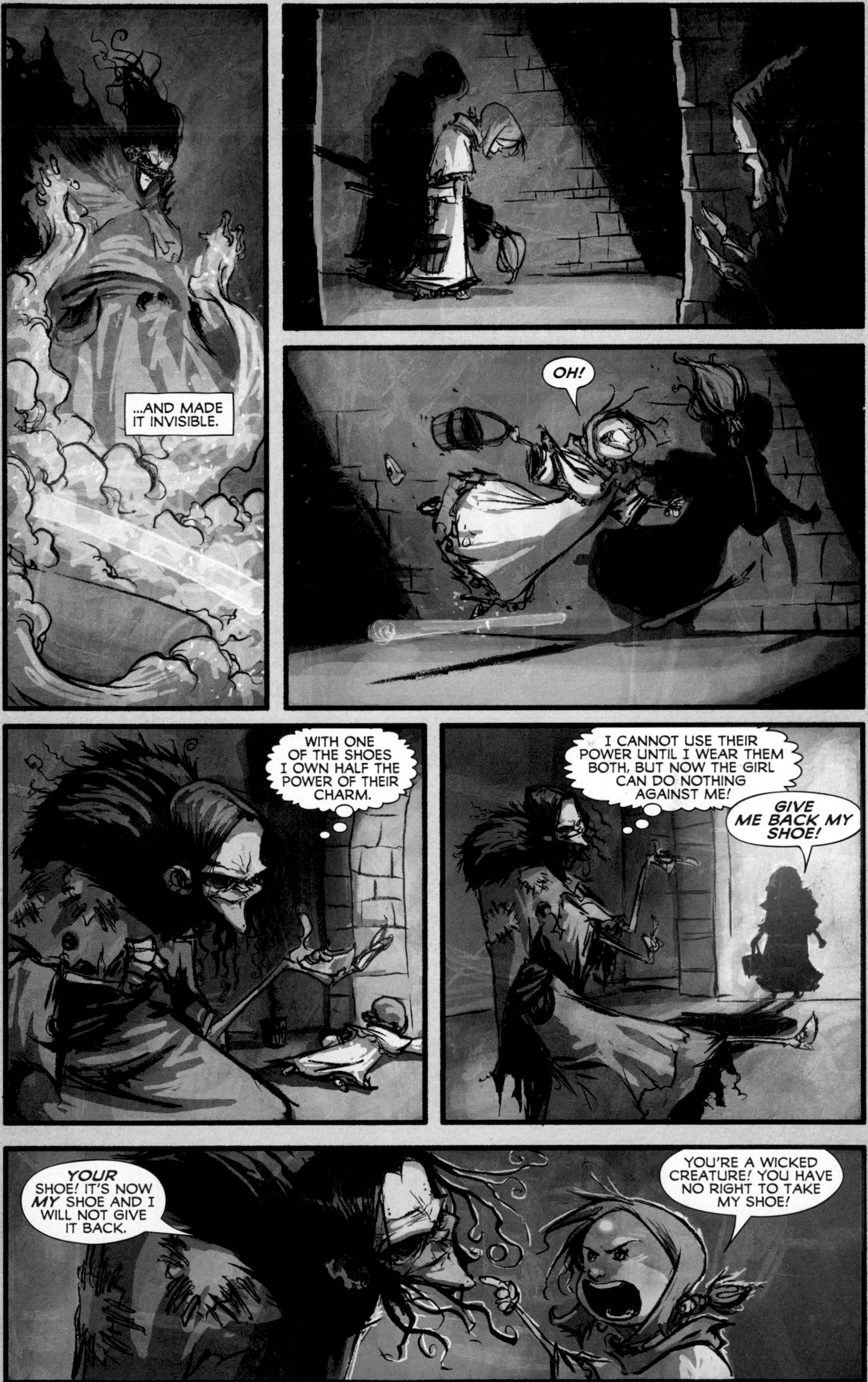

...AND MADE IT INVISIBLE.
OH!
WITH ONE OF THE SHOES I OWN HALF THE POWER OF THEIR CHARM.
I CANNOT USE THEIR POWER UNTIL I WEAR THEM BOTH, BUT NOW THE GIRL CAN DO NOTHING AGAINST ME!
GIVE ME BACK MY SHOE!
YOUR SHOE! IT'S NOW MY SHOE AND I WILL NOT GIVE IT BACK.
YOU'RE A WICKED CREATURE! YOU HAVE NO RIGHT TO TAKE MY SHOE!

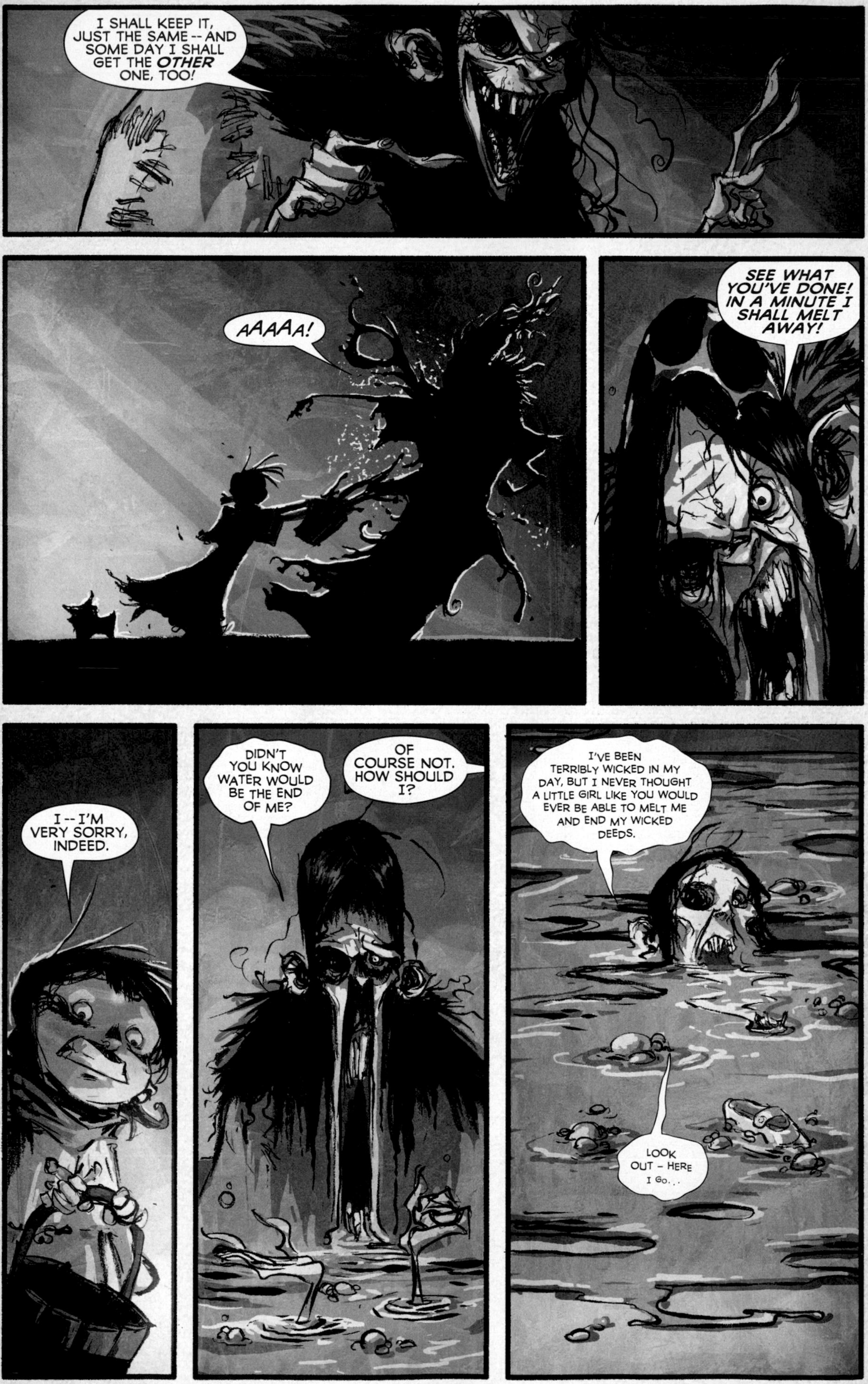
I SHALL KEEP IT, JUST THE SAME -- AND SOME DAY I SHALL GET THE *OTHER* ONE, TOO!
AAAAA!
SEE WHAT YOU'VE DONE! IN A MINUTE I SHALL MELT AWAY!
I -- I'M VERY SORRY, INDEED.
DIDN'T YOU KNOW WATER WOULD BE THE END OF ME?
OF COURSE NOT. HOW SHOULD I?
I'VE BEEN TERRIBLY WICKED IN MY DAY, BUT I NEVER THOUGHT A LITTLE GIRL LIKE YOU WOULD EVER BE ABLE TO MELT ME AND END MY WICKED DEEDS.
LOOK OUT - HERE I GO. . .

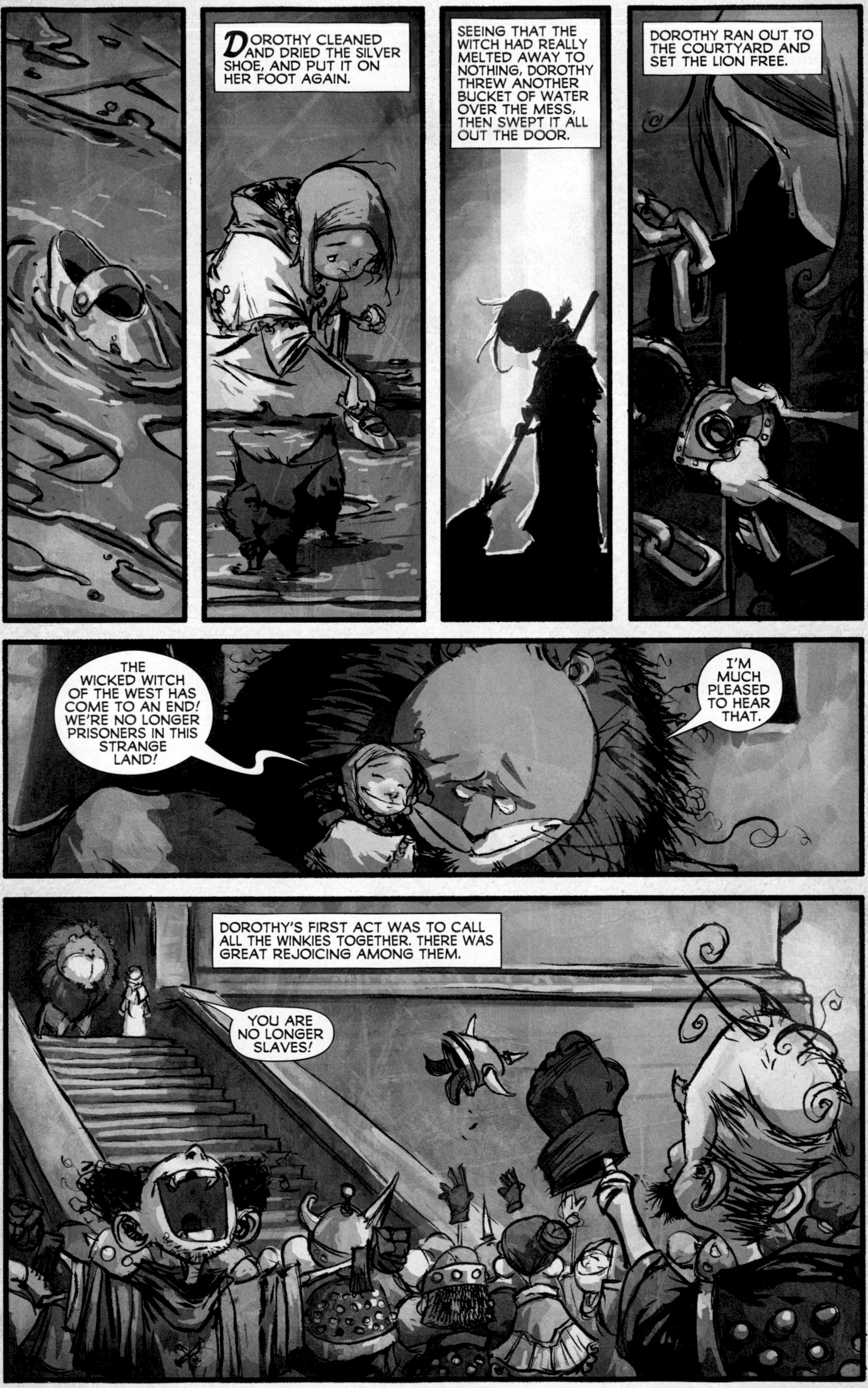
DOROTHY CLEANED AND DRIED THE SILVER SHOE, AND PUT IT ON HER FOOT AGAIN.
SEEING THAT THE WITCH HAD REALLY MELTED AWAY TO NOTHING, DOROTHY THREW ANOTHER BUCKET OF WATER OVER THE MESS, THEN SWEPT IT ALL OUT THE DOOR.
DOROTHY RAN OUT TO THE COURTYARD AND SET THE LION FREE.
THE WICKED WITCH OF THE WEST HAS COME TO AN END! WE'RE NO LONGER PRISONERS IN THIS STRANGE LAND!
I'M MUCH PLEASED TO HEAR THAT.
DOROTHY'S FIRST ACT WAS TO CALL ALL THE WINKIES TOGETHER. THERE WAS GREAT REJOICING AMONG THEM.
YOU ARE NO LONGER SLAVES!

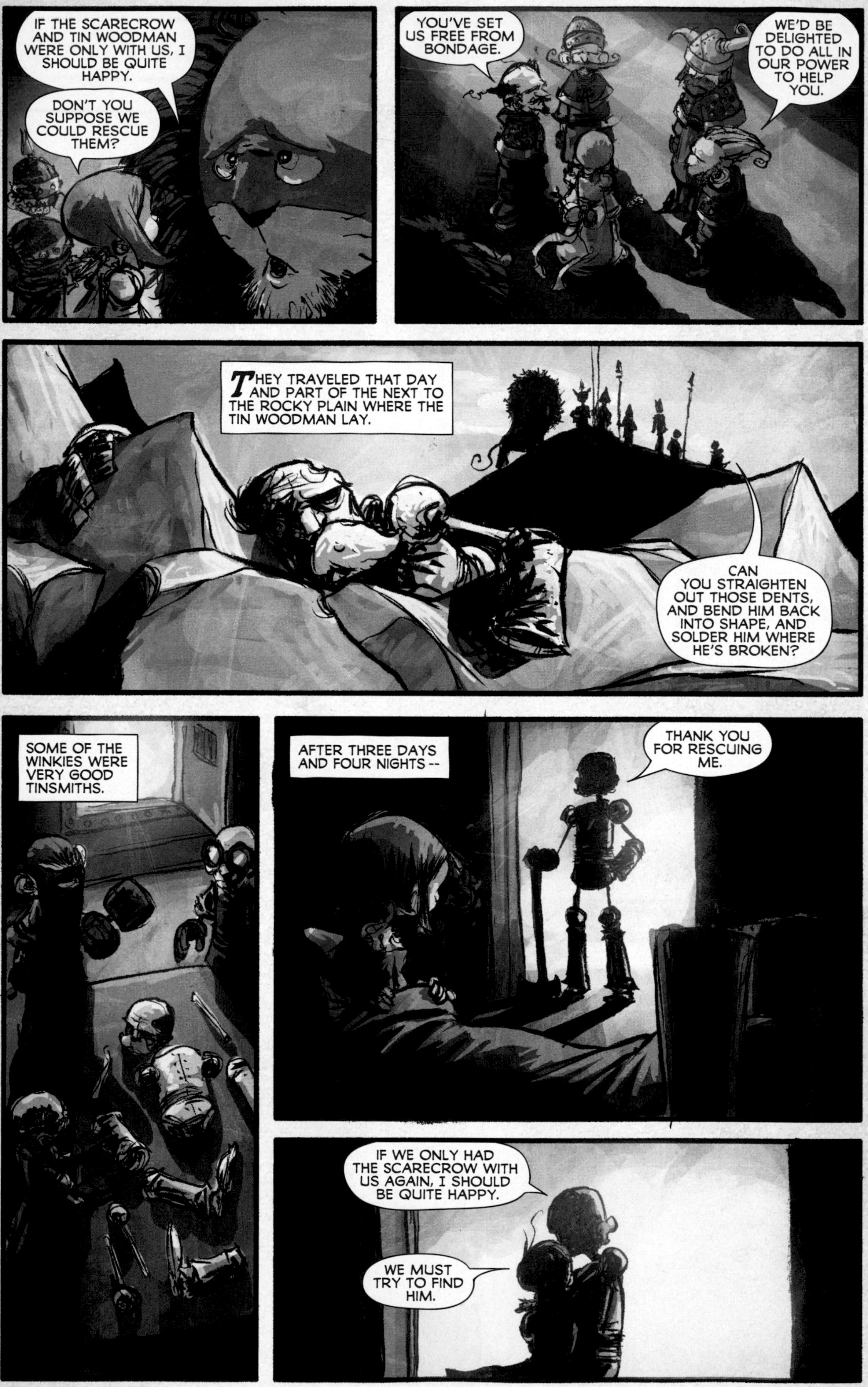
IF THE SCARECROW AND TIN WOODMAN WERE ONLY WITH US, I SHOULD BE QUITE HAPPY.
DON'T YOU SUPPOSE WE COULD RESCUE THEM?
YOU'VE SET US FREE FROM BONDAGE.
WE'D BE DELIGHTED TO DO ALL IN OUR POWER TO HELP YOU.
THEY TRAVELED THAT DAY AND PART OF THE NEXT TO THE ROCKY PLAIN WHERE THE TIN WOODMAN LAY.
CAN YOU STRAIGHTEN OUT THOSE DENTS, AND BEND HIM BACK INTO SHAPE, AND SOLDER HIM WHERE HE'S BROKEN?
SOME OF THE WINKIES WERE VERY GOOD TINSMITHS.
AFTER THREE DAYS AND FOUR NIGHTS --
THANK YOU FOR RESCUING ME.
IF WE ONLY HAD THE SCARECROW WITH US AGAIN, I SHOULD BE QUITE HAPPY.
WE MUST TRY TO FIND HIM.

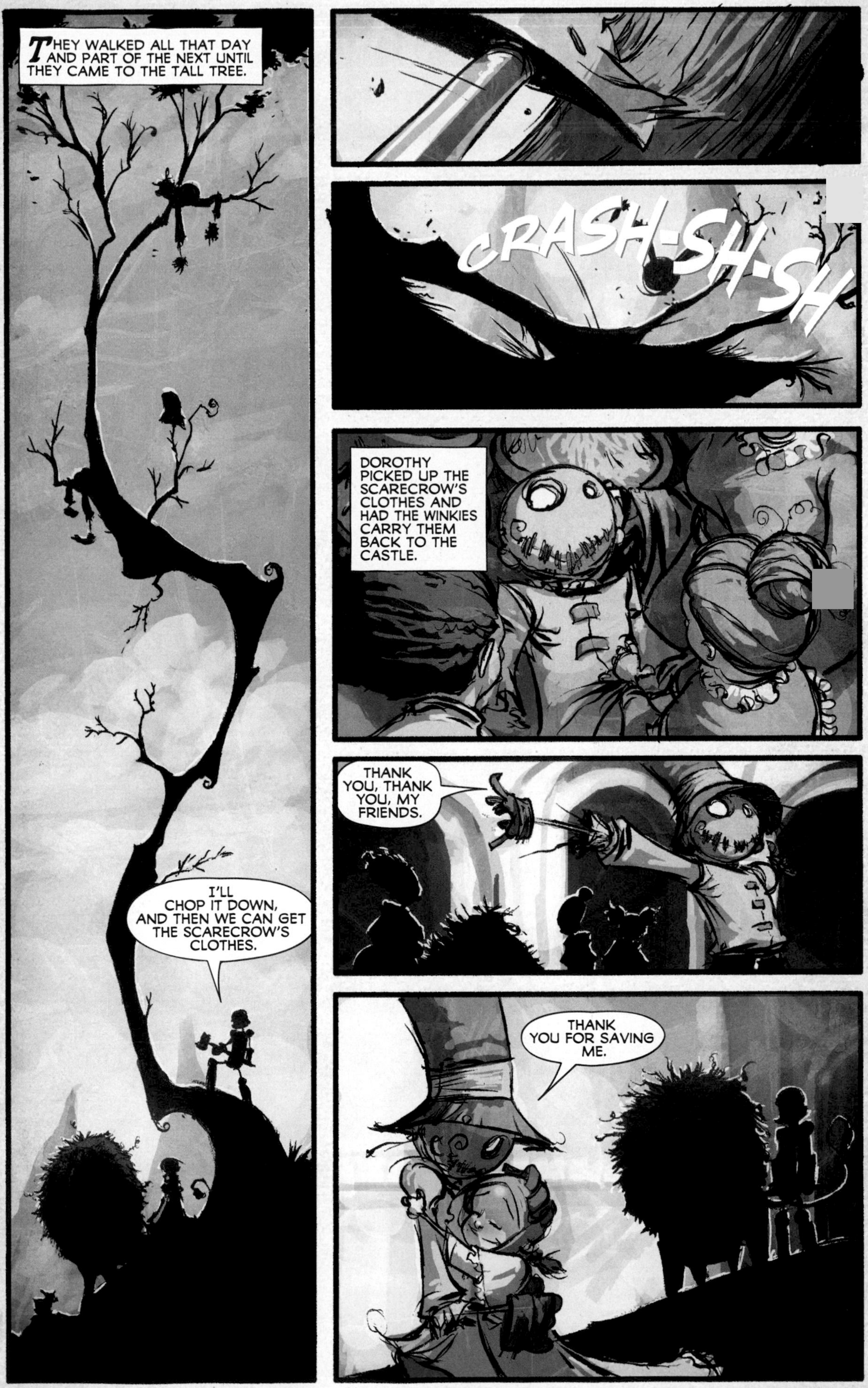
THEY WALKED ALL THAT DAY AND PART OF THE NEXT UNTIL THEY CAME TO THE TALL TREE.
I'LL CHOP IT DOWN, AND THEN WE CAN GET THE SCARECROW'S CLOTHES.
CRASH-SH-SH
DOROTHY PICKED UP THE SCARECROW'S CLOTHES AND HAD THE WINKIES CARRY THEM BACK TO THE CASTLE.
THANK YOU, THANK YOU, MY FRIENDS.
THANK YOU FOR SAVING ME.

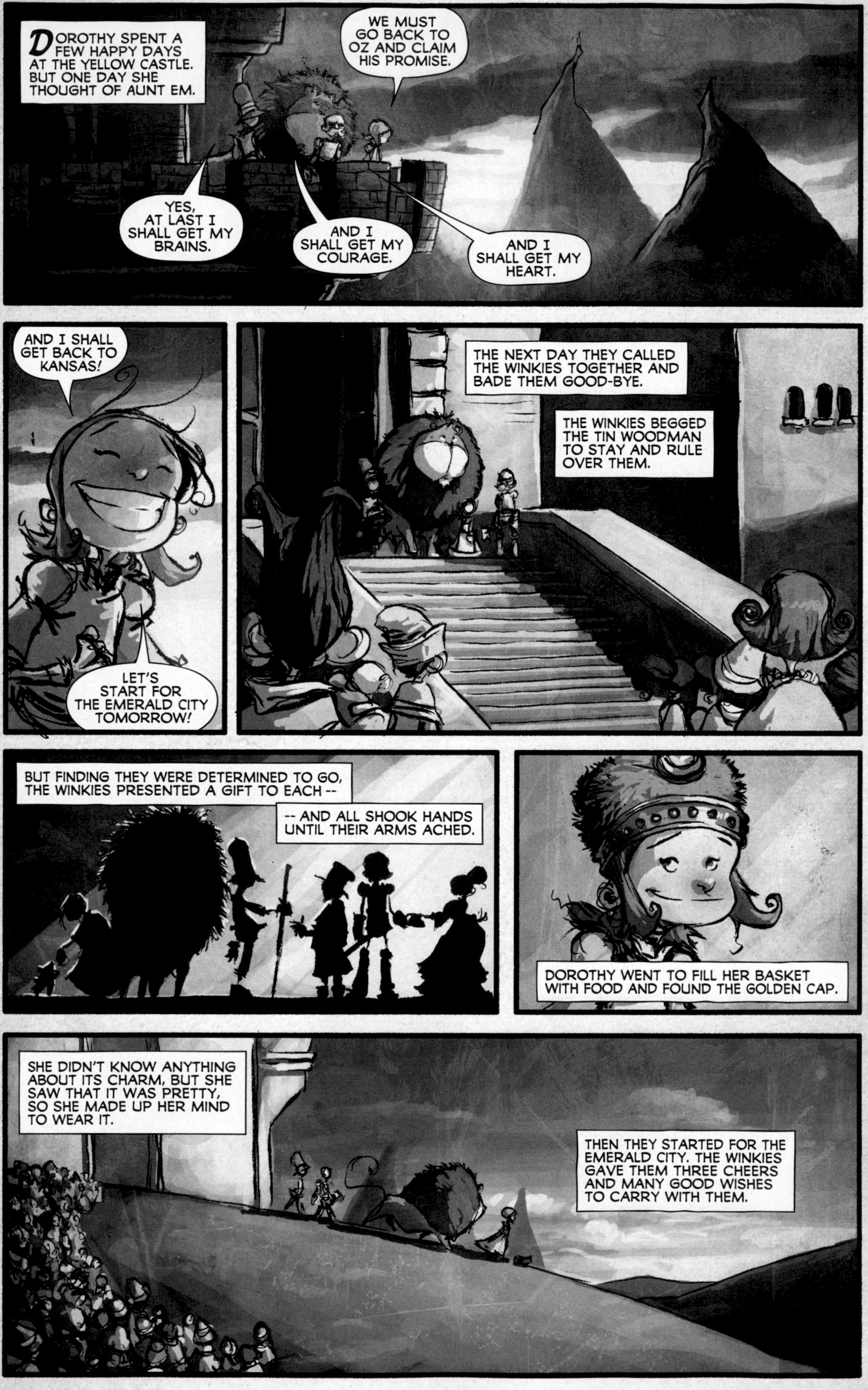
DOROTHY SPENT A FEW HAPPY DAYS AT THE YELLOW CASTLE. BUT ONE DAY SHE THOUGHT OF AUNT EM.
WE MUST GO BACK TO OZ AND CLAIM HIS PROMISE.
YES, AT LAST I SHALL GET MY BRAINS.
AND I SHALL GET MY COURAGE.
AND I SHALL GET MY HEART.
AND I SHALL GET BACK TO KANSAS!
LET'S START FOR THE EMERALD CITY TOMORROW!
THE NEXT DAY THEY CALLED THE WINKIES TOGETHER AND BADE THEM GOOD-BYE.
THE WINKIES BEGGED THE TIN WOODMAN TO STAY AND RULE OVER THEM.
BUT FINDING THEY WERE DETERMINED TO GO, THE WINKIES PRESENTED A GIFT TO EACH --
-- AND ALL SHOOK HANDS UNTIL THEIR ARMS ACHED.
DOROTHY WENT TO FILL HER BASKET WITH FOOD AND FOUND THE GOLDEN CAP.
SHE DIDN'T KNOW ANYTHING ABOUT ITS CHARM, BUT SHE SAW THAT IT WAS PRETTY, SO SHE MADE UP HER MIND TO WEAR IT.
THEN THEY STARTED FOR THE EMERALD CITY. THE WINKIES GAVE THEM THREE CHEERS AND MANY GOOD WISHES TO CARRY WITH THEM.

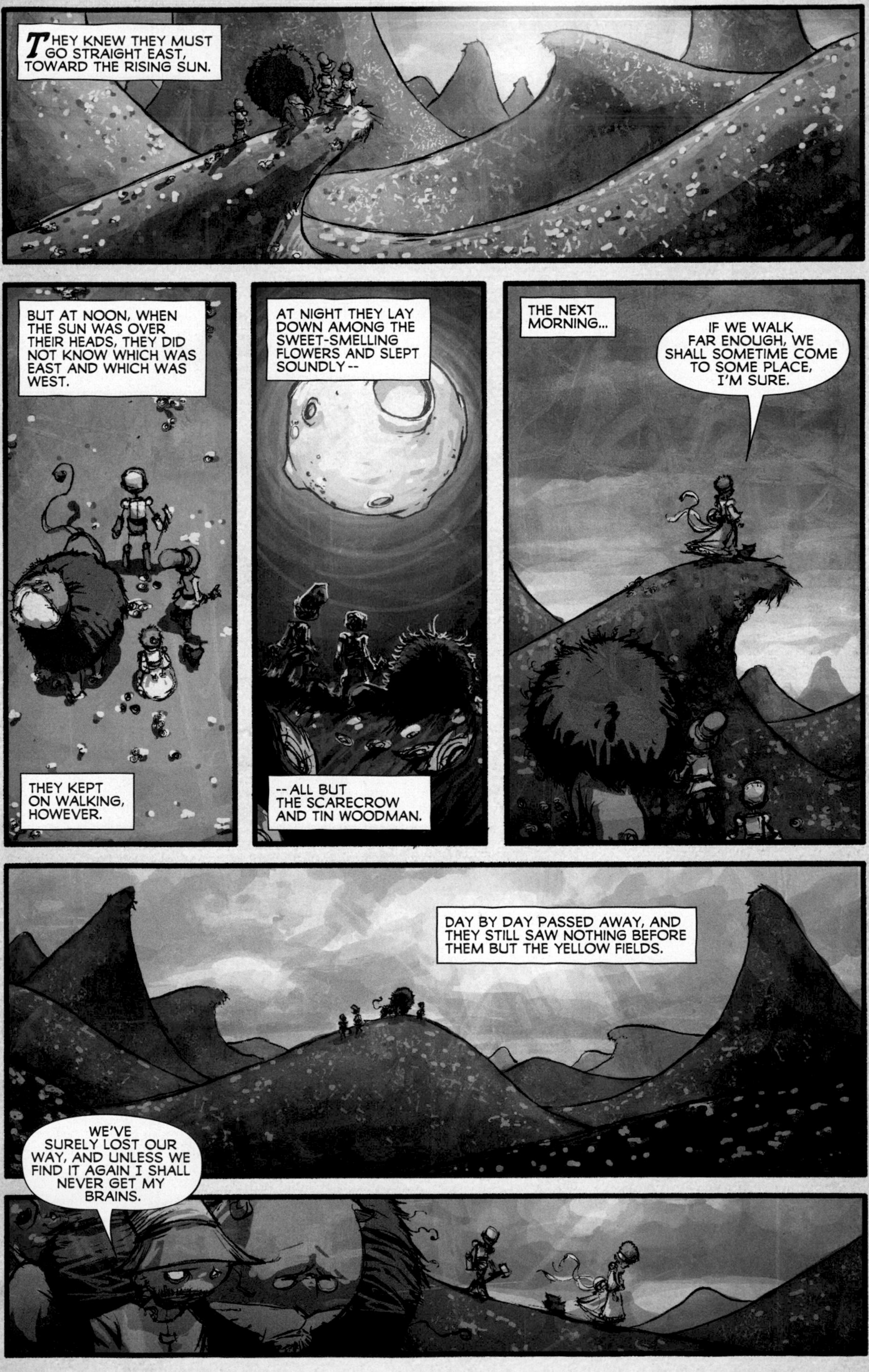
THEY KNEW THEY MUST GO STRAIGHT EAST, TOWARD THE RISING SUN.
BUT AT NOON, WHEN THE SUN WAS OVER THEIR HEADS, THEY DID NOT KNOW WHICH WAS EAST AND WHICH WAS WEST.
THEY KEPT ON WALKING, HOWEVER.
AT NIGHT THEY LAY DOWN AMONG THE SWEET-SMELLING FLOWERS AND SLEPT SOUNDLY --
-- ALL BUT THE SCARECROW AND TIN WOODMAN.
THE NEXT MORNING...
IF WE WALK FAR ENOUGH, WE SHALL SOMETIME COME TO SOME PLACE, I'M SURE.
DAY BY DAY PASSED AWAY, AND THEY STILL SAW NOTHING BEFORE THEM BUT THE YELLOW FIELDS.
WE'VE SURELY LOST OUR WAY, AND UNLESS WE FIND IT AGAIN I SHALL NEVER GET MY BRAINS.

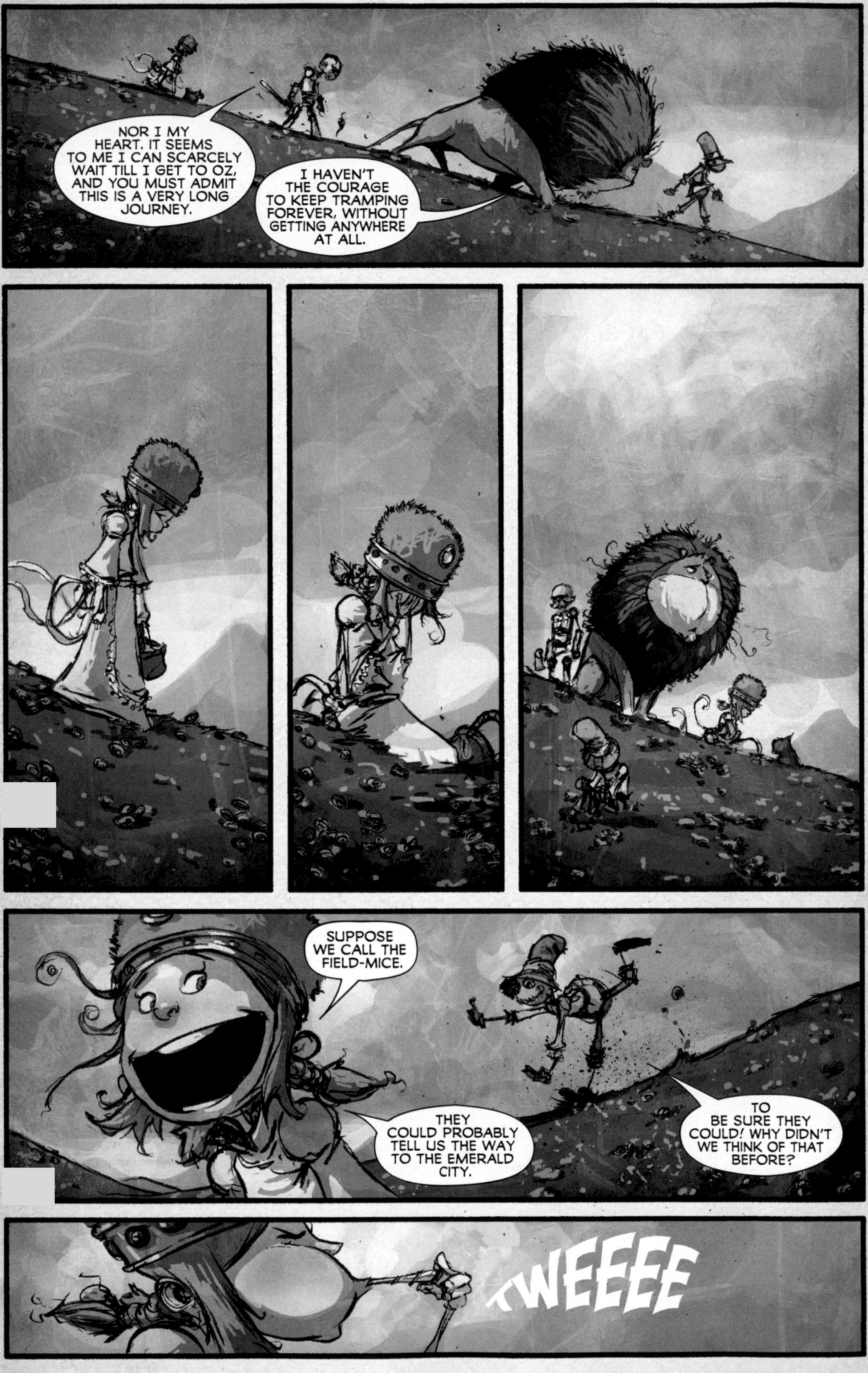
NOR I MY HEART. IT SEEMS TO ME I CAN SCARCELY WAIT TILL I GET TO OZ, AND YOU MUST ADMIT THIS IS A VERY LONG JOURNEY.
I HAVEN'T THE COURAGE TO KEEP TRAMPING FOREVER, WITHOUT GETTING ANYWHERE AT ALL.
SUPPOSE WE CALL THE FIELD-MICE.
THEY COULD PROBABLY TELL US THE WAY TO THE EMERALD CITY.
TO BE SURE THEY COULD! WHY DIDN'T WE THINK OF THAT BEFORE?
TWEEEE

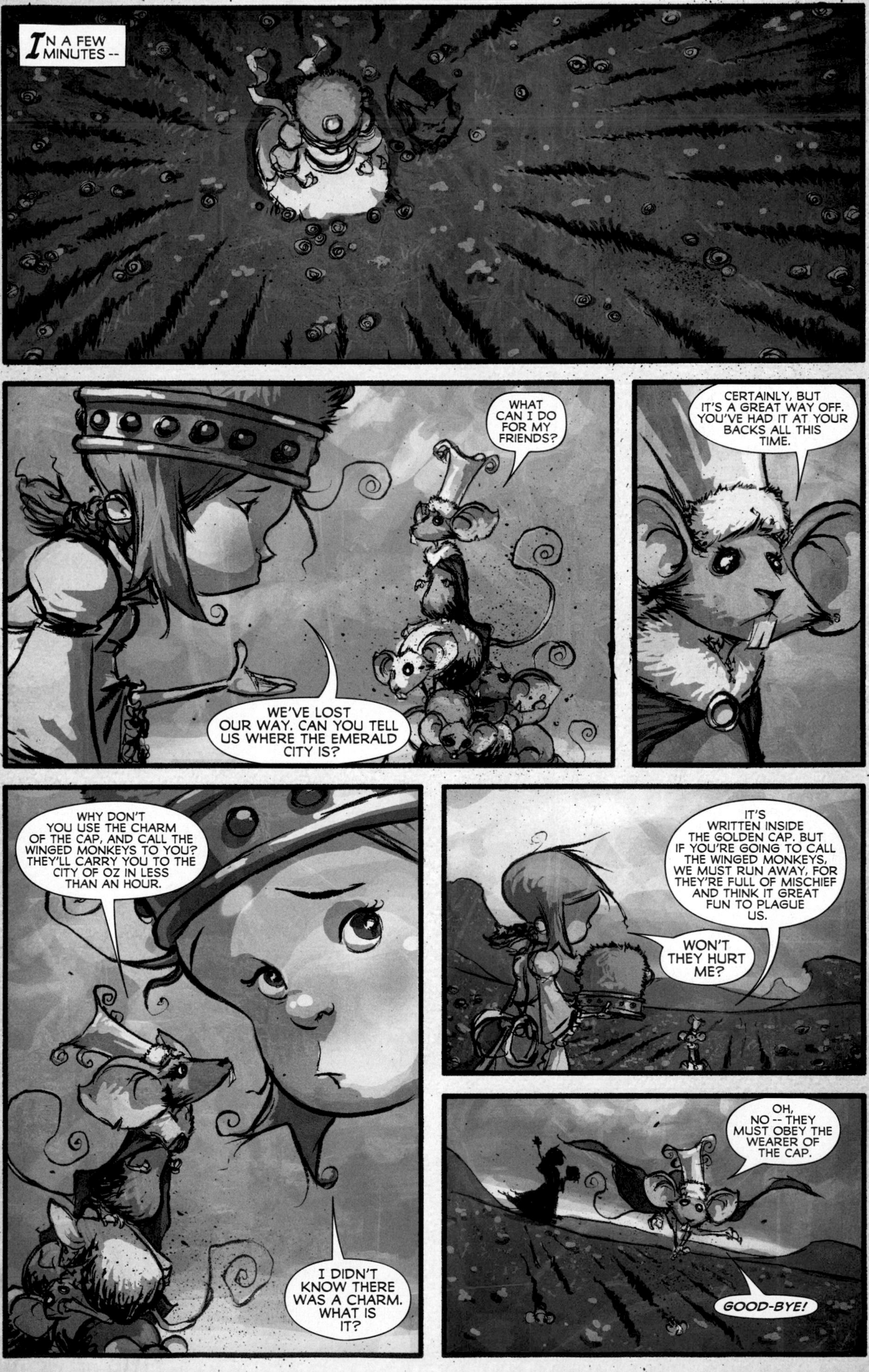
IN A FEW MINUTES --
WHAT CAN I DO FOR MY FRIENDS?
WE'VE LOST OUR WAY. CAN YOU TELL US WHERE THE EMERALD CITY IS?
CERTAINLY, BUT IT'S A GREAT WAY OFF. YOU'VE HAD IT AT YOUR BACKS ALL THIS TIME.
WHY DON'T YOU USE THE CHARM OF THE CAP, AND CALL THE WINGED MONKEYS TO YOU? THEY'LL CARRY YOU TO THE CITY OF OZ IN LESS THAN AN HOUR.
I DIDN'T KNOW THERE WAS A CHARM. WHAT IS IT?
IT'S WRITTEN INSIDE THE GOLDEN CAP. BUT IF YOU'RE GOING TO CALL THE WINGED MONKEYS, WE MUST RUN AWAY, FOR THEY'RE FULL OF MISCHIEF AND THINK IT GREAT FUN TO PLAGUE US.
WON'T THEY HURT ME?
OH, NO -- THEY MUST OBEY THE WEARER OF THE CAP.
GOOD-BYE!

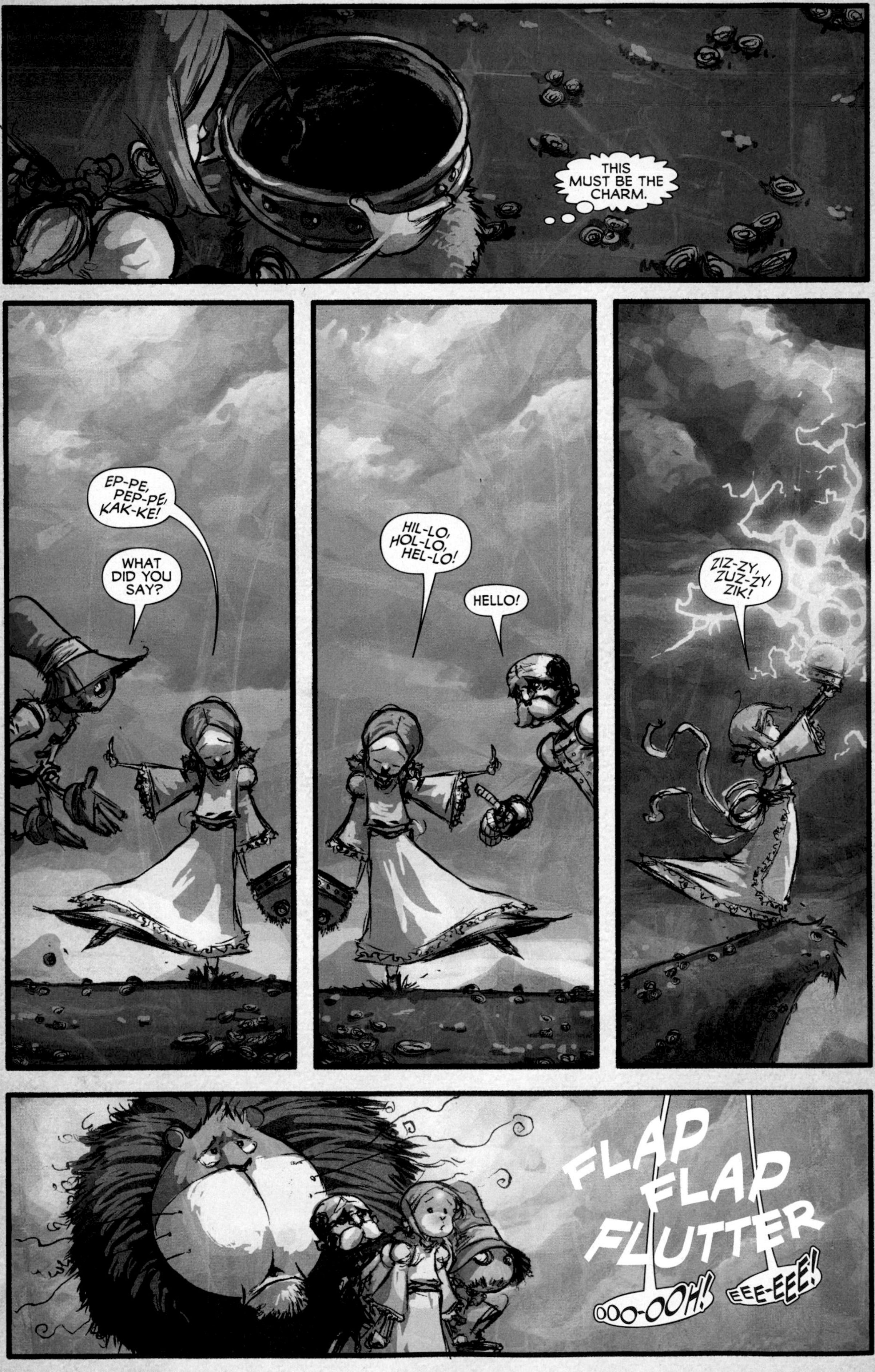
THIS MUST BE THE CHARM.
EP-PE, PEP-PE, KAK-KE!
WHAT DID YOU SAY?
HIL-LO, HOL-LO, HEL-LO!
HELLO!
ZIZ-ZY, ZUZ-ZY, ZIK!
FLAP FLAP FLUTTER
OOO-OOH!
EEE-EEE!

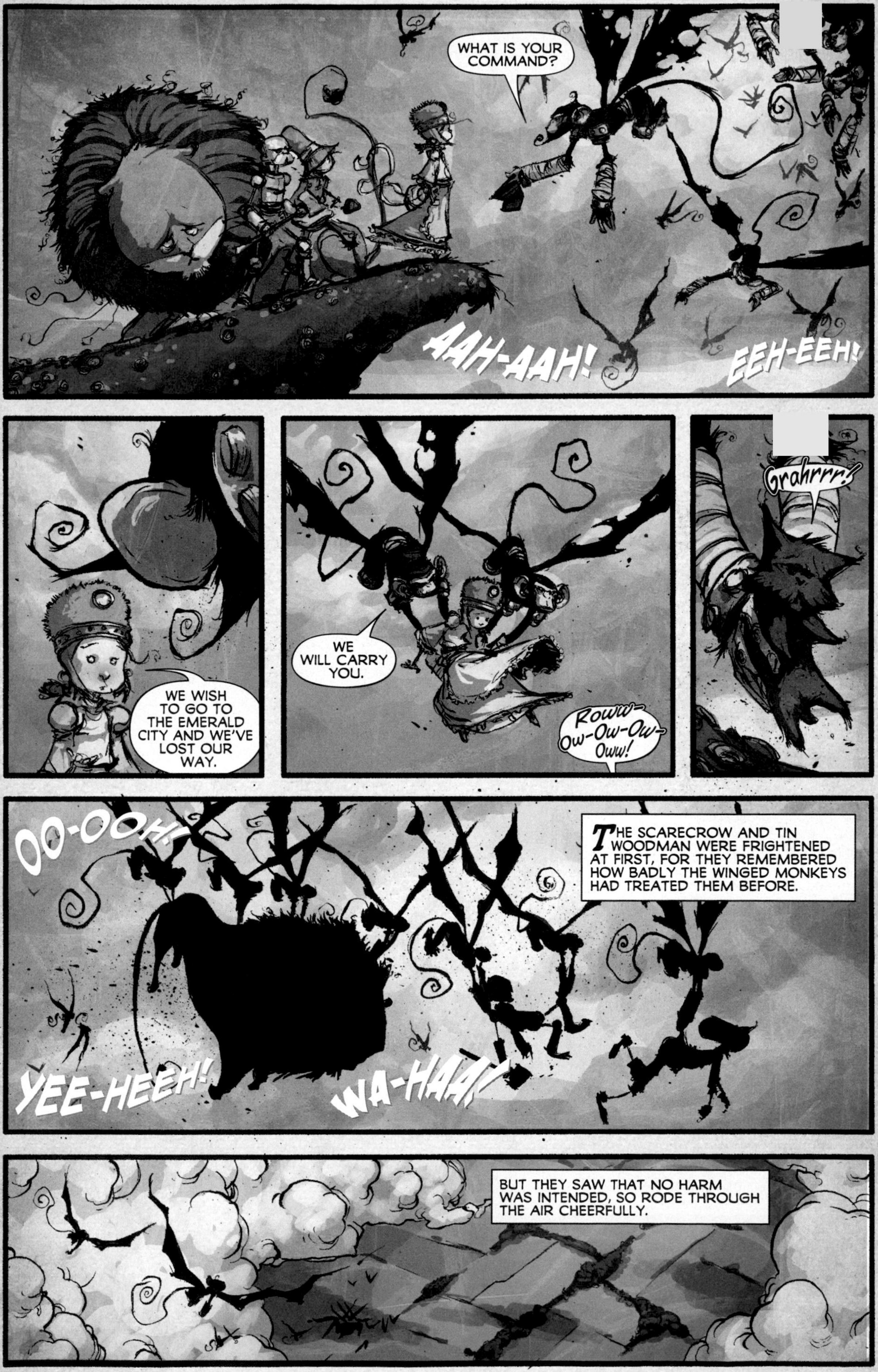
WHAT IS YOUR COMMAND?
AAH-AAH!
EEH-EEH!
WE WISH TO GO TO THE EMERALD CITY AND WE'VE LOST OUR WAY.
WE WILL CARRY YOU.
Roww-Ow-Ow-Ow-Oww!
Grahrrr!
OO-OOH!
THE SCARECROW AND TIN WOODMAN WERE FRIGHTENED AT FIRST, FOR THEY REMEMBERED HOW BADLY THE WINGED MONKEYS HAD TREATED THEM BEFORE.
YEE-HEEH!
WA-HAA!
BUT THEY SAW THAT NO HARM WAS INTENDED, SO RODE THROUGH THE AIR CHEERFULLY.

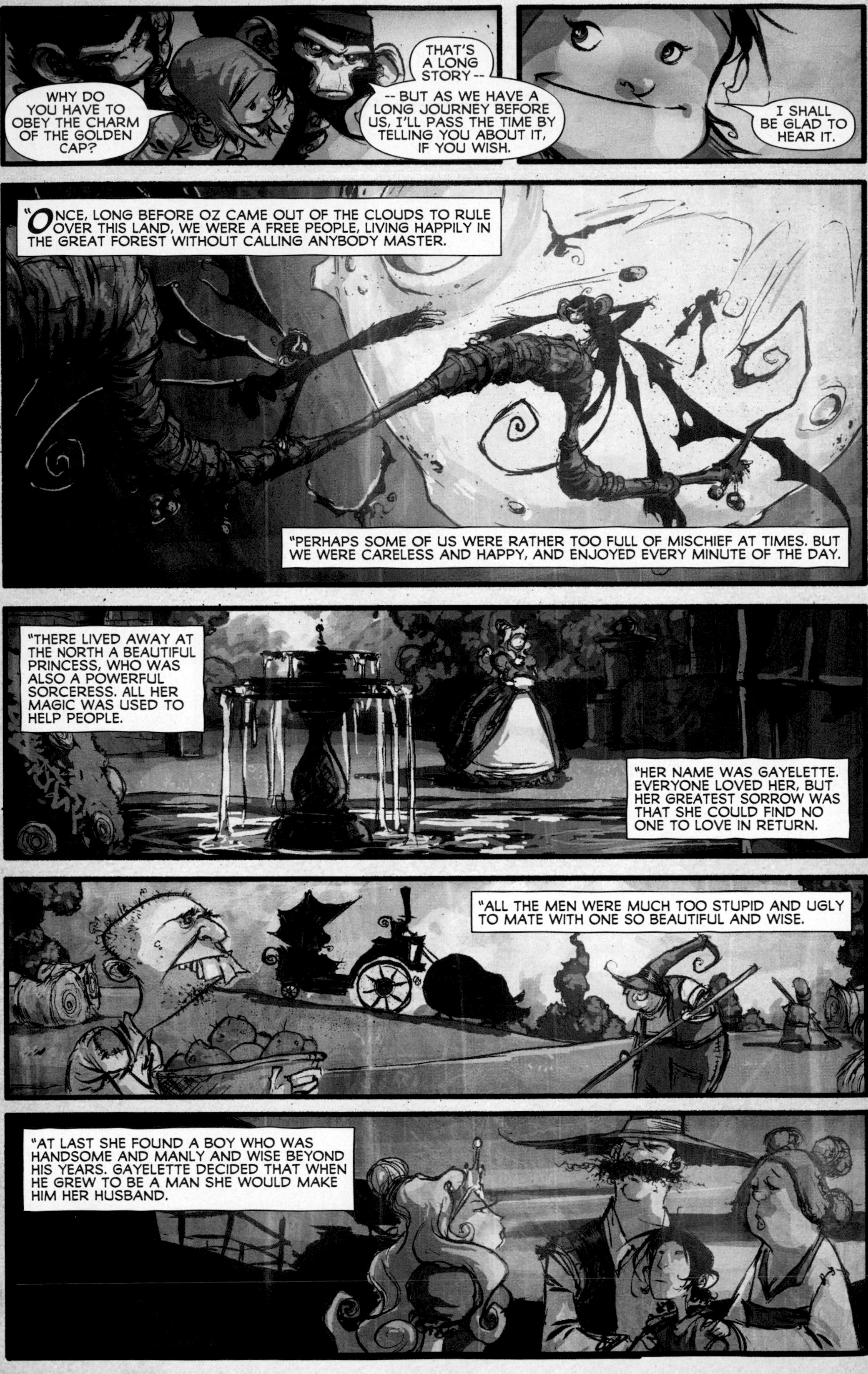
WHY DO YOU HAVE TO OBEY THE CHARM OF THE GOLDEN CAP?
THAT'S A LONG STORY --
-- BUT AS WE HAVE A LONG JOURNEY BEFORE US, I'LL PASS THE TIME BY TELLING YOU ABOUT IT, IF YOU WISH.
I SHALL BE GLAD TO HEAR IT.
"ONCE, LONG BEFORE OZ CAME OUT OF THE CLOUDS TO RULE OVER THIS LAND, WE WERE A FREE PEOPLE, LIVING HAPPILY IN THE GREAT FOREST WITHOUT CALLING ANYBODY MASTER.
"PERHAPS SOME OF US WERE RATHER TOO FULL OF MISCHIEF AT TIMES. BUT WE WERE CARELESS AND HAPPY, AND ENJOYED EVERY MINUTE OF THE DAY.
"THERE LIVED AWAY AT THE NORTH A BEAUTIFUL PRINCESS, WHO WAS ALSO A POWERFUL SORCERESS. ALL HER MAGIC WAS USED TO HELP PEOPLE.
"HER NAME WAS GAYELETTE. EVERYONE LOVED HER, BUT HER GREATEST SORROW WAS THAT SHE COULD FIND NO ONE TO LOVE IN RETURN.
"ALL THE MEN WERE MUCH TOO STUPID AND UGLY TO MATE WITH ONE SO BEAUTIFUL AND WISE.
"AT LAST SHE FOUND A BOY WHO WAS HANDSOME AND MANLY AND WISE BEYOND HIS YEARS. GAYELETTE DECIDED THAT WHEN HE GREW TO BE A MAN SHE WOULD MAKE HIM HER HUSBAND.

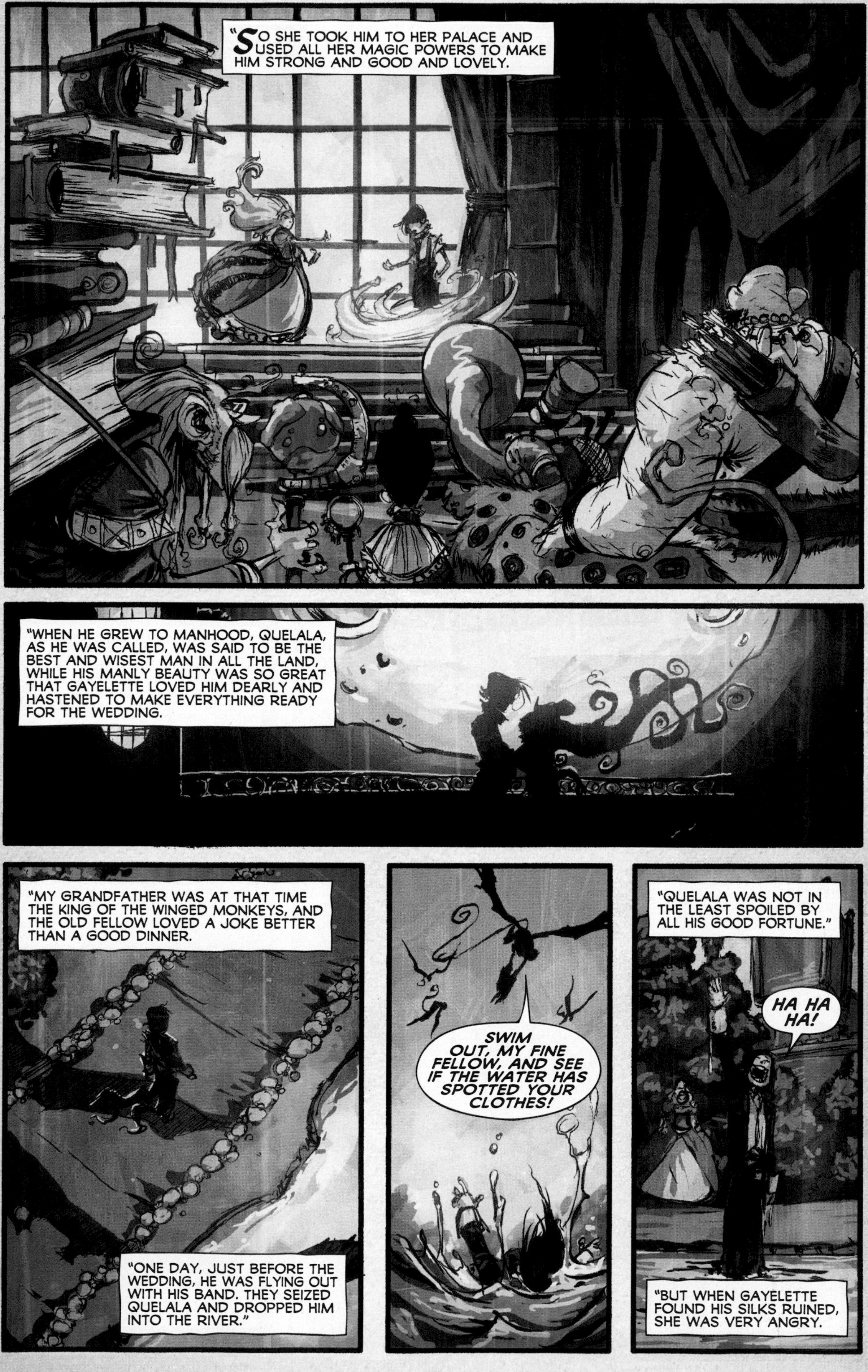
"SO SHE TOOK HIM TO HER PALACE AND USED ALL HER MAGIC POWERS TO MAKE HIM STRONG AND GOOD AND LOVELY.
"WHEN HE GREW TO MANHOOD, QUELALA, AS HE WAS CALLED, WAS SAID TO BE THE BEST AND WISEST MAN IN ALL THE LAND, WHILE HIS MANLY BEAUTY WAS SO GREAT THAT GAYELETTE LOVED HIM DEARLY AND HASTENED TO MAKE EVERYTHING READY FOR THE WEDDING.
"MY GRANDFATHER WAS AT THAT TIME THE KING OF THE WINGED MONKEYS, AND THE OLD FELLOW LOVED A JOKE BETTER THAN A GOOD DINNER.
"ONE DAY, JUST BEFORE THE WEDDING, HE WAS FLYING OUT WITH HIS BAND. THEY SEIZED QUELALA AND DROPPED HIM INTO THE RIVER."
SWIM OUT, MY FINE FELLOW, AND SEE IF THE WATER HAS SPOTTED YOUR CLOTHES!
"QUELALA WAS NOT IN THE LEAST SPOILED BY ALL HIS GOOD FORTUNE."
HA HA HA!
"BUT WHEN GAYELETTE FOUND HIS SILKS RUINED, SHE WAS VERY ANGRY.

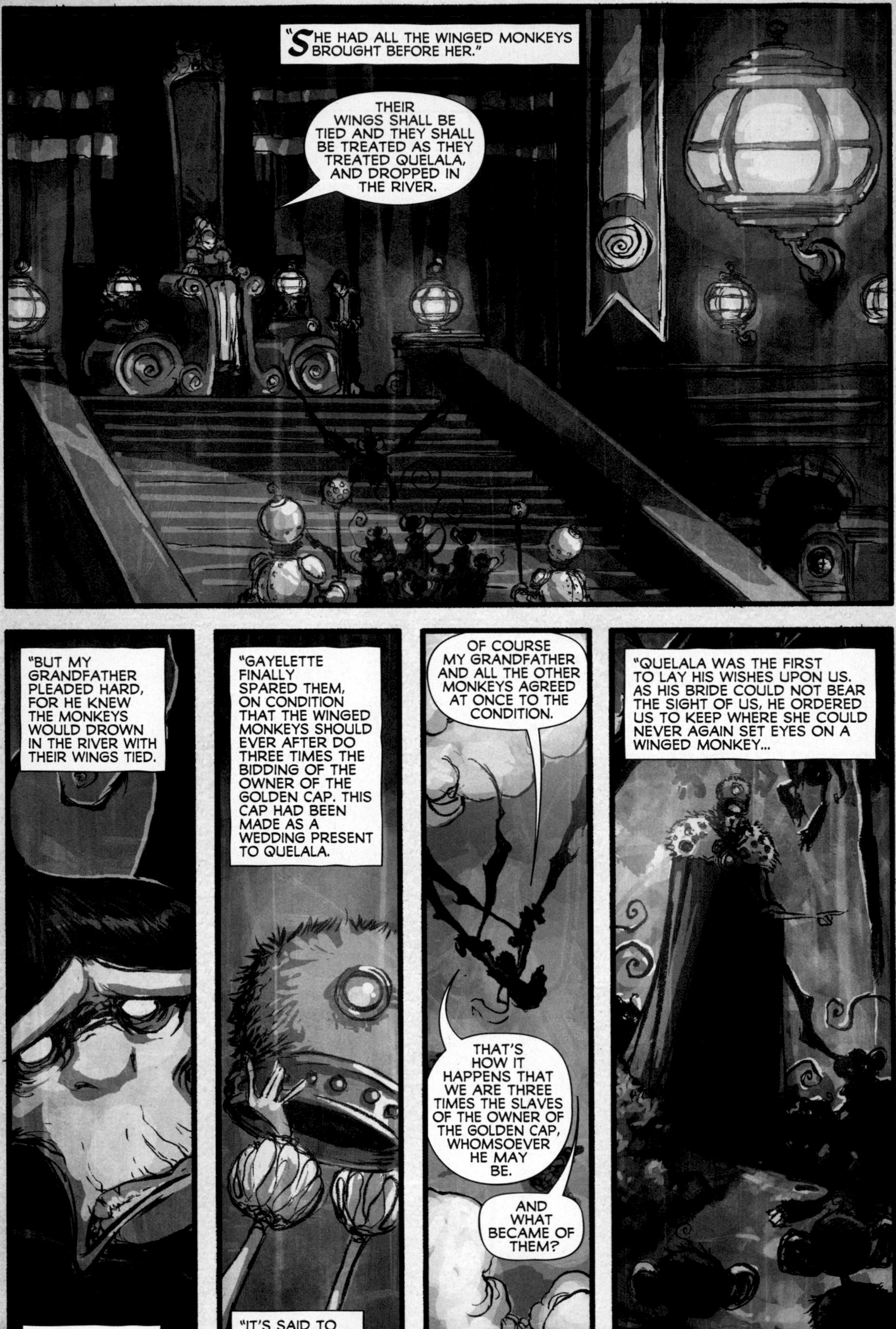
"SHE HAD ALL THE WINGED MONKEYS BROUGHT BEFORE HER."
THEIR WINGS SHALL BE TIED AND THEY SHALL BE TREATED AS THEY TREATED QUELALA, AND DROPPED IN THE RIVER.
"BUT MY GRANDFATHER PLEADED HARD, FOR HE KNEW THE MONKEYS WOULD DROWN IN THE RIVER WITH THEIR WINGS TIED.
"QUELALA SAID A KIND WORD FOR THEM ALSO.
"GAYELETTE FINALLY SPARED THEM, ON CONDITION THAT THE WINGED MONKEYS SHOULD EVER AFTER DO THREE TIMES THE BIDDING OF THE OWNER OF THE GOLDEN CAP. THIS CAP HAD BEEN MADE AS A WEDDING PRESENT TO QUELALA.
"IT'S SAID TO HAVE COST THE PRINCESS HALF HER KINGDOM."
OF COURSE MY GRANDFATHER AND ALL THE OTHER MONKEYS AGREED AT ONCE TO THE CONDITION.
THAT'S HOW IT HAPPENS THAT WE ARE THREE TIMES THE SLAVES OF THE OWNER OF THE GOLDEN CAP, WHOMSOEVER HE MAY BE.
AND WHAT BECAME OF THEM?
"QUELALA WAS THE FIRST TO LAY HIS WISHES UPON US. AS HIS BRIDE COULD NOT BEAR THE SIGHT OF US, HE ORDERED US TO KEEP WHERE SHE COULD NEVER AGAIN SET EYES ON A WINGED MONKEY...
"...WHICH WE WERE GLAD TO DO."

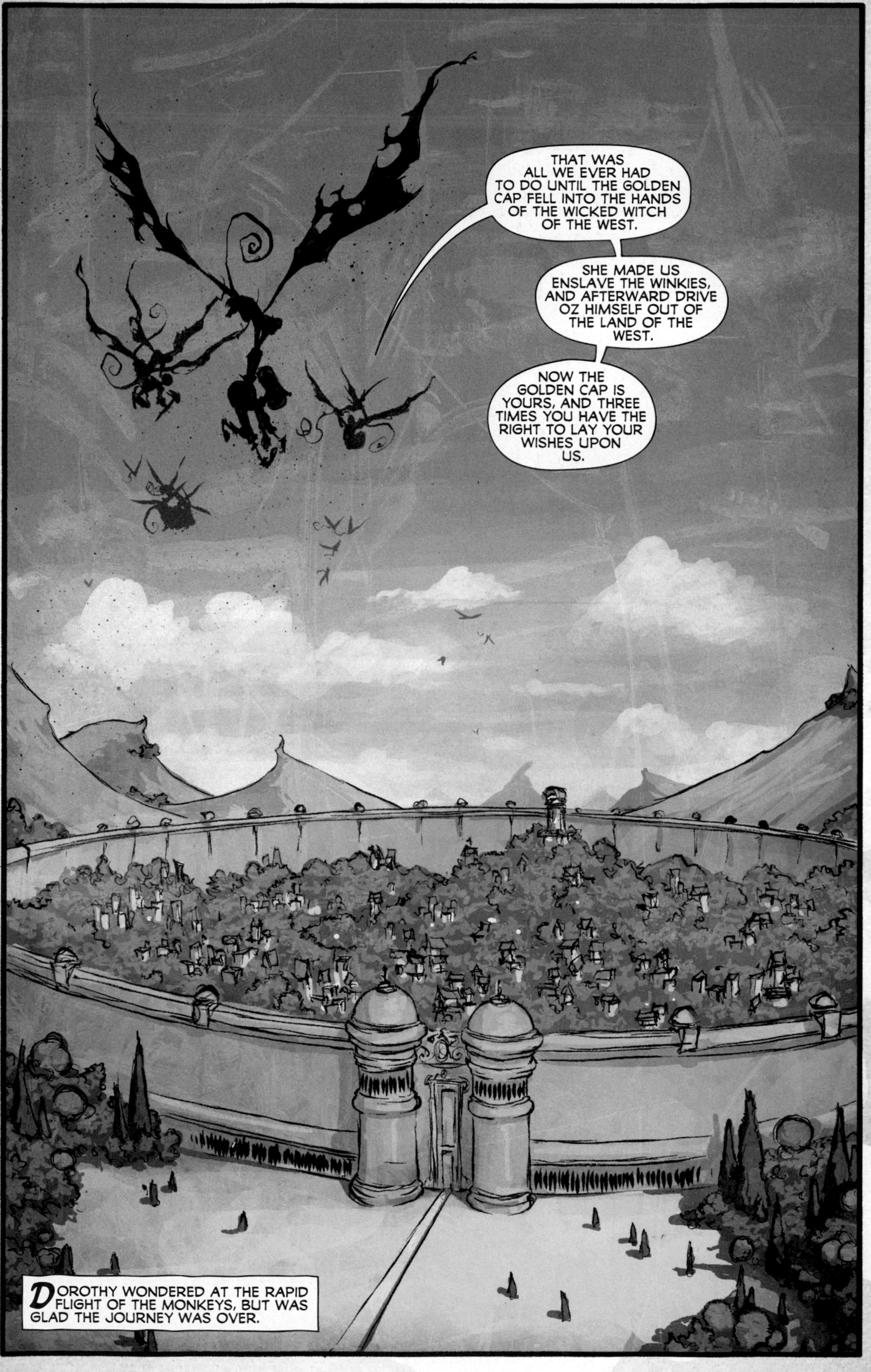
THAT WAS ALL WE EVER HAD TO DO UNTIL THE GOLDEN CAP FELL INTO THE HANDS OF THE WICKED WITCH OF THE WEST.
SHE MADE US ENSLAVE THE WINKIES, AND AFTERWARD DRIVE OZ HIMSELF OUT OF THE LAND OF THE WEST.
NOW THE GOLDEN CAP IS YOURS, AND THREE TIMES YOU HAVE THE RIGHT TO LAY YOUR WISHES UPON US.
DOROTHY WONDERED AT THE RAPID FLIGHT OF THE MONKEYS, BUT WAS GLAD THE JOURNEY WAS OVER.

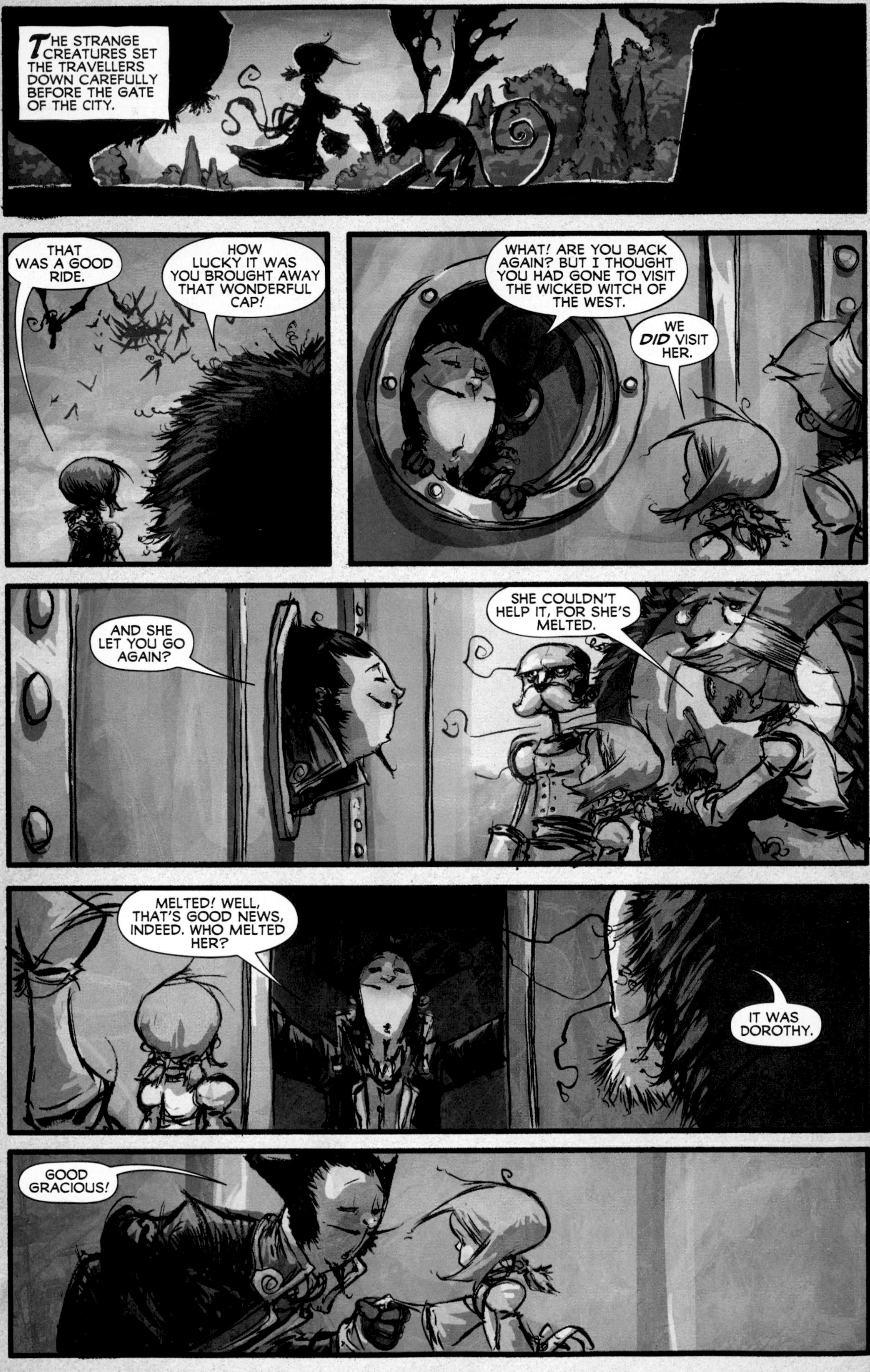
THE STRANGE CREATURES SET THE TRAVELLERS DOWN CAREFULLY BEFORE THE GATE OF THE CITY.
THAT WAS A GOOD RIDE.
HOW LUCKY IT WAS YOU BROUGHT AWAY THAT WONDERFUL CAP!
WHAT! ARE YOU BACK AGAIN? BUT I THOUGHT YOU HAD GONE TO VISIT THE WICKED WITCH OF THE WEST.
WE DID VISIT HER.
AND SHE LET YOU GO AGAIN?
SHE COULDN'T HELP IT, FOR SHE'S MELTED.
MELTED! WELL, THAT'S GOOD NEWS, INDEED. WHO MELTED HER?
IT WAS DOROTHY.
GOOD GRACIOUS!

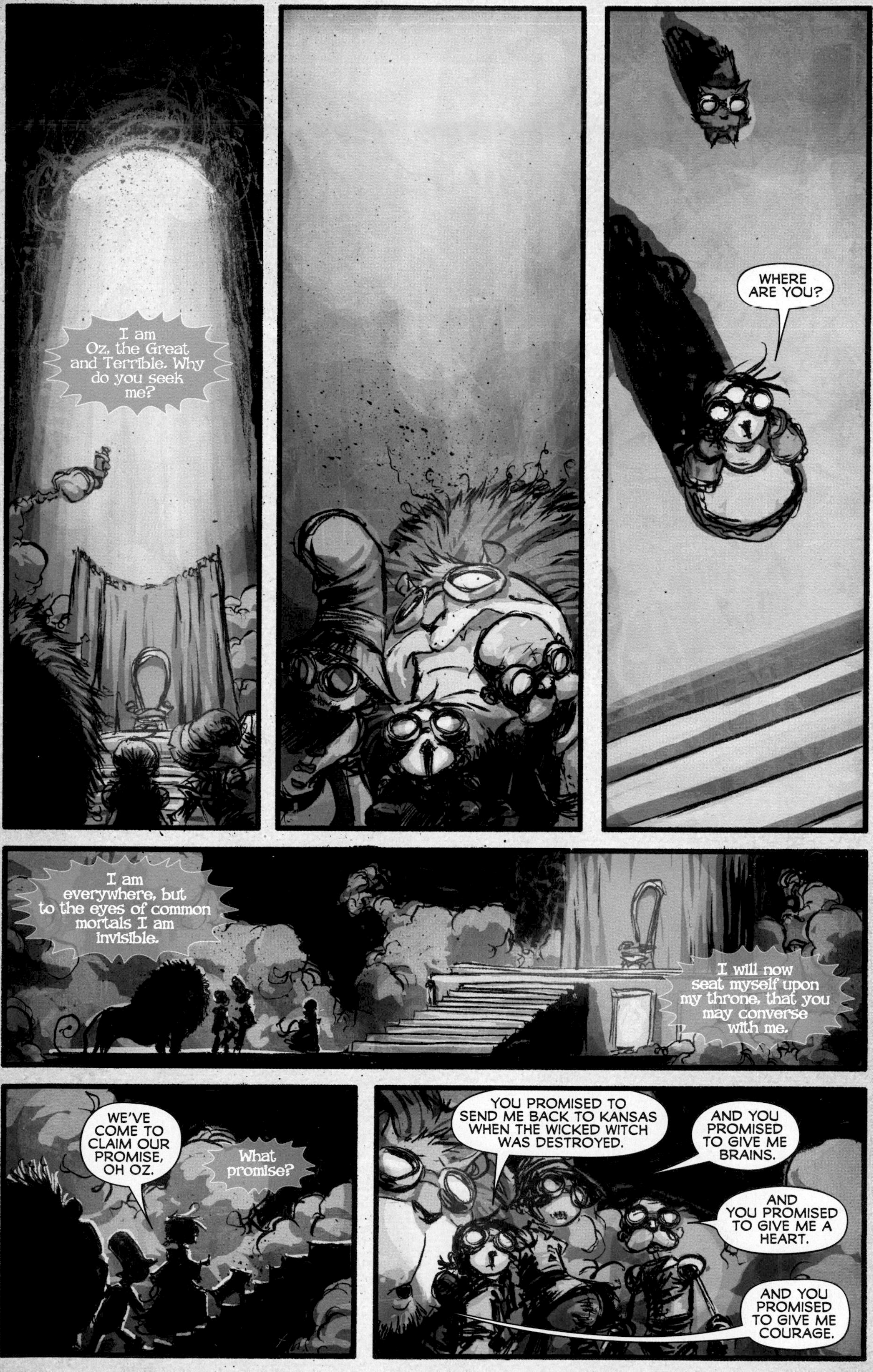
I am Oz, the Great and Terrible. Why do you seek me?
WHERE ARE YOU?
I am everywhere, but to the eyes of common mortals I am invisible.
I will now seat myself upon my throne, that you may converse with me.
WE'VE COME TO CLAIM OUR PROMISE, OH OZ.
What promise?
YOU PROMISED TO SEND ME BACK TO KANSAS WHEN THE WICKED WITCH WAS DESTROYED.
AND YOU PROMISED TO GIVE ME BRAINS.
AND YOU PROMISED TO GIVE ME A HEART.
AND YOU PROMISED TO GIVE ME COURAGE.

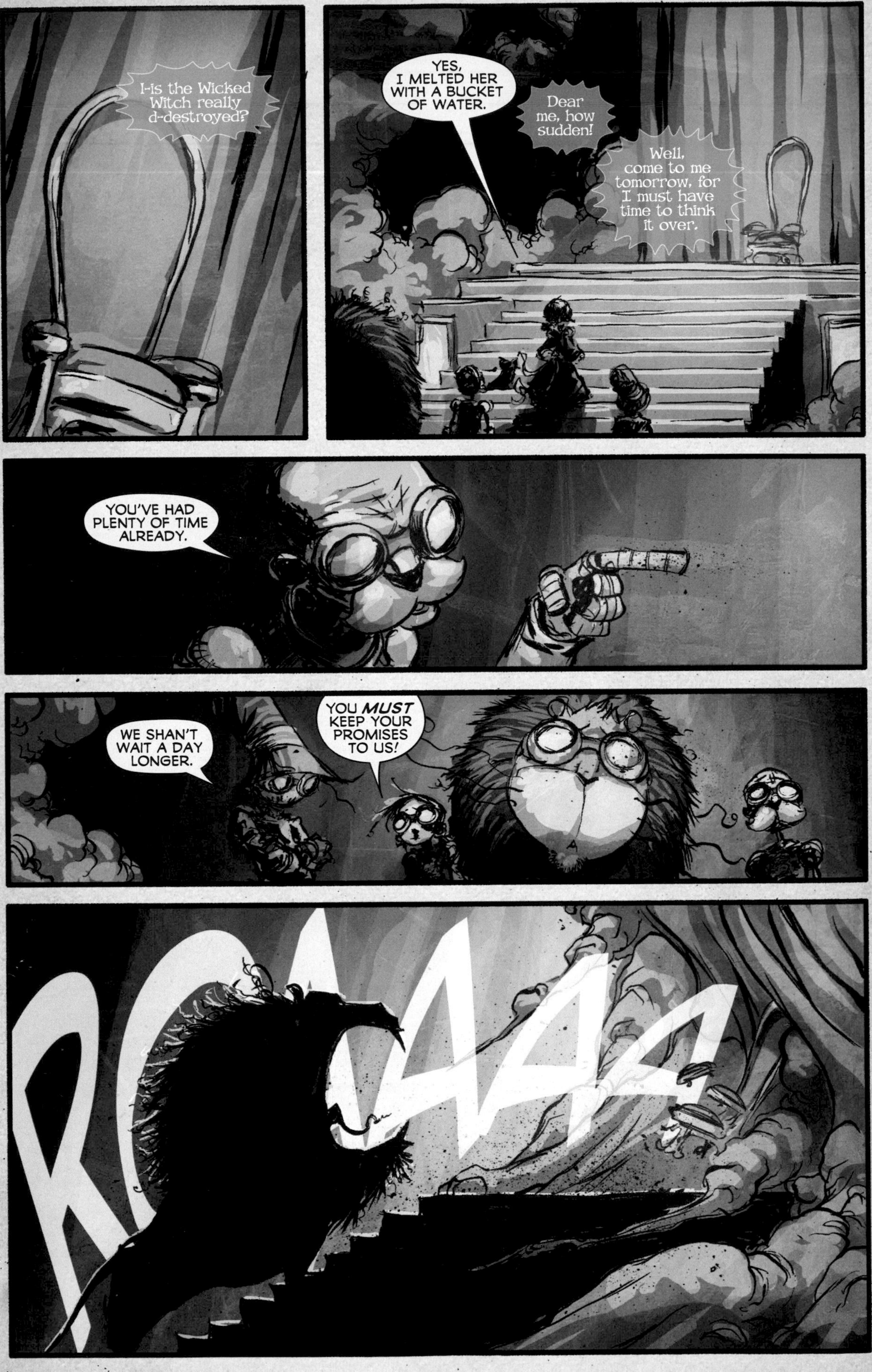

I-is the Wicked Witch really d-destroyed?
YES, I MELTED HER WITH A BUCKET OF WATER.
Dear me, how sudden!
Well, come to me tomorrow, for I must have time to think it over.
YOU'VE HAD PLENTY OF TIME ALREADY.
WE SHAN'T WAIT A DAY LONGER.
YOU MUST KEEP YOUR PROMISES TO US!

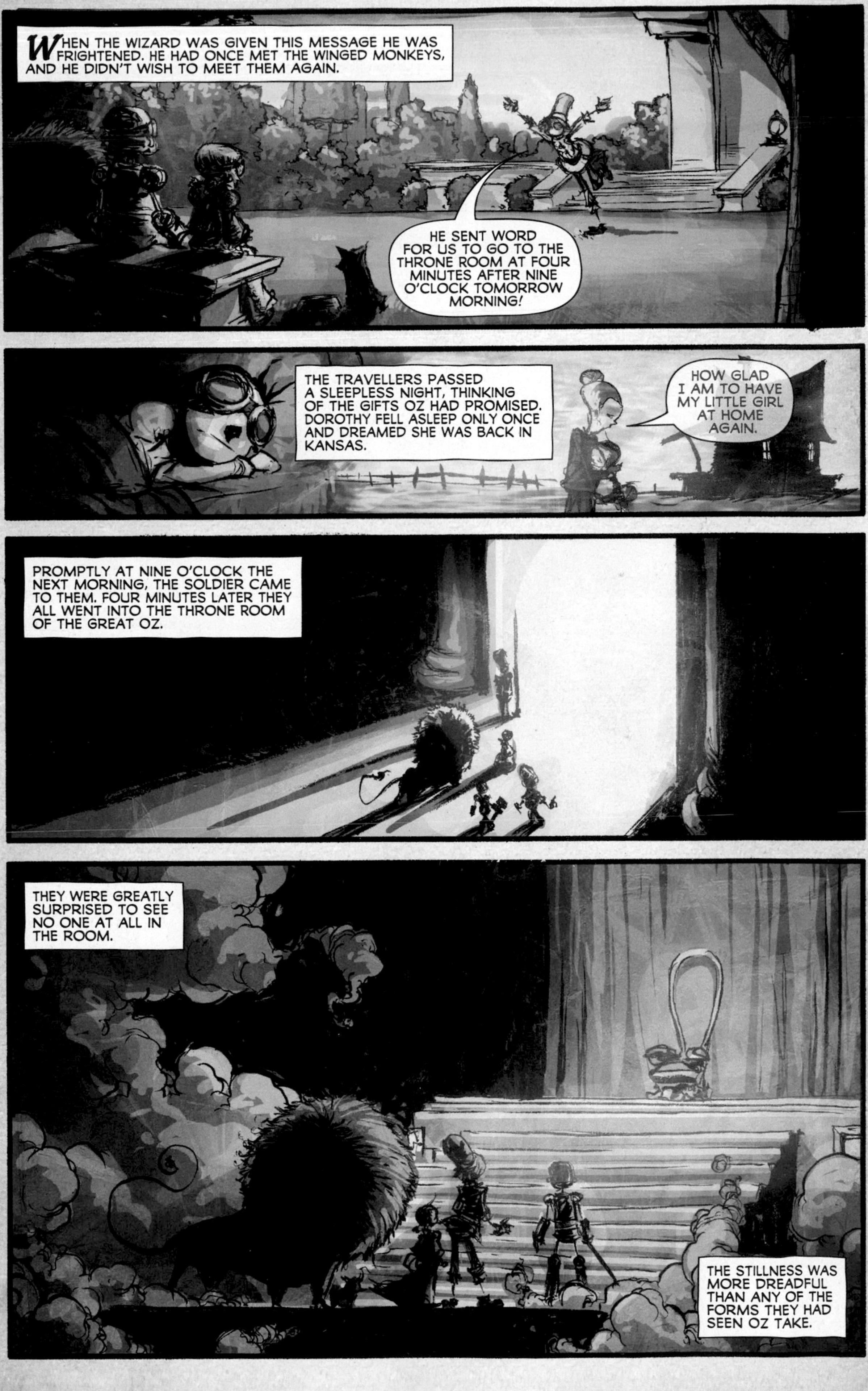

WHEN THE WIZARD WAS GIVEN THIS MESSAGE HE WAS FRIGHTENED. HE HAD ONCE MET THE WINGED MONKEYS, AND HE DIDN'T WISH TO MEET THEM AGAIN.
HE SENT WORD FOR US TO GO TO THE THRONE ROOM AT FOUR MINUTES AFTER NINE O'CLOCK TOMORROW MORNING!
THE TRAVELLERS PASSED A SLEEPLESS NIGHT, THINKING OF THE GIFTS OZ HAD PROMISED. DOROTHY FELL ASLEEP ONLY ONCE AND DREAMED SHE WAS BACK IN KANSAS.
HOW GLAD I AM TO HAVE MY LITTLE GIRL AT HOME AGAIN.
PROMPTLY AT NINE O'CLOCK THE NEXT MORNING, THE SOLDIER CAME TO THEM. FOUR MINUTES LATER THEY ALL WENT INTO THE THRONE ROOM OF THE GREAT OZ.
THEY WERE GREATLY SURPRISED TO SEE NO ONE AT ALL IN THE ROOM.
THE STILLNESS WAS MORE DREADFUL THAN ANY OF THE FORMS THEY HAD SEEN OZ TAKE.

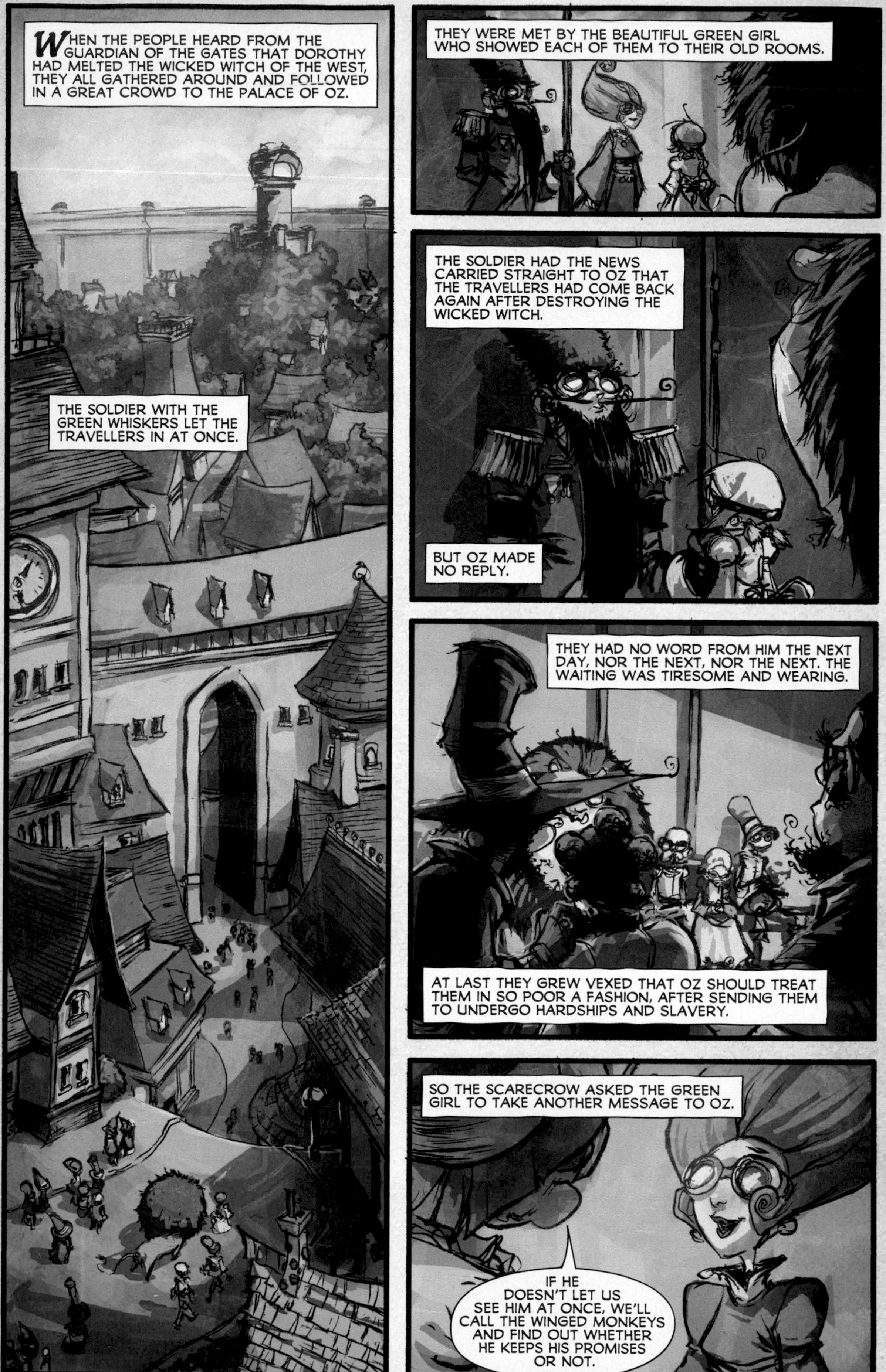
WHEN THE PEOPLE HEARD FROM THE GUARDIAN OF THE GATES THAT DOROTHY HAD MELTED THE WICKED WITCH OF THE WEST, THEY ALL GATHERED AROUND AND FOLLOWED IN A GREAT CROWD TO THE PALACE OF OZ.
THE SOLDIER WITH THE GREEN WHISKERS LET THE TRAVELLERS IN AT ONCE.
THEY WERE MET BY THE BEAUTIFUL GREEN GIRL WHO SHOWED EACH OF THEM TO THEIR OLD ROOMS.
THE SOLDIER HAD THE NEWS CARRIED STRAIGHT TO OZ THAT THE TRAVELLERS HAD COME BACK AGAIN AFTER DESTROYING THE WICKED WITCH.
BUT OZ MADE NO REPLY.
THEY HAD NO WORD FROM HIM THE NEXT DAY, NOR THE NEXT, NOR THE NEXT. THE WAITING WAS TIRESOME AND WEARING.
AT LAST THEY GREW VEXED THAT OZ SHOULD TREAT THEM IN SO POOR A FASHION, AFTER SENDING THEM TO UNDERGO HARDSHIPS AND SLAVERY.
SO THE SCARECROW ASKED THE GREEN GIRL TO TAKE ANOTHER MESSAGE TO OZ.
IF HE DOESN'T LET US SEE HIM AT ONCE, WE'LL CALL THE WINGED MONKEYS AND FIND OUT WHETHER HE KEEPS HIS PROMISES OR NOT.

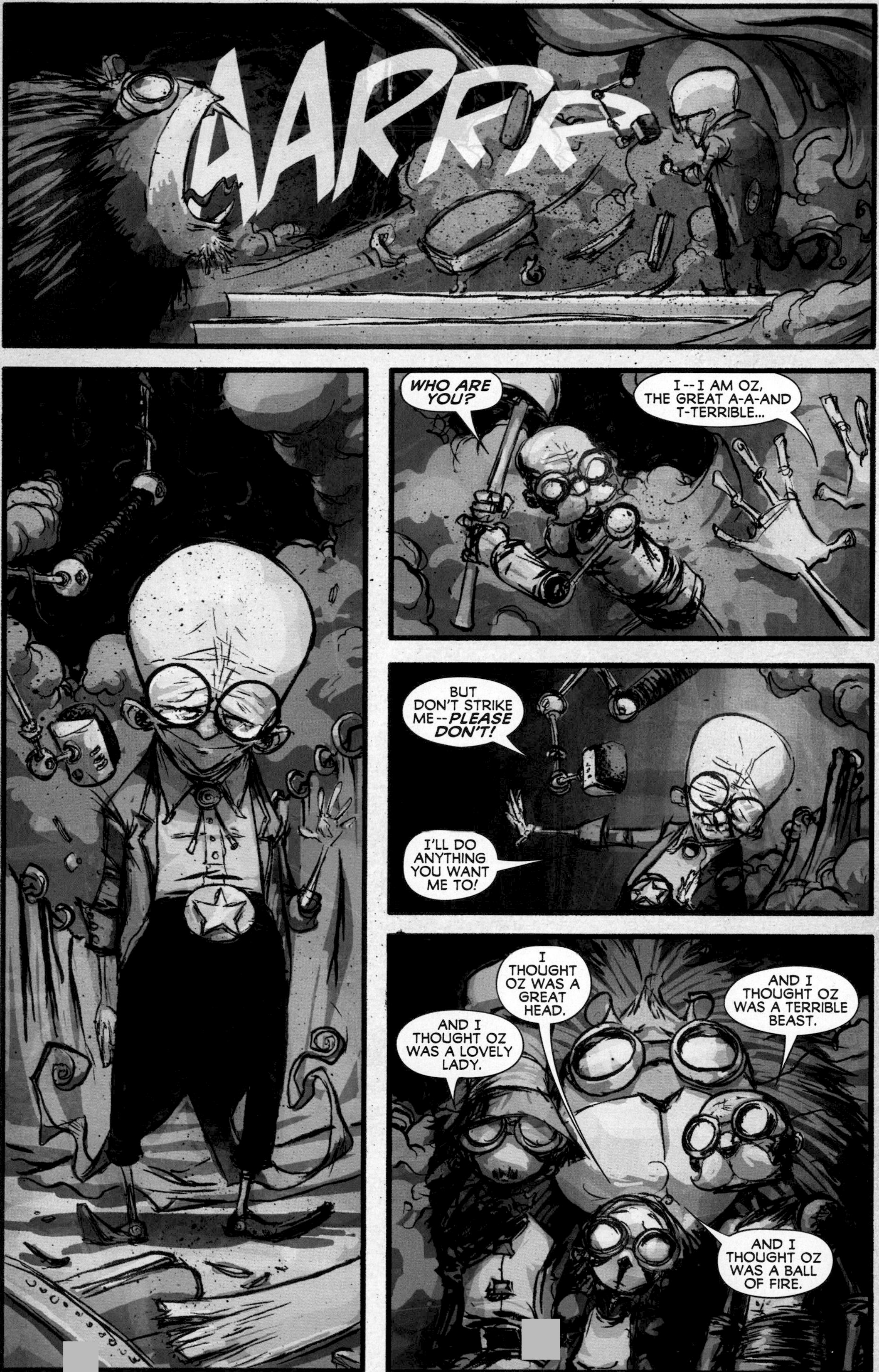
AARRR
WHO ARE YOU?
I -- I AM OZ, THE GREAT A-A-AND T-TERRIBLE...
BUT DON'T STRIKE ME -- *PLEASE DON'T!*
I'LL DO ANYTHING YOU WANT ME TO!
I THOUGHT OZ WAS A GREAT HEAD.
AND I THOUGHT OZ WAS A LOVELY LADY.
AND I THOUGHT OZ WAS A TERRIBLE BEAST.
AND I THOUGHT OZ WAS A BALL OF FIRE.

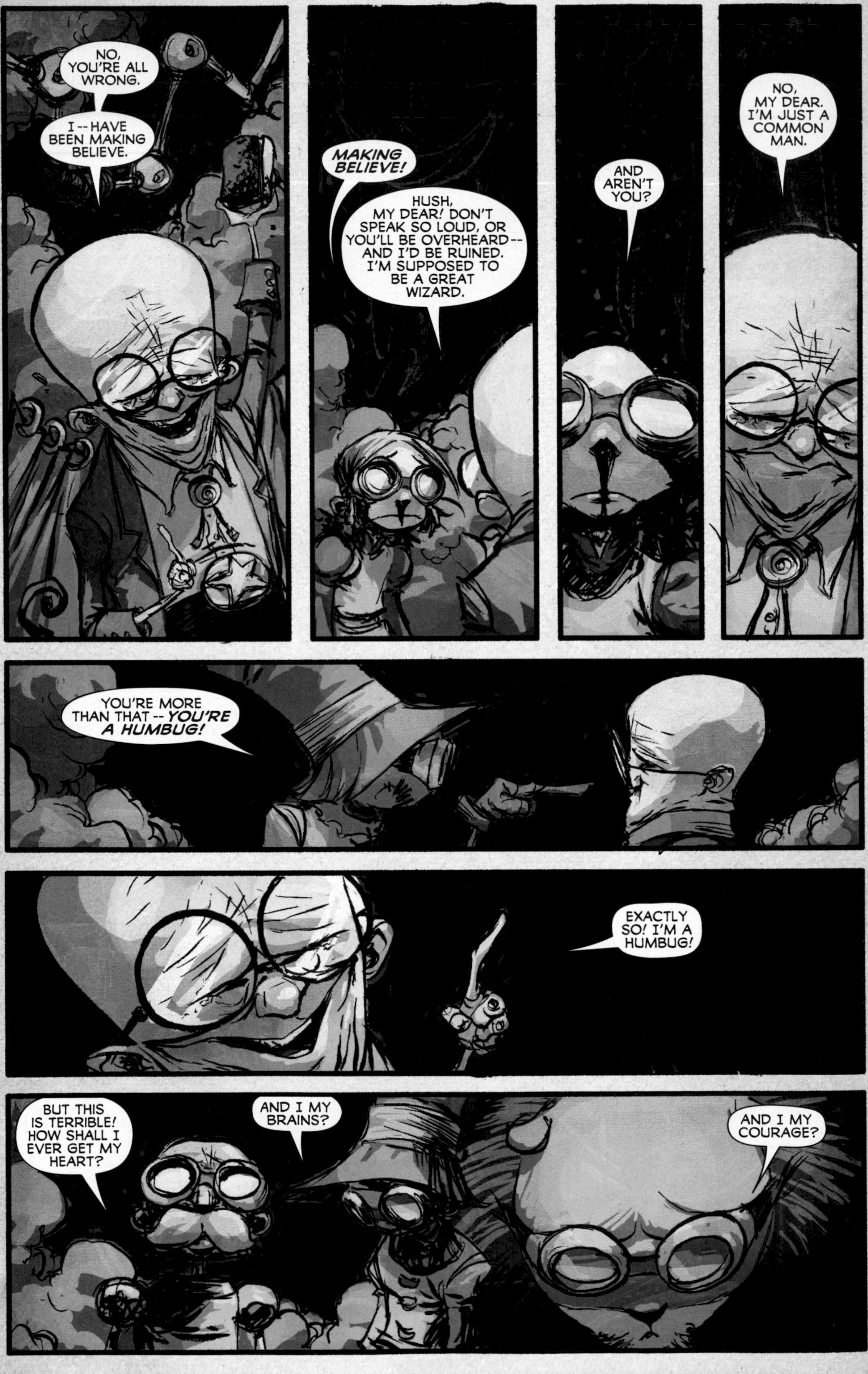
NO, YOU'RE ALL WRONG.
I -- HAVE BEEN MAKING BELIEVE.
MAKING BELIEVE!
HUSH, MY DEAR! DON'T SPEAK SO LOUD, OR YOU'LL BE OVERHEARD -- AND I'D BE RUINED. I'M SUPPOSED TO BE A GREAT WIZARD.
AND AREN'T YOU?
NO, MY DEAR. I'M JUST A COMMON MAN.
YOU'RE MORE THAN THAT -- YOU'RE A HUMBUG!
EXACTLY SO! I'M A HUMBUG!
BUT THIS IS TERRIBLE! HOW SHALL I EVER GET MY HEART?
AND I MY BRAINS?
AND I MY COURAGE?

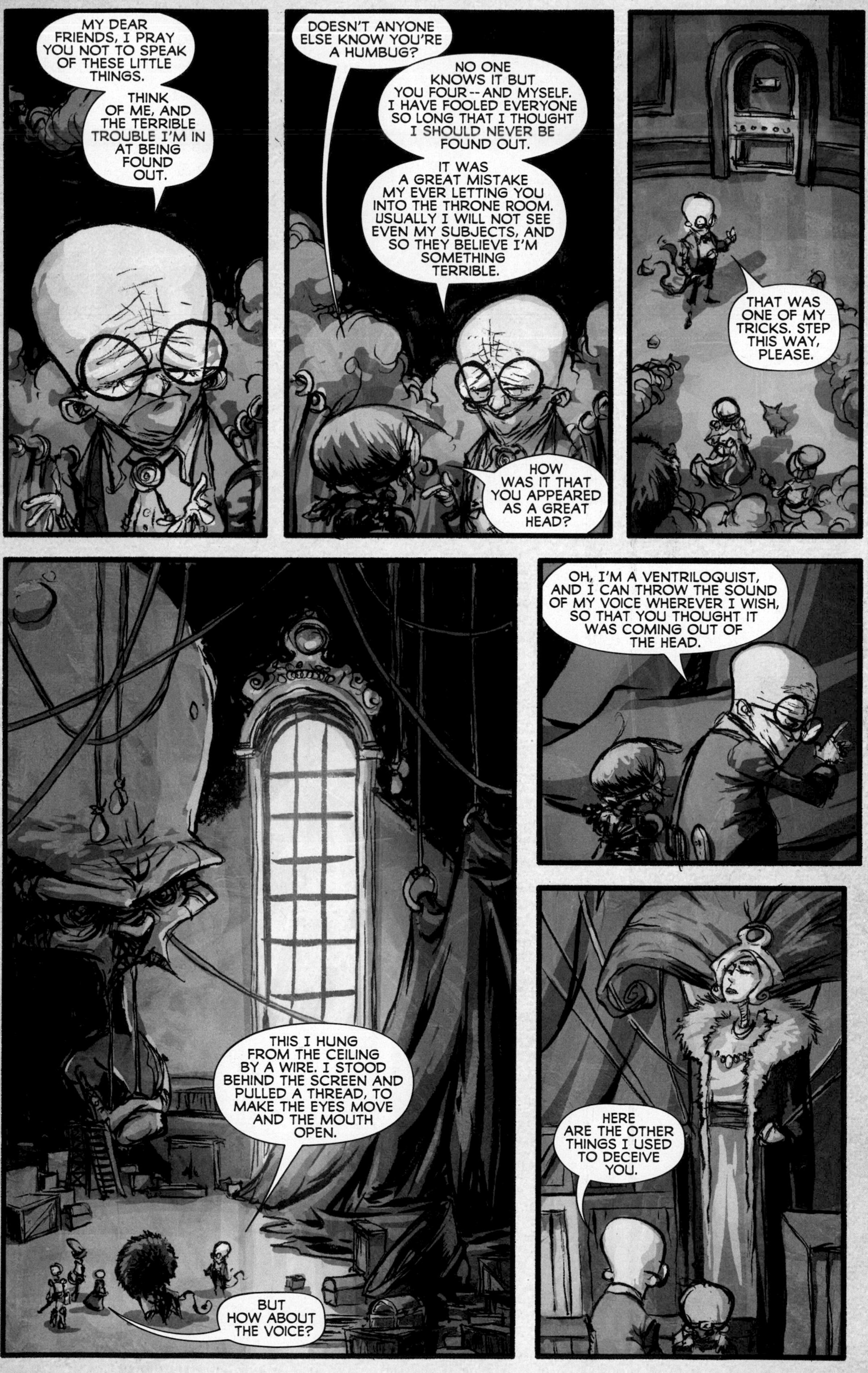
MY DEAR FRIENDS, I PRAY YOU NOT TO SPEAK OF THESE LITTLE THINGS.
THINK OF ME, AND THE TERRIBLE TROUBLE I'M IN AT BEING FOUND OUT.
DOESN'T ANYONE ELSE KNOW YOU'RE A HUMBUG?
NO ONE KNOWS IT BUT YOU FOUR--AND MYSELF. I HAVE FOOLED EVERYONE SO LONG THAT I THOUGHT I SHOULD NEVER BE FOUND OUT.
IT WAS A GREAT MISTAKE MY EVER LETTING YOU INTO THE THRONE ROOM. USUALLY I WILL NOT SEE EVEN MY SUBJECTS, AND SO THEY BELIEVE I'M SOMETHING TERRIBLE.
HOW WAS IT THAT YOU APPEARED AS A GREAT HEAD?
THAT WAS ONE OF MY TRICKS. STEP THIS WAY, PLEASE.
THIS I HUNG FROM THE CEILING BY A WIRE. I STOOD BEHIND THE SCREEN AND PULLED A THREAD, TO MAKE THE EYES MOVE AND THE MOUTH OPEN.
BUT HOW ABOUT THE VOICE?
OH, I'M A VENTRILOQUIST, AND I CAN THROW THE SOUND OF MY VOICE WHEREVER I WISH, SO THAT YOU THOUGHT IT WAS COMING OUT OF THE HEAD.
HERE ARE THE OTHER THINGS I USED TO DECEIVE YOU.

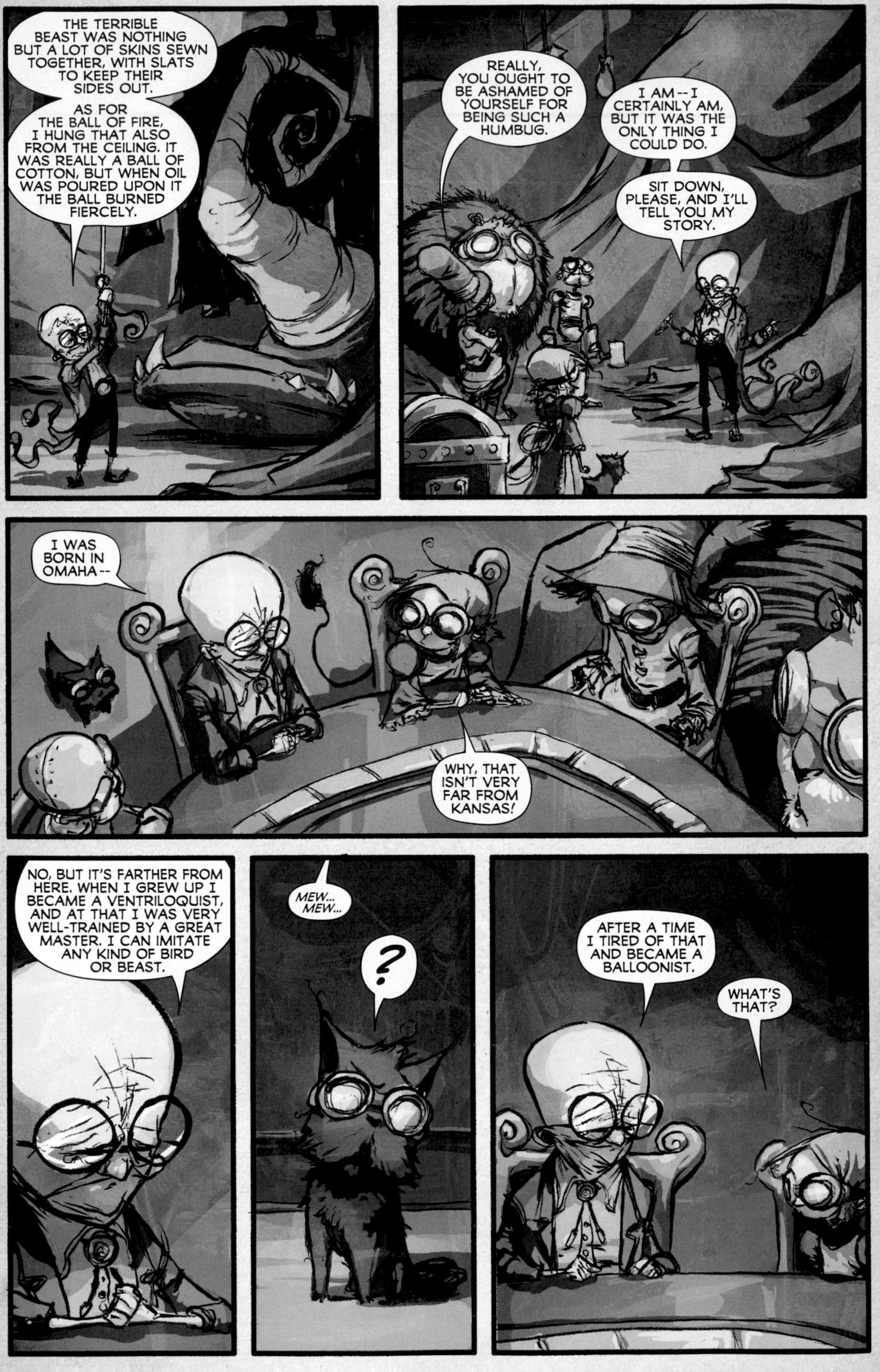
THE TERRIBLE BEAST WAS NOTHING BUT A LOT OF SKINS SEWN TOGETHER, WITH SLATS TO KEEP THEIR SIDES OUT.
AS FOR THE BALL OF FIRE, I HUNG THAT ALSO FROM THE CEILING. IT WAS REALLY A BALL OF COTTON, BUT WHEN OIL WAS POURED UPON IT THE BALL BURNED FIERCELY.
REALLY, YOU OUGHT TO BE ASHAMED OF YOURSELF FOR BEING SUCH A HUMBUG.
I AM -- I CERTAINLY AM, BUT IT WAS THE ONLY THING I COULD DO.
SIT DOWN, PLEASE, AND I'LL TELL YOU MY STORY.
I WAS BORN IN OMAHA--
WHY, THAT ISN'T VERY FAR FROM KANSAS!
NO, BUT IT'S FARTHER FROM HERE. WHEN I GREW UP I BECAME A VENTRILOQUIST, AND AT THAT I WAS VERY WELL-TRAINED BY A GREAT MASTER. I CAN IMITATE ANY KIND OF BIRD OR BEAST.
MEW... MEW...
?
AFTER A TIME I TIRED OF THAT AND BECAME A BALLOONIST.
WHAT'S THAT?

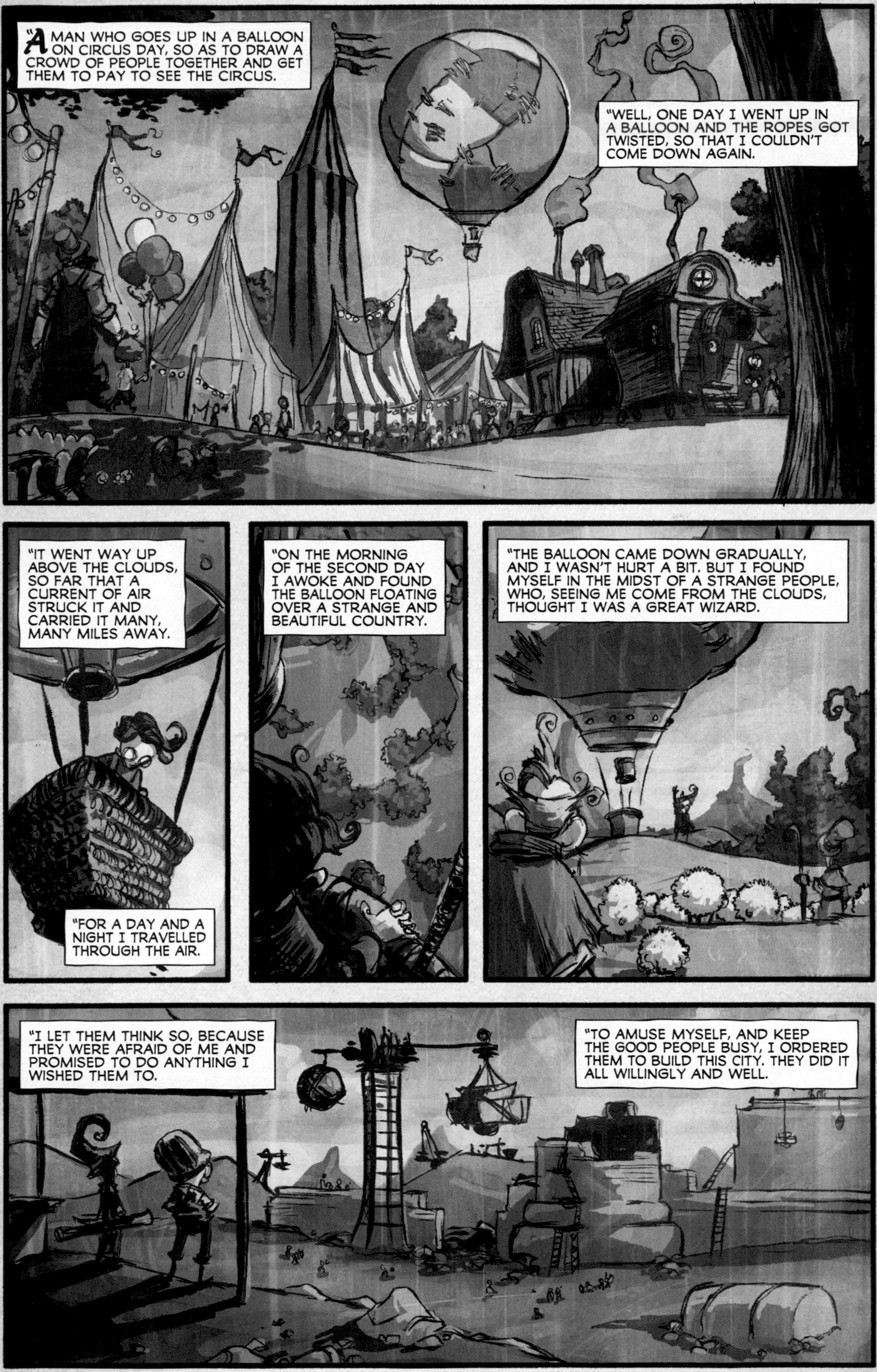
"A MAN WHO GOES UP IN A BALLOON ON CIRCUS DAY, SO AS TO DRAW A CROWD OF PEOPLE TOGETHER AND GET THEM TO PAY TO SEE THE CIRCUS.
"WELL, ONE DAY I WENT UP IN A BALLOON AND THE ROPES GOT TWISTED, SO THAT I COULDN'T COME DOWN AGAIN.
"IT WENT WAY UP ABOVE THE CLOUDS, SO FAR THAT A CURRENT OF AIR STRUCK IT AND CARRIED IT MANY, MANY MILES AWAY.
"FOR A DAY AND A NIGHT I TRAVELLED THROUGH THE AIR.
"ON THE MORNING OF THE SECOND DAY I AWOKE AND FOUND THE BALLOON FLOATING OVER A STRANGE AND BEAUTIFUL COUNTRY.
"THE BALLOON CAME DOWN GRADUALLY, AND I WASN'T HURT A BIT. BUT I FOUND MYSELF IN THE MIDST OF A STRANGE PEOPLE, WHO, SEEING ME COME FROM THE CLOUDS, THOUGHT I WAS A GREAT WIZARD.
"I LET THEM THINK SO, BECAUSE THEY WERE AFRAID OF ME AND PROMISED TO DO ANYTHING I WISHED THEM TO.
"TO AMUSE MYSELF, AND KEEP THE GOOD PEOPLE BUSY, I ORDERED THEM TO BUILD THIS CITY. THEY DID IT ALL WILLINGLY AND WELL.

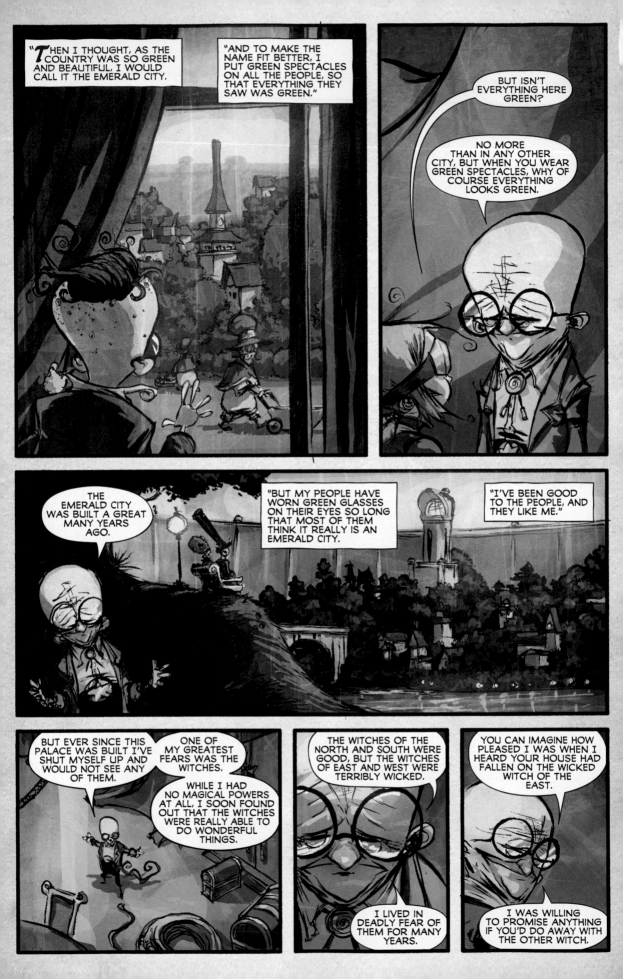

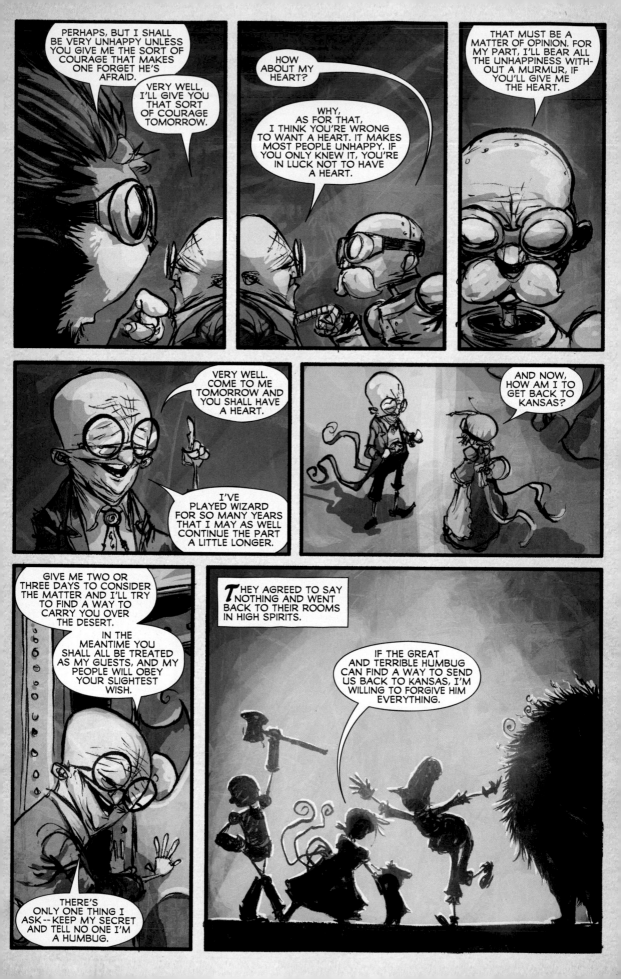

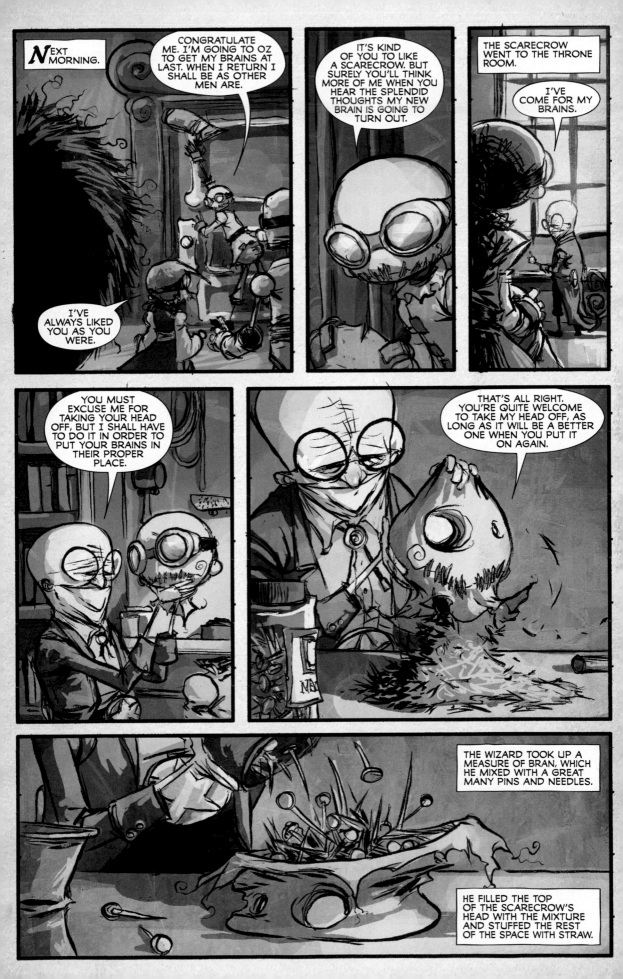

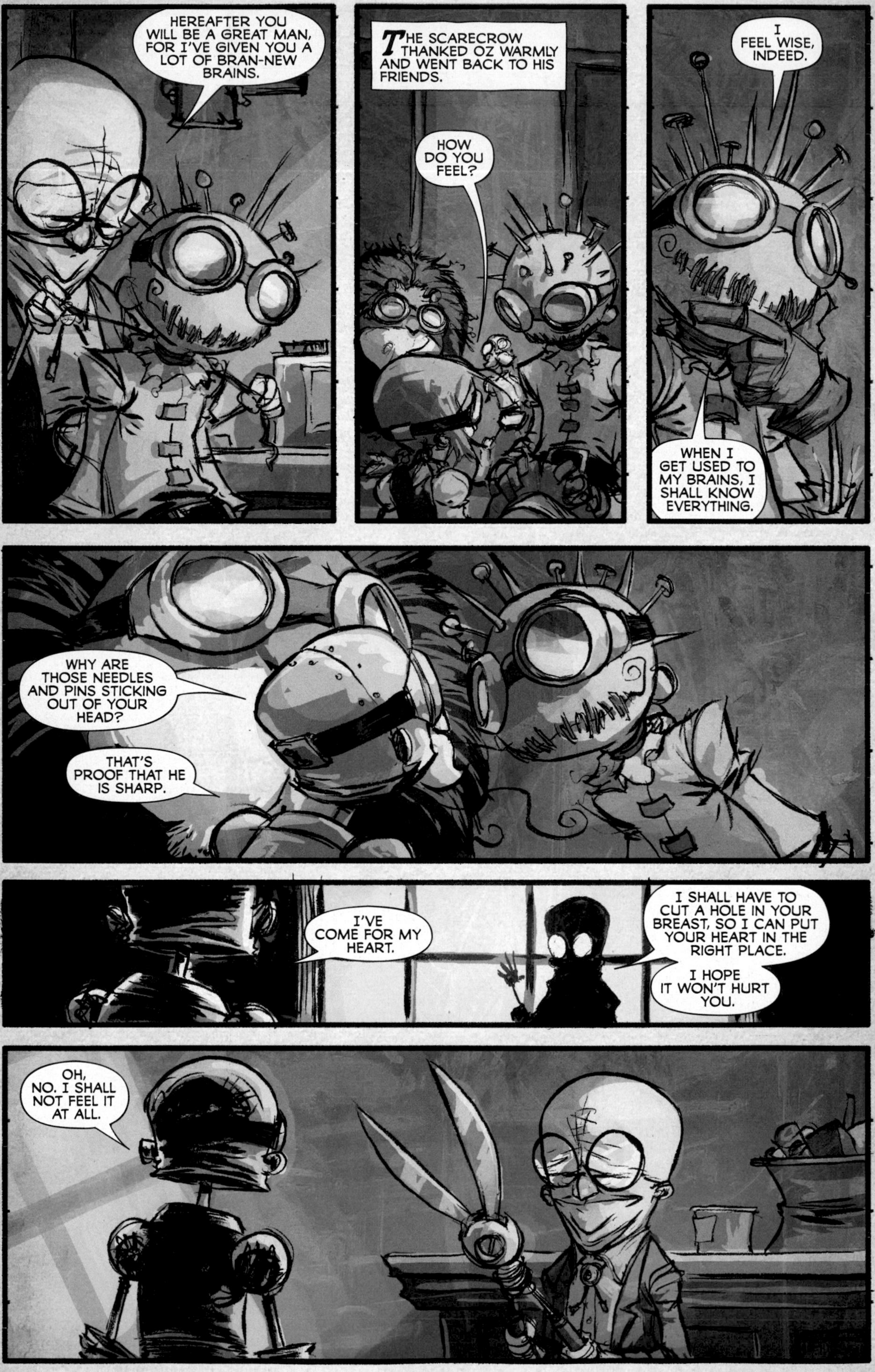
HEREAFTER YOU WILL BE A GREAT MAN, FOR I'VE GIVEN YOU A LOT OF BRAN-NEW BRAINS.
THE SCARECROW THANKED OZ WARMLY AND WENT BACK TO HIS FRIENDS.
HOW DO YOU FEEL?
I FEEL WISE, INDEED.
WHEN I GET USED TO MY BRAINS, I SHALL KNOW EVERYTHING.
WHY ARE THOSE NEEDLES AND PINS STICKING OUT OF YOUR HEAD?
THAT'S PROOF THAT HE IS SHARP.
I'VE COME FOR MY HEART.
I SHALL HAVE TO CUT A HOLE IN YOUR BREAST, SO I CAN PUT YOUR HEART IN THE RIGHT PLACE.
I HOPE IT WON'T HURT YOU.
OH, NO. I SHALL NOT FEEL IT AT ALL.

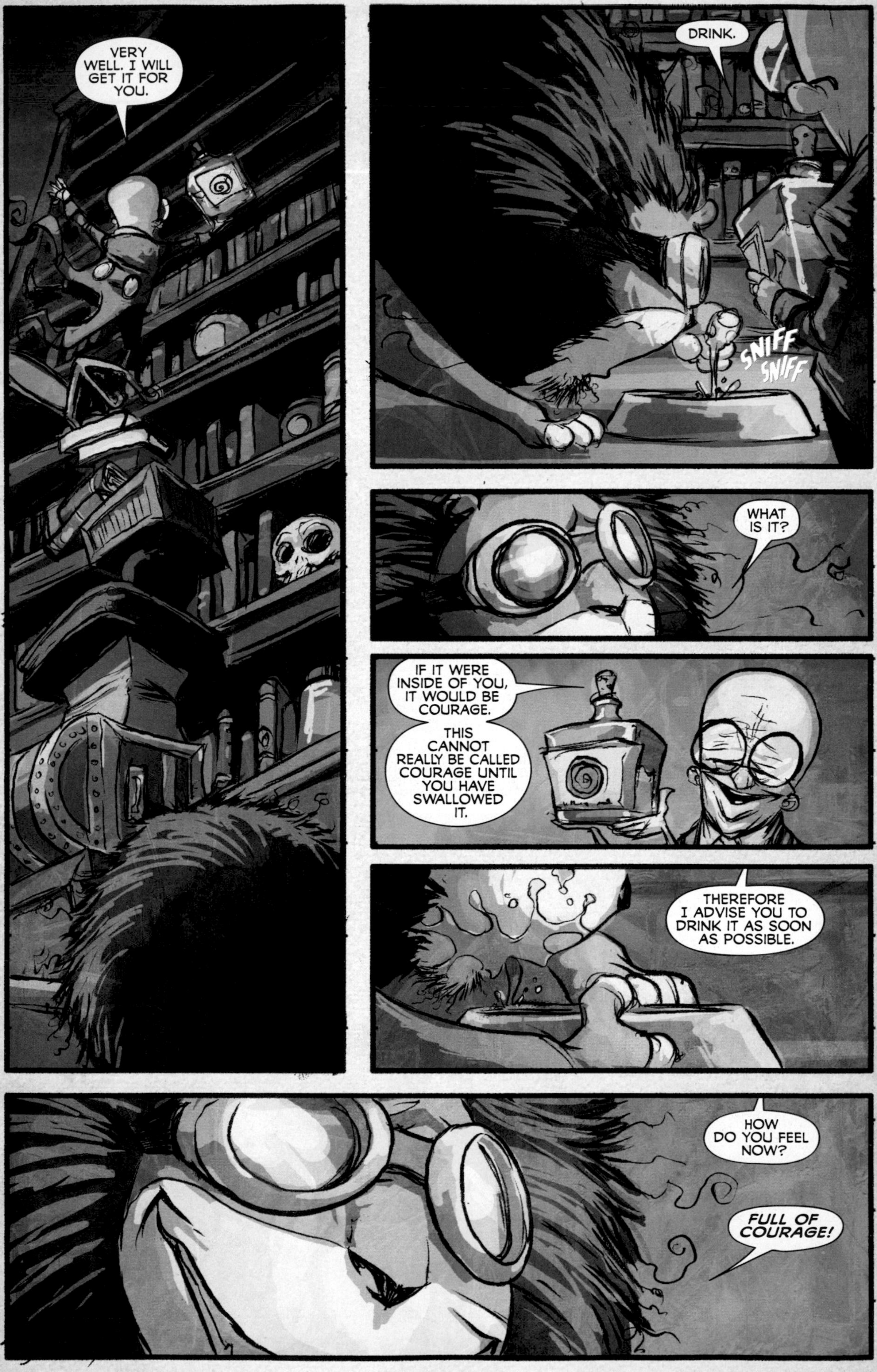
VERY WELL. I WILL GET IT FOR YOU.
DRINK.
SNIFF SNIFF
WHAT IS IT?
IF IT WERE INSIDE OF YOU, IT WOULD BE COURAGE.
THIS CANNOT REALLY BE CALLED COURAGE UNTIL YOU HAVE SWALLOWED IT.
THEREFORE I ADVISE YOU TO DRINK IT AS SOON AS POSSIBLE.
HOW DO YOU FEEL NOW?
FULL OF COURAGE!

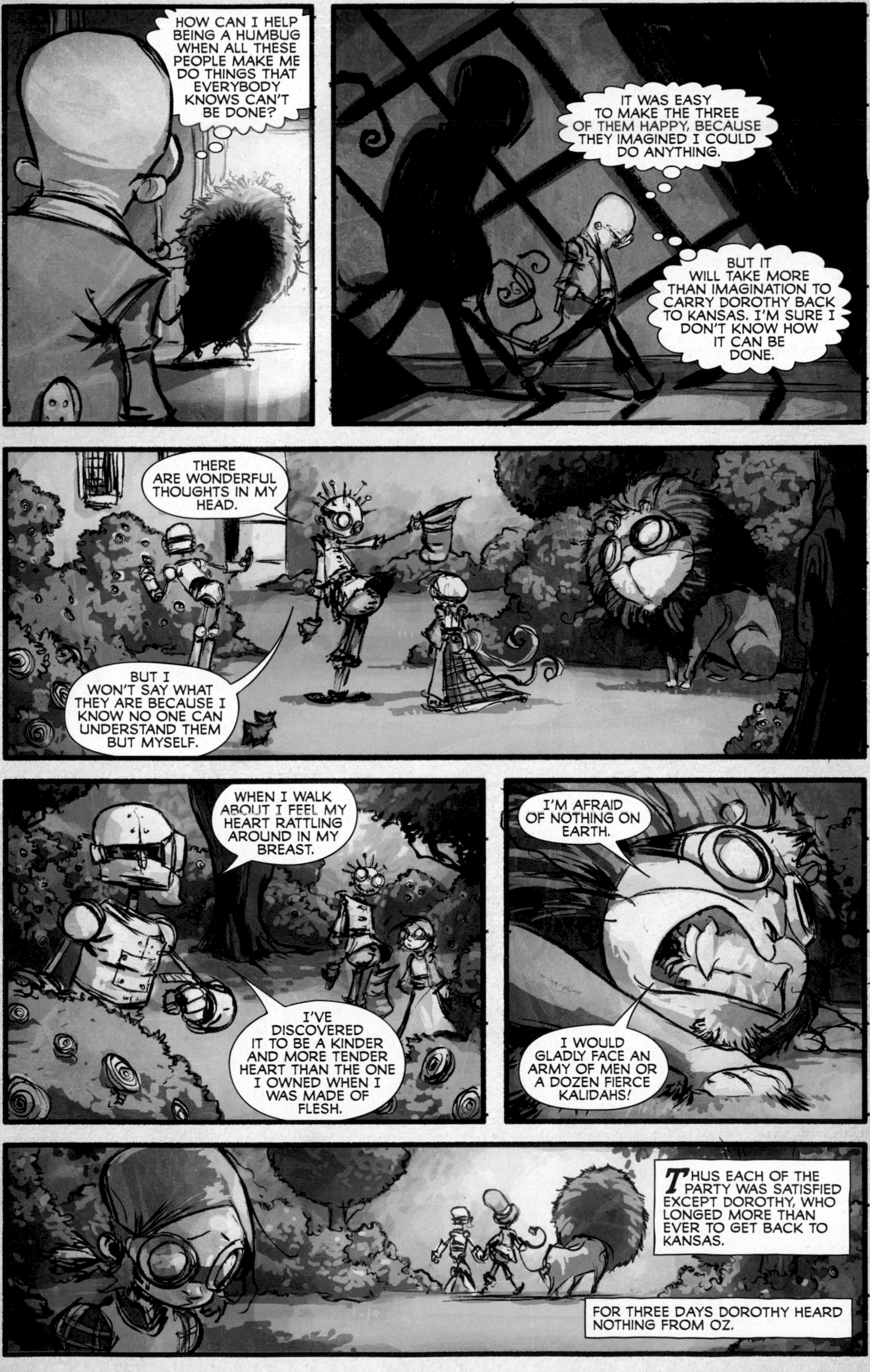
HOW CAN I HELP BEING A HUMBUG WHEN ALL THESE PEOPLE MAKE ME DO THINGS THAT EVERYBODY KNOWS CAN'T BE DONE?
IT WAS EASY TO MAKE THE THREE OF THEM HAPPY, BECAUSE THEY IMAGINED I COULD DO ANYTHING.
BUT IT WILL TAKE MORE THAN IMAGINATION TO CARRY DOROTHY BACK TO KANSAS. I'M SURE I DON'T KNOW HOW IT CAN BE DONE.
THERE ARE WONDERFUL THOUGHTS IN MY HEAD.
BUT I WON'T SAY WHAT THEY ARE BECAUSE I KNOW NO ONE CAN UNDERSTAND THEM BUT MYSELF.
WHEN I WALK ABOUT I FEEL MY HEART RATTLING AROUND IN MY BREAST.
I'VE DISCOVERED IT TO BE A KINDER AND MORE TENDER HEART THAN THE ONE I OWNED WHEN I WAS MADE OF FLESH.
I'M AFRAID OF NOTHING ON EARTH.
I WOULD GLADLY FACE AN ARMY OF MEN OR A DOZEN FIERCE KALIDAHS!
THUS EACH OF THE PARTY WAS SATISFIED EXCEPT DOROTHY, WHO LONGED MORE THAN EVER TO GET BACK TO KANSAS.
FOR THREE DAYS DOROTHY HEARD NOTHING FROM OZ.

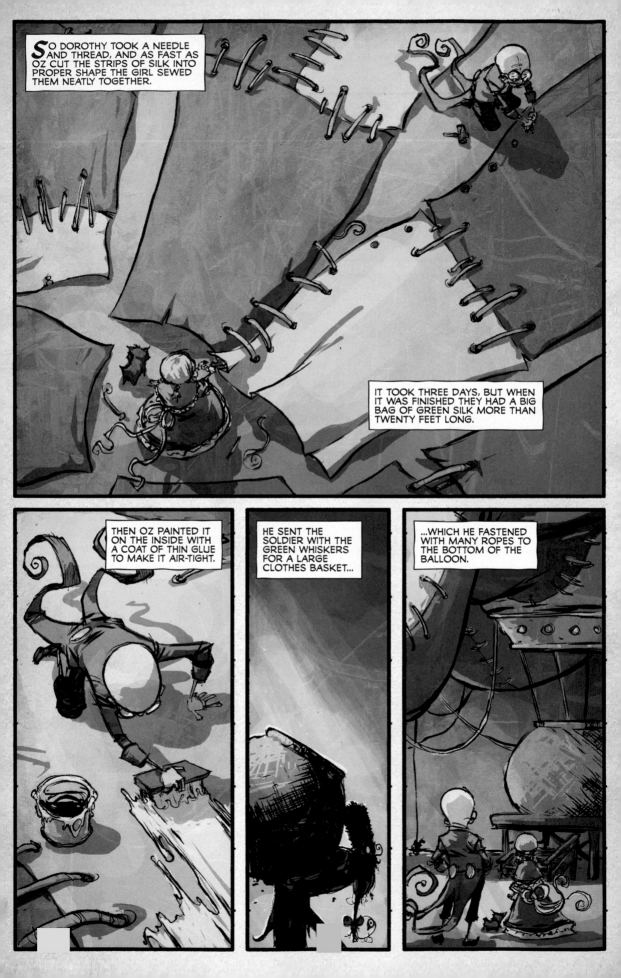

SO DOROTHY TOOK A NEEDLE AND THREAD, AND AS FAST AS OZ CUT THE STRIPS OF SILK INTO PROPER SHAPE THE GIRL SEWED THEM NEATLY TOGETHER.

IT TOOK THREE DAYS, BUT WHEN IT WAS FINISHED THEY HAD A BIG BAG OF GREEN SILK MORE THAN TWENTY FEET LONG.

THEN OZ PAINTED IT ON THE INSIDE WITH A COAT OF THIN GLUE TO MAKE IT AIR-TIGHT.

HE SENT THE SOLDIER WITH THE GREEN WHISKERS FOR A LARGE CLOTHES BASKET...

...WHICH HE FASTENED WITH MANY ROPES TO THE BOTTOM OF THE BALLOON.

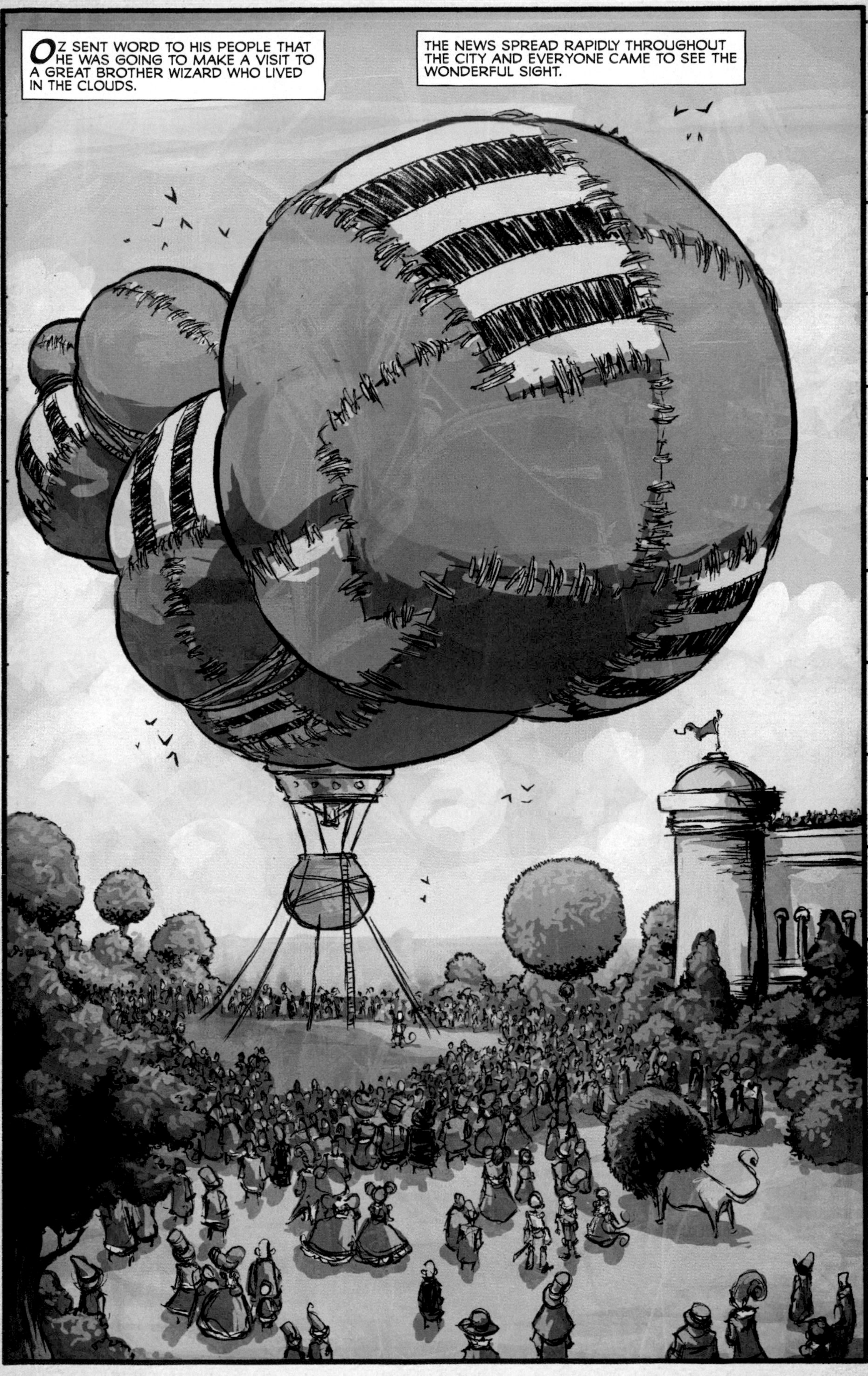
OZ SENT WORD TO HIS PEOPLE THAT HE WAS GOING TO MAKE A VISIT TO A GREAT BROTHER WIZARD WHO LIVED IN THE CLOUDS.
THE NEWS SPREAD RAPIDLY THROUGHOUT THE CITY AND EVERYONE CAME TO SEE THE WONDERFUL SIGHT.

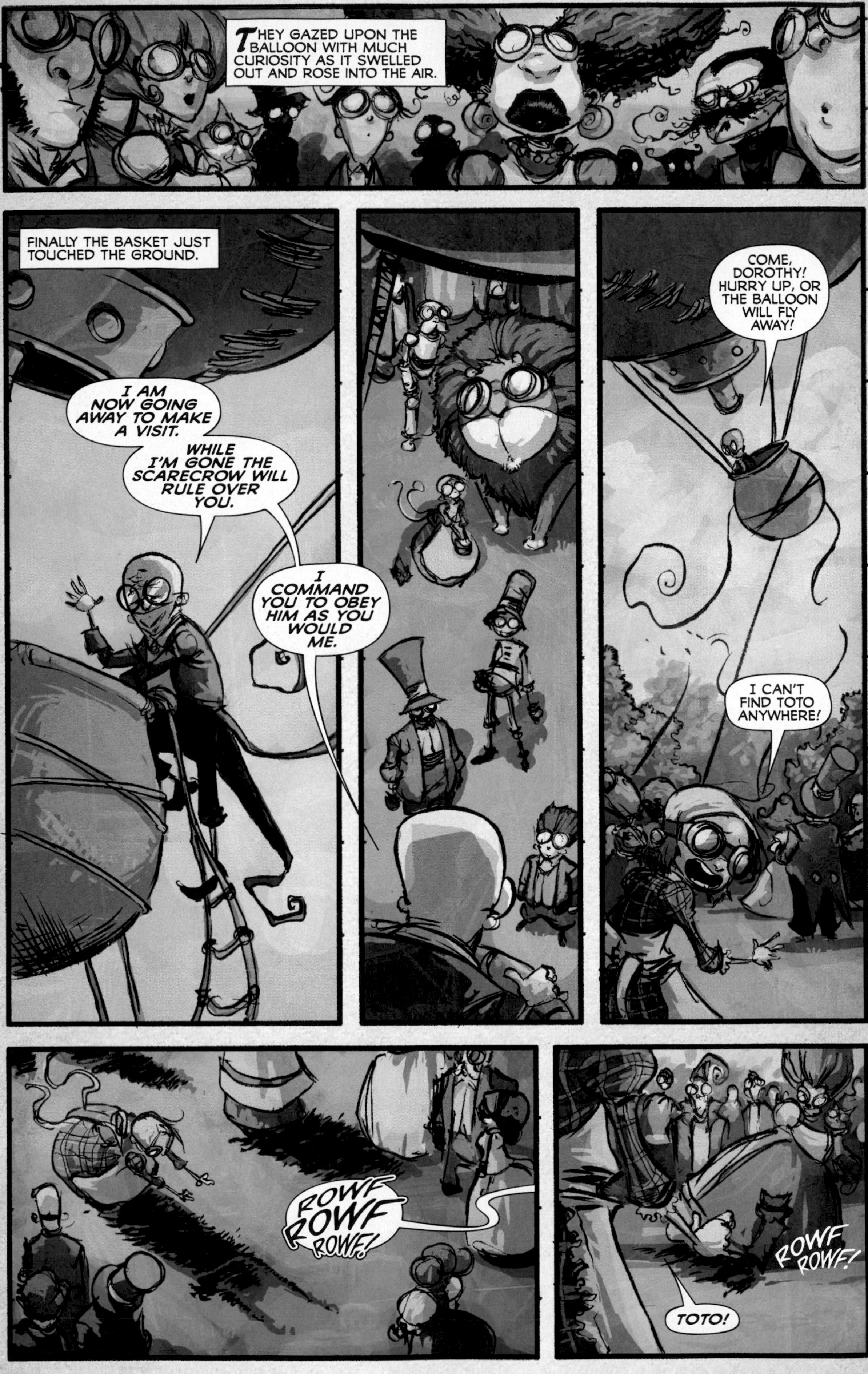
THEY GAZED UPON THE BALLOON WITH MUCH CURIOSITY AS IT SWELLED OUT AND ROSE INTO THE AIR.
FINALLY THE BASKET JUST TOUCHED THE GROUND.
I AM NOW GOING AWAY TO MAKE A VISIT.
WHILE I'M GONE THE SCARECROW WILL RULE OVER YOU.
I COMMAND YOU TO OBEY HIM AS YOU WOULD ME.
COME, DOROTHY! HURRY UP, OR THE BALLOON WILL FLY AWAY!
I CAN'T FIND TOTO ANYWHERE!
ROWF ROWF ROWF!
ROWF ROWF!
TOTO!

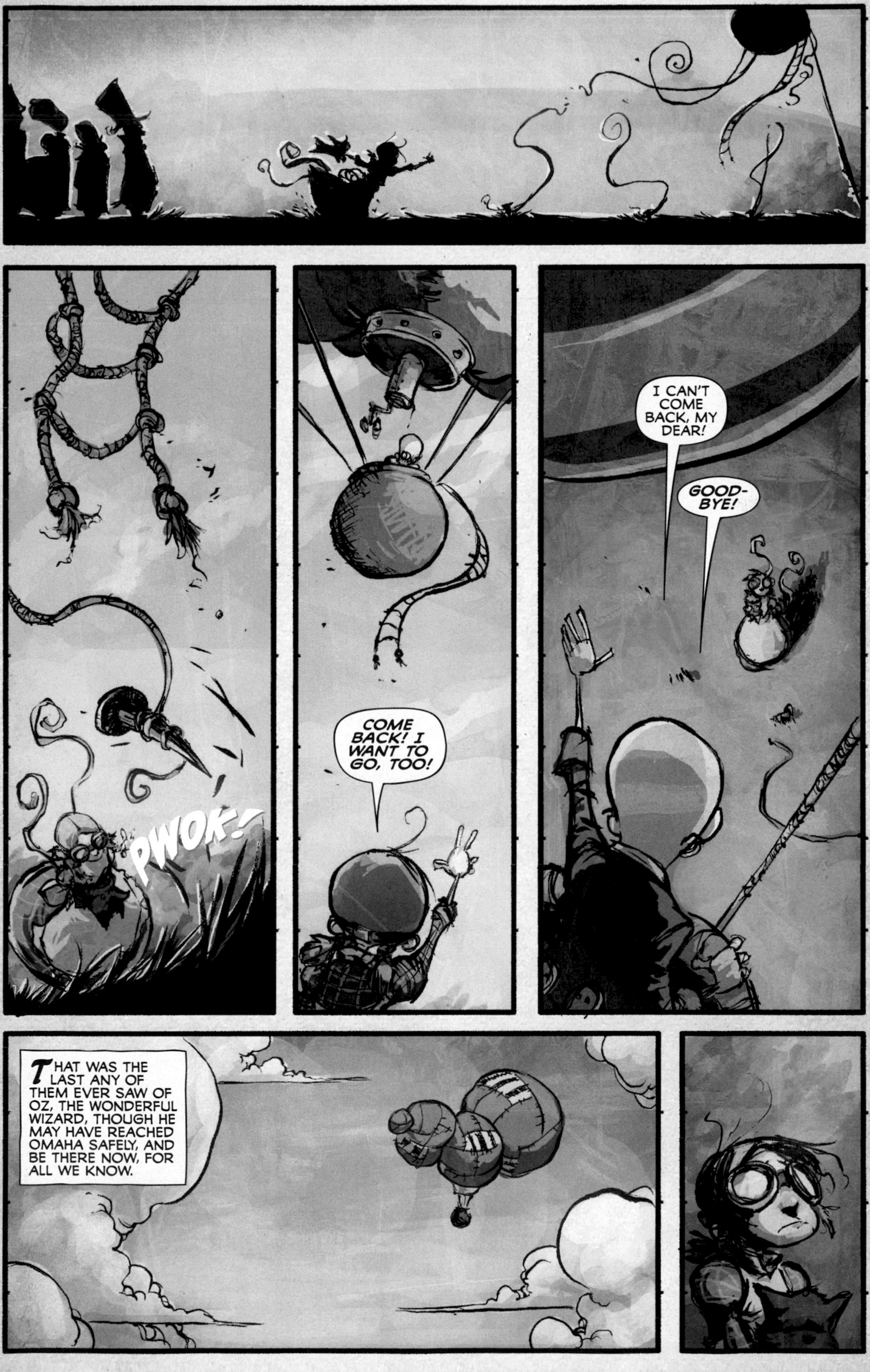
PWOK!
COME BACK! I WANT TO GO, TOO!
I CAN'T COME BACK, MY DEAR!
GOOD-BYE!
THAT WAS THE LAST ANY OF THEM EVER SAW OF OZ, THE WONDERFUL WIZARD, THOUGH HE MAY HAVE REACHED OMAHA SAFELY, AND BE THERE NOW, FOR ALL WE KNOW.

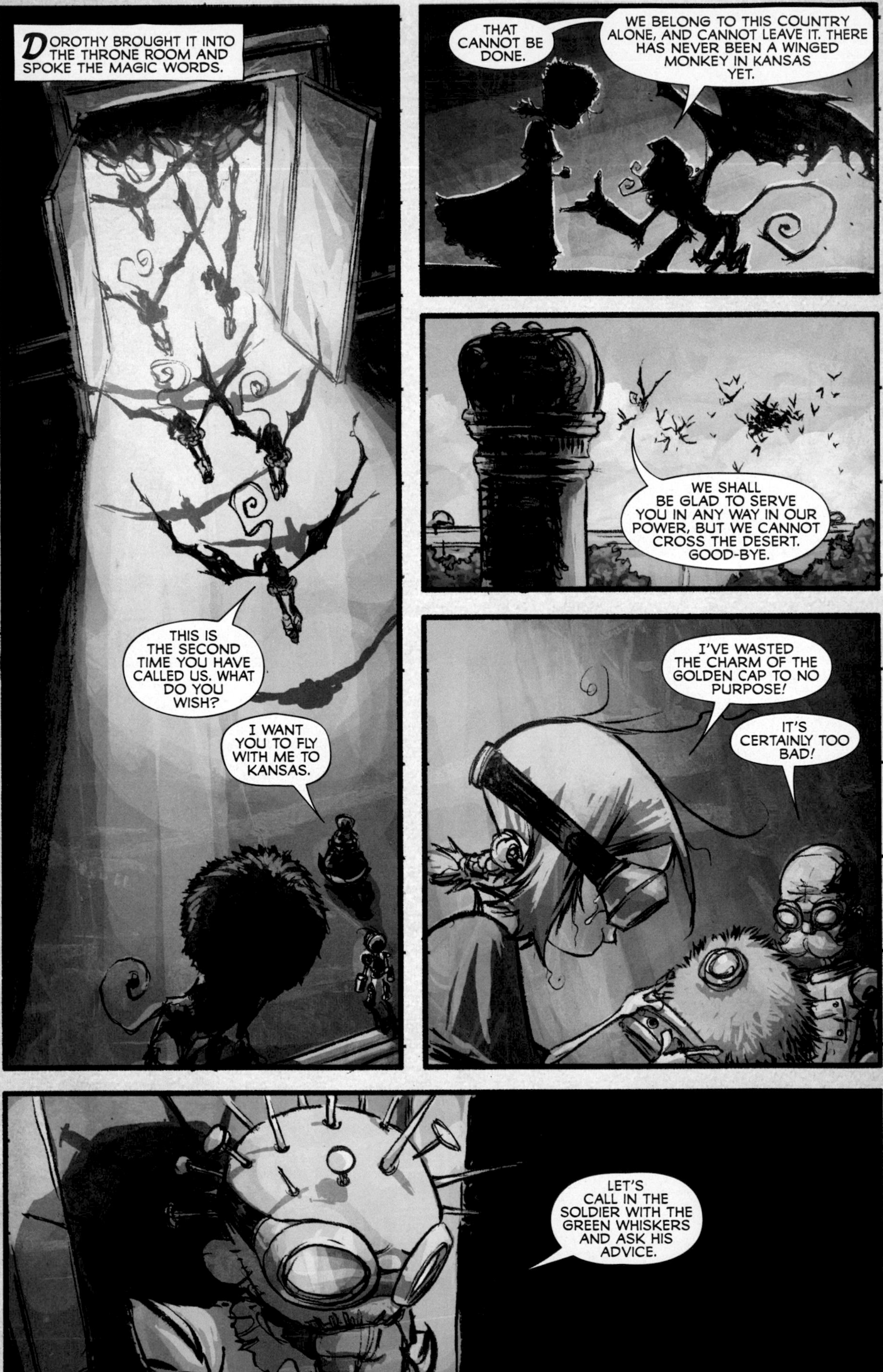
DOROTHY BROUGHT IT INTO THE THRONE ROOM AND SPOKE THE MAGIC WORDS.
THIS IS THE SECOND TIME YOU HAVE CALLED US. WHAT DO YOU WISH?
I WANT YOU TO FLY WITH ME TO KANSAS.
WE BELONG TO THIS COUNTRY ALONE, AND CANNOT LEAVE IT. THERE HAS NEVER BEEN A WINGED MONKEY IN KANSAS YET.
THAT CANNOT BE DONE.
WE SHALL BE GLAD TO SERVE YOU IN ANY WAY IN OUR POWER, BUT WE CANNOT CROSS THE DESERT. GOOD-BYE.
I'VE WASTED THE CHARM OF THE GOLDEN CAP TO NO PURPOSE!
IT'S CERTAINLY TOO BAD!
LET'S CALL IN THE SOLDIER WITH THE GREEN WHISKERS AND ASK HIS ADVICE.

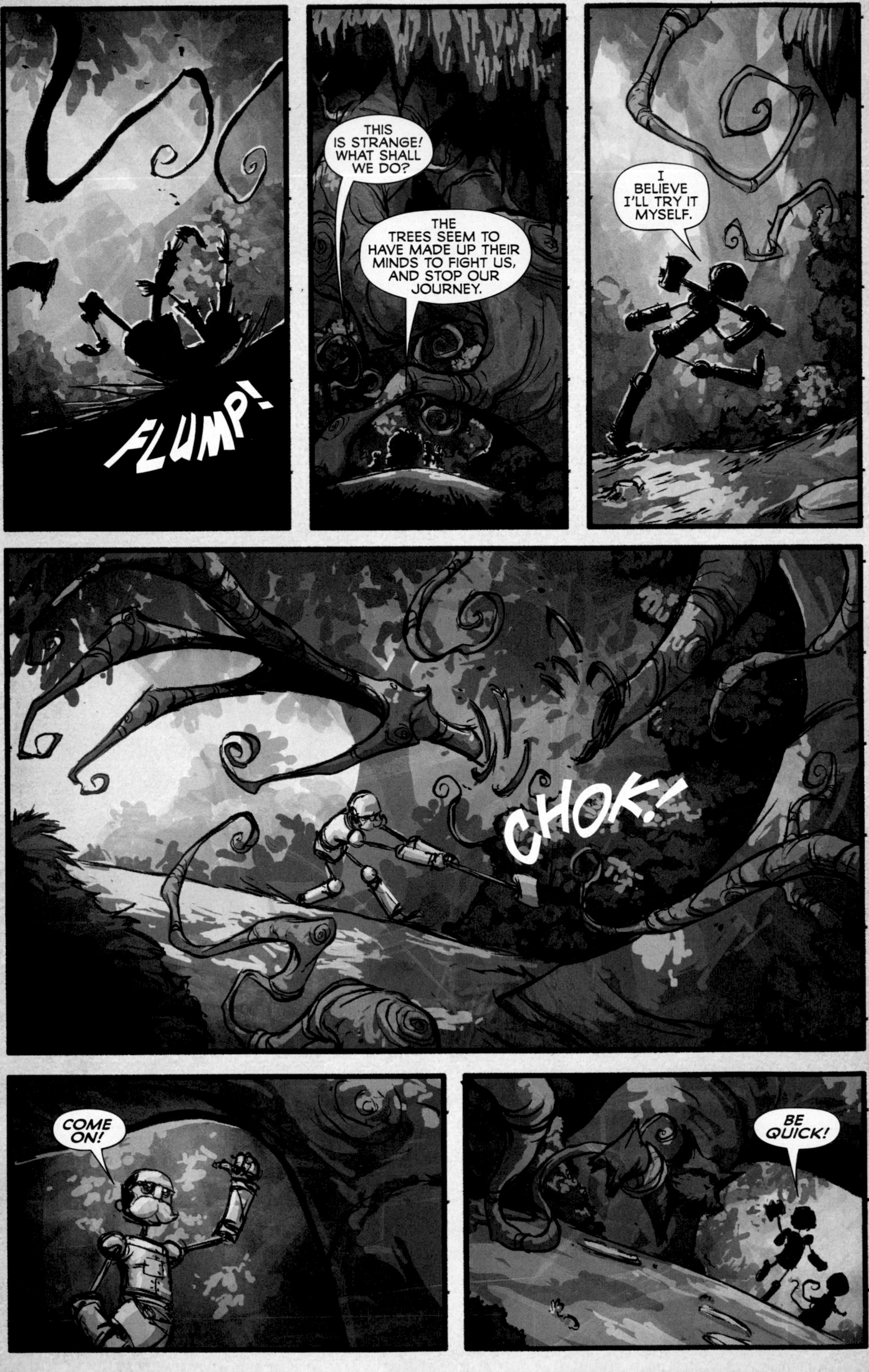
FLUMP!
THIS IS STRANGE! WHAT SHALL WE DO?
THE TREES SEEM TO HAVE MADE UP THEIR MINDS TO FIGHT US, AND STOP OUR JOURNEY.
I BELIEVE I'LL TRY IT MYSELF.
CHOK!
COME ON!
BE QUICK!

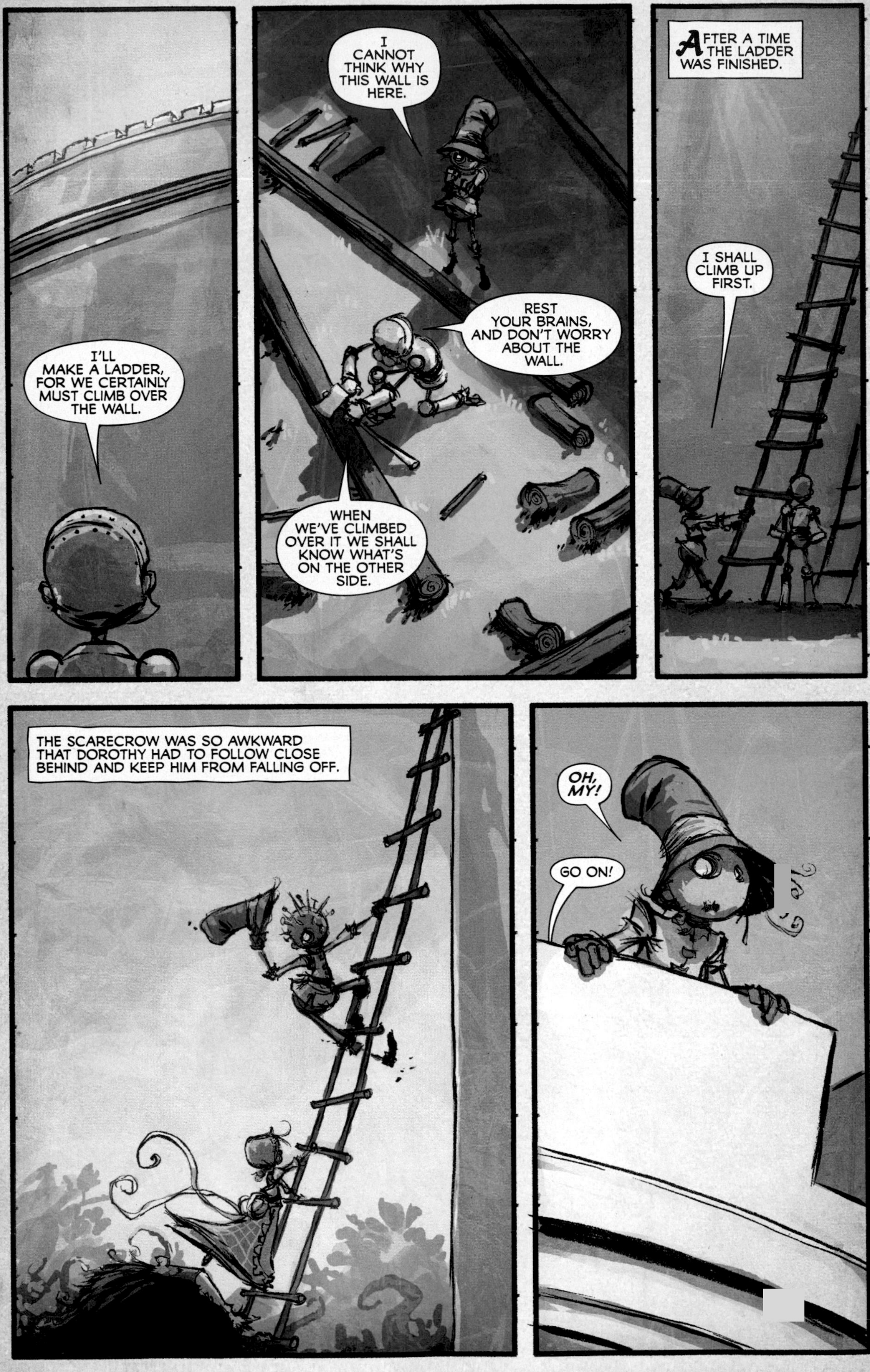
I'LL MAKE A LADDER, FOR WE CERTAINLY MUST CLIMB OVER THE WALL.
I CANNOT THINK WHY THIS WALL IS HERE.
REST YOUR BRAINS, AND DON'T WORRY ABOUT THE WALL.
WHEN WE'VE CLIMBED OVER IT WE SHALL KNOW WHAT'S ON THE OTHER SIDE.
AFTER A TIME THE LADDER WAS FINISHED.
I SHALL CLIMB UP FIRST.
THE SCARECROW WAS SO AWKWARD THAT DOROTHY HAD TO FOLLOW CLOSE BEHIND AND KEEP HIM FROM FALLING OFF.
OH, MY!
GO ON!

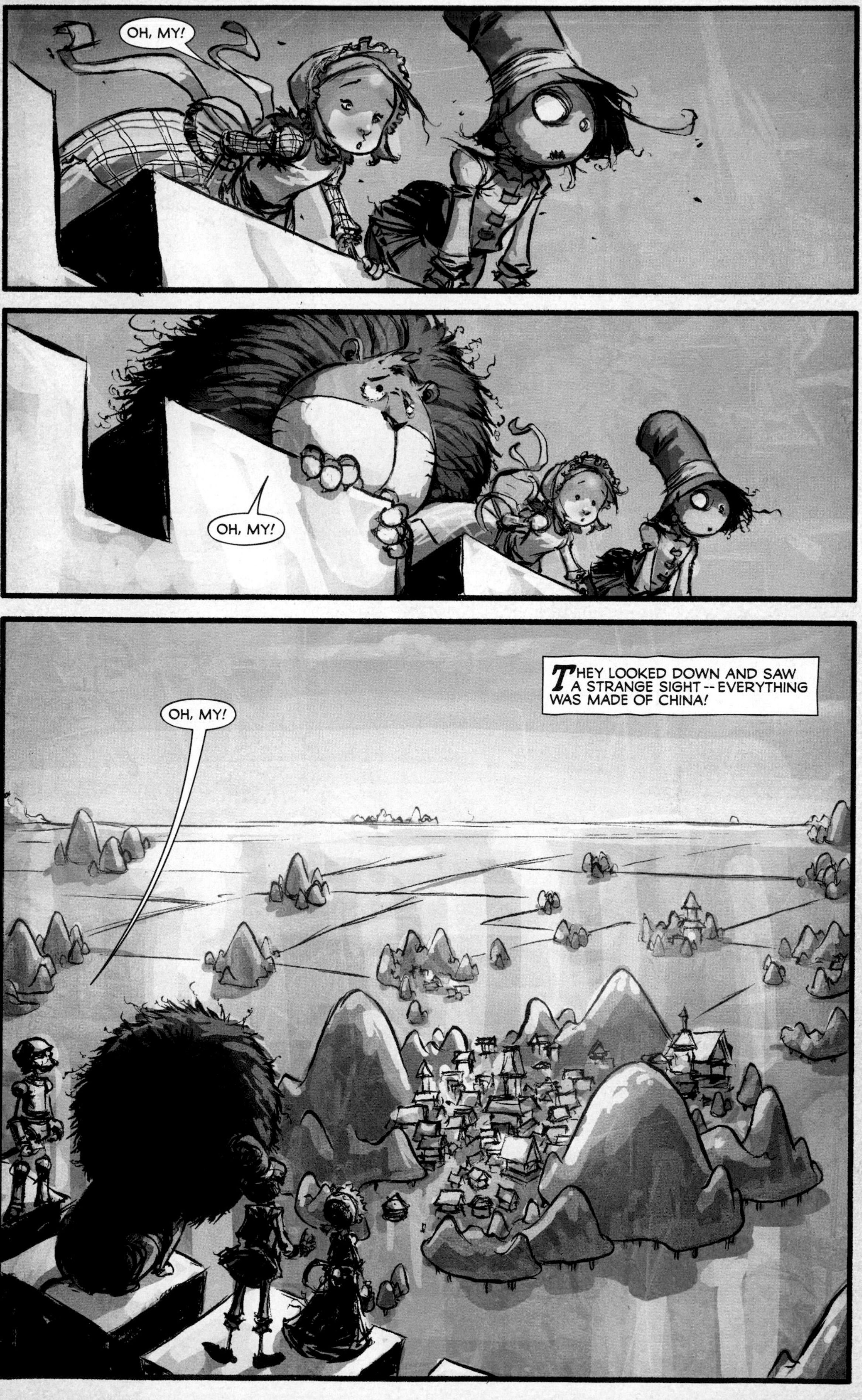
OH, MY!
OH, MY!
THEY LOOKED DOWN AND SAW A STRANGE SIGHT -- EVERYTHING WAS MADE OF CHINA!
OH, MY!

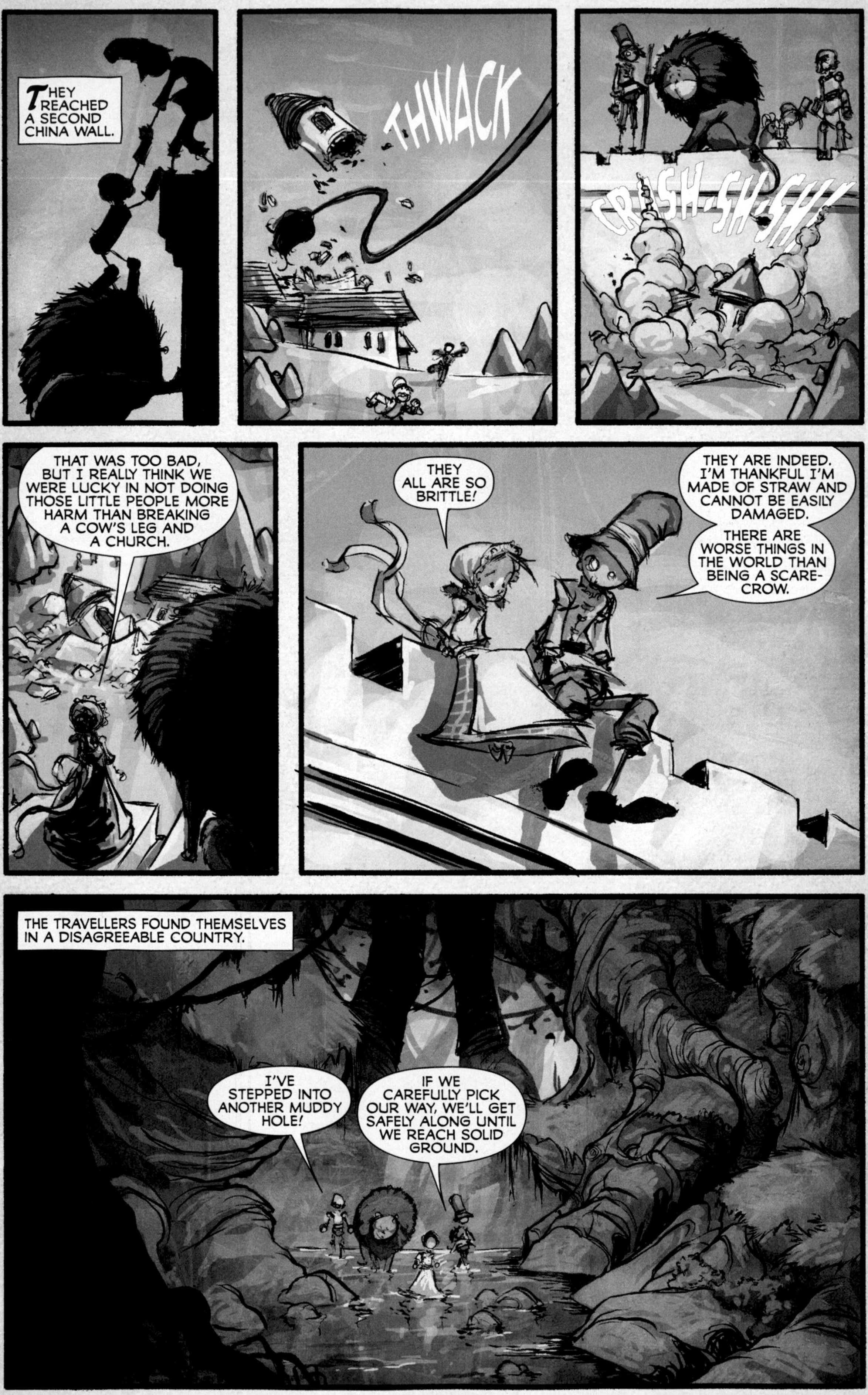
THEY REACHED A SECOND CHINA WALL.
THWACK
CRASH-SH-SH!
THAT WAS TOO BAD, BUT I REALLY THINK WE WERE LUCKY IN NOT DOING THOSE LITTLE PEOPLE MORE HARM THAN BREAKING A COW'S LEG AND A CHURCH.
THEY ALL ARE SO BRITTLE!
THEY ARE INDEED. I'M THANKFUL I'M MADE OF STRAW AND CANNOT BE EASILY DAMAGED.
THERE ARE WORSE THINGS IN THE WORLD THAN BEING A SCARE-CROW.
THE TRAVELLERS FOUND THEMSELVES IN A DISAGREEABLE COUNTRY.
I'VE STEPPED INTO ANOTHER MUDDY HOLE!
IF WE CAREFULLY PICK OUR WAY, WE'LL GET SAFELY ALONG UNTIL WE REACH SOLID GROUND.

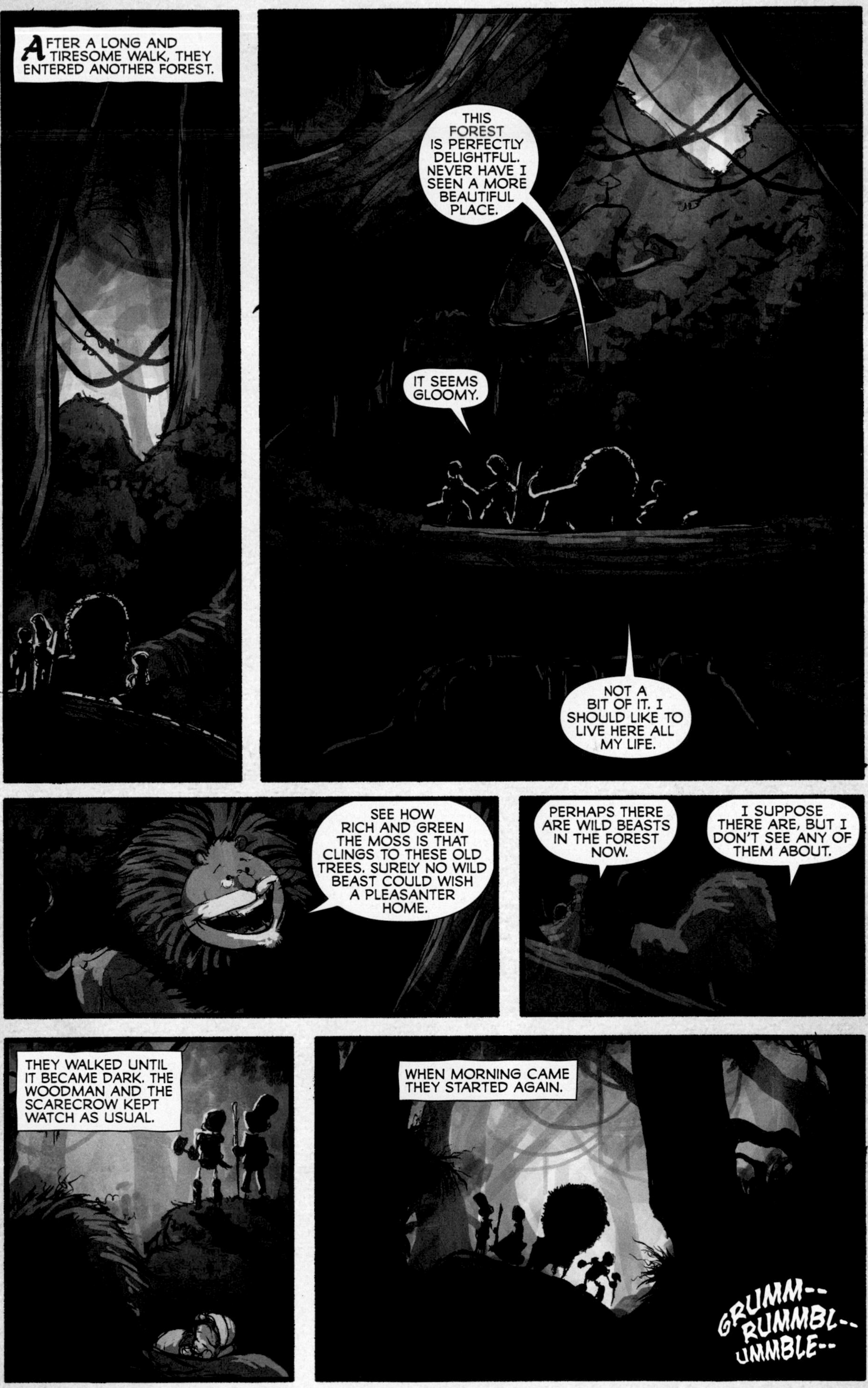
AFTER A LONG AND TIRESOME WALK, THEY ENTERED ANOTHER FOREST.
THIS FOREST IS PERFECTLY DELIGHTFUL. NEVER HAVE I SEEN A MORE BEAUTIFUL PLACE.
IT SEEMS GLOOMY.
NOT A BIT OF IT. I SHOULD LIKE TO LIVE HERE ALL MY LIFE.
SEE HOW RICH AND GREEN THE MOSS IS THAT CLINGS TO THESE OLD TREES. SURELY NO WILD BEAST COULD WISH A PLEASANTER HOME.
PERHAPS THERE ARE WILD BEASTS IN THE FOREST NOW.
I SUPPOSE THERE ARE, BUT I DON'T SEE ANY OF THEM ABOUT.
THEY WALKED UNTIL IT BECAME DARK. THE WOODMAN AND THE SCARECROW KEPT WATCH AS USUAL.
WHEN MORNING CAME THEY STARTED AGAIN.
GRUMM-- RUMMBL-- UMMBLE--

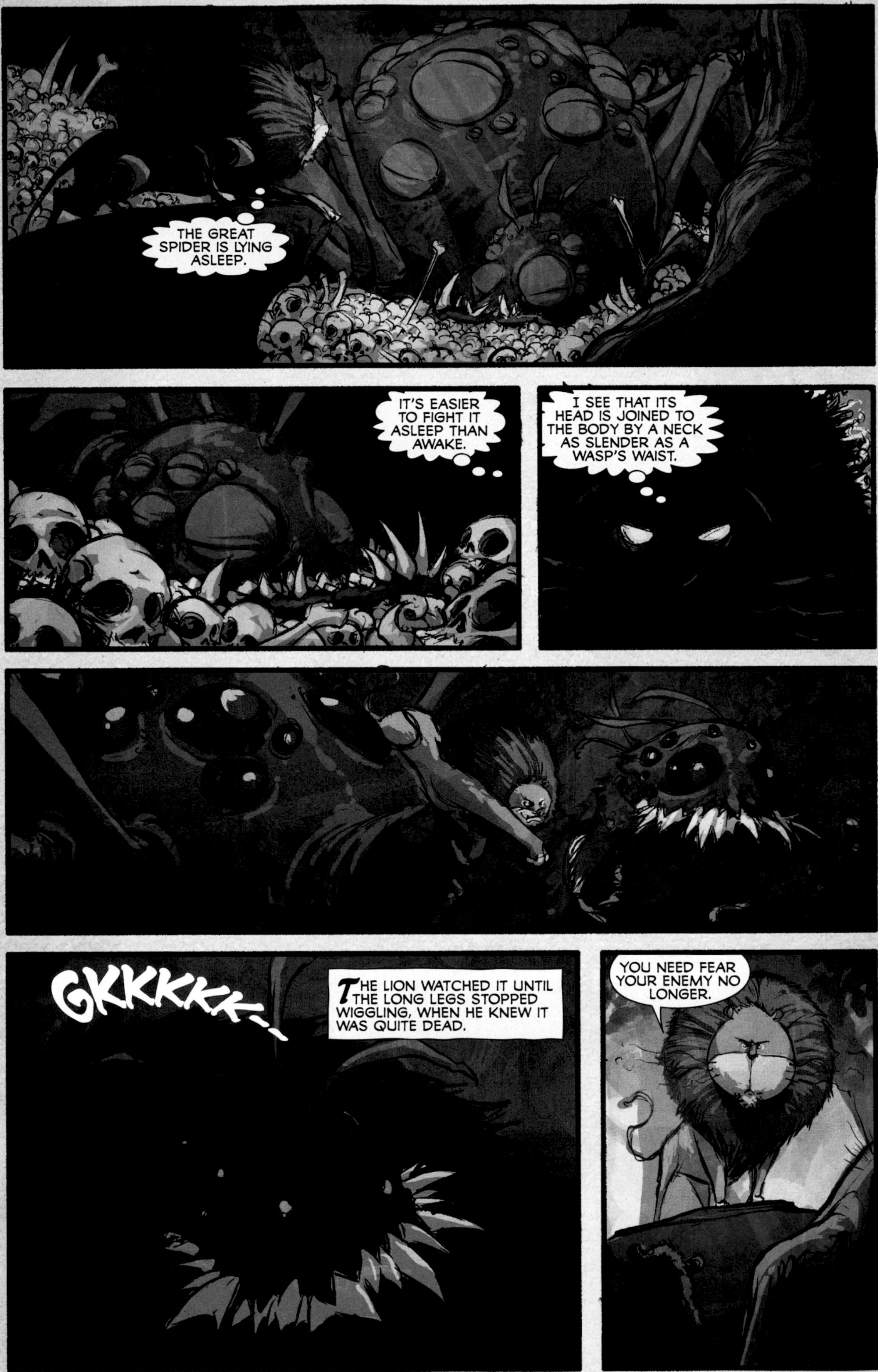
THE GREAT SPIDER IS LYING ASLEEP.
IT'S EASIER TO FIGHT IT ASLEEP THAN AWAKE.
I SEE THAT ITS HEAD IS JOINED TO THE BODY BY A NECK AS SLENDER AS A WASP'S WAIST.
GKKKKK--
THE LION WATCHED IT UNTIL THE LONG LEGS STOPPED WIGGLING, WHEN HE KNEW IT WAS QUITE DEAD.
YOU NEED FEAR YOUR ENEMY NO LONGER.

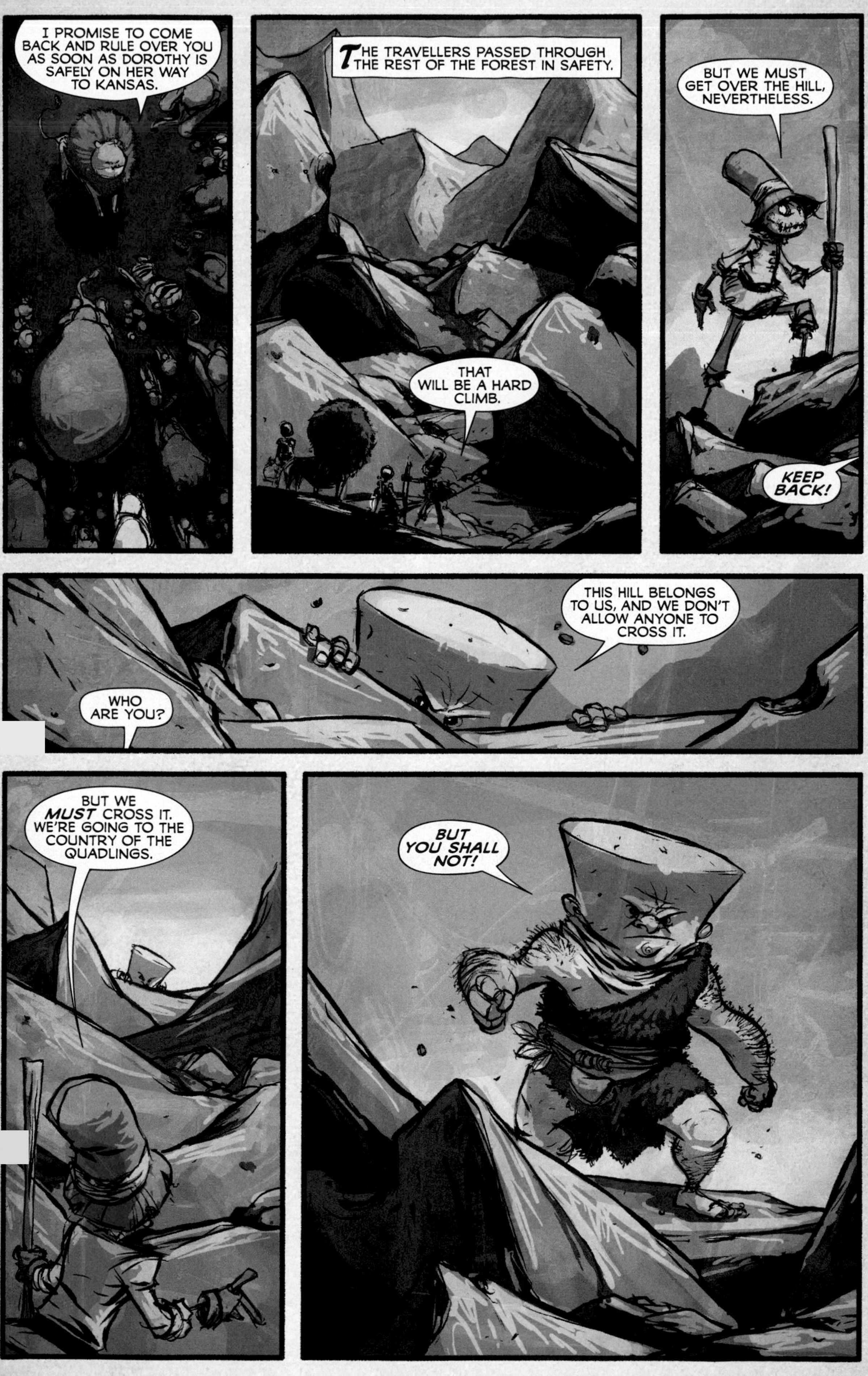
I PROMISE TO COME BACK AND RULE OVER YOU AS SOON AS DOROTHY IS SAFELY ON HER WAY TO KANSAS.
THE TRAVELLERS PASSED THROUGH THE REST OF THE FOREST IN SAFETY.
THAT WILL BE A HARD CLIMB.
BUT WE MUST GET OVER THE HILL, NEVERTHELESS.
KEEP BACK!
WHO ARE YOU?
THIS HILL BELONGS TO US, AND WE DON'T ALLOW ANYONE TO CROSS IT.
BUT WE *MUST* CROSS IT. WE'RE GOING TO THE COUNTRY OF THE QUADLINGS.
BUT YOU SHALL NOT!

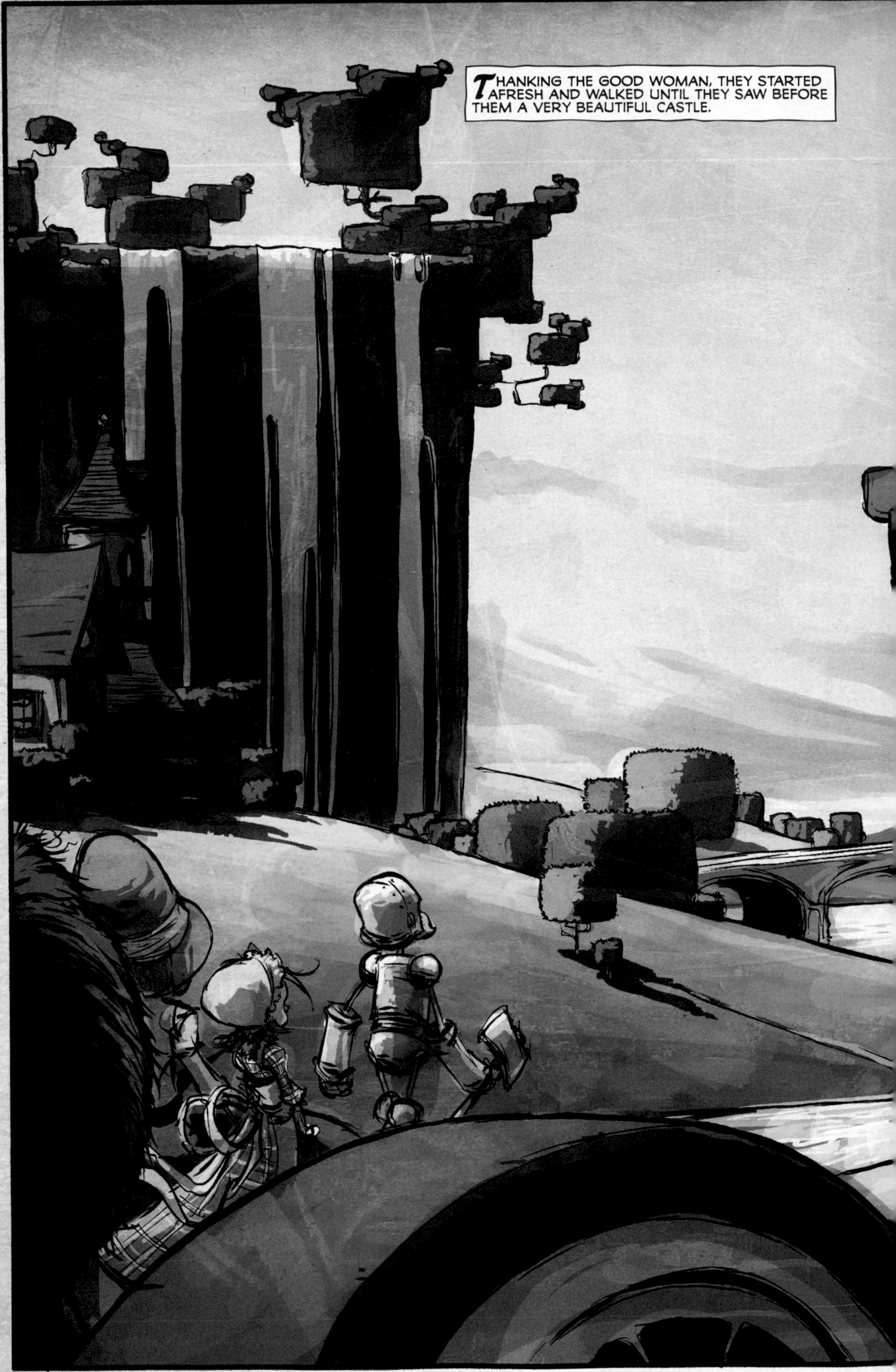
THANKING THE GOOD WOMAN, THEY STARTED AFRESH AND WALKED UNTIL THEY SAW BEFORE THEM A VERY BEAUTIFUL CASTLE.

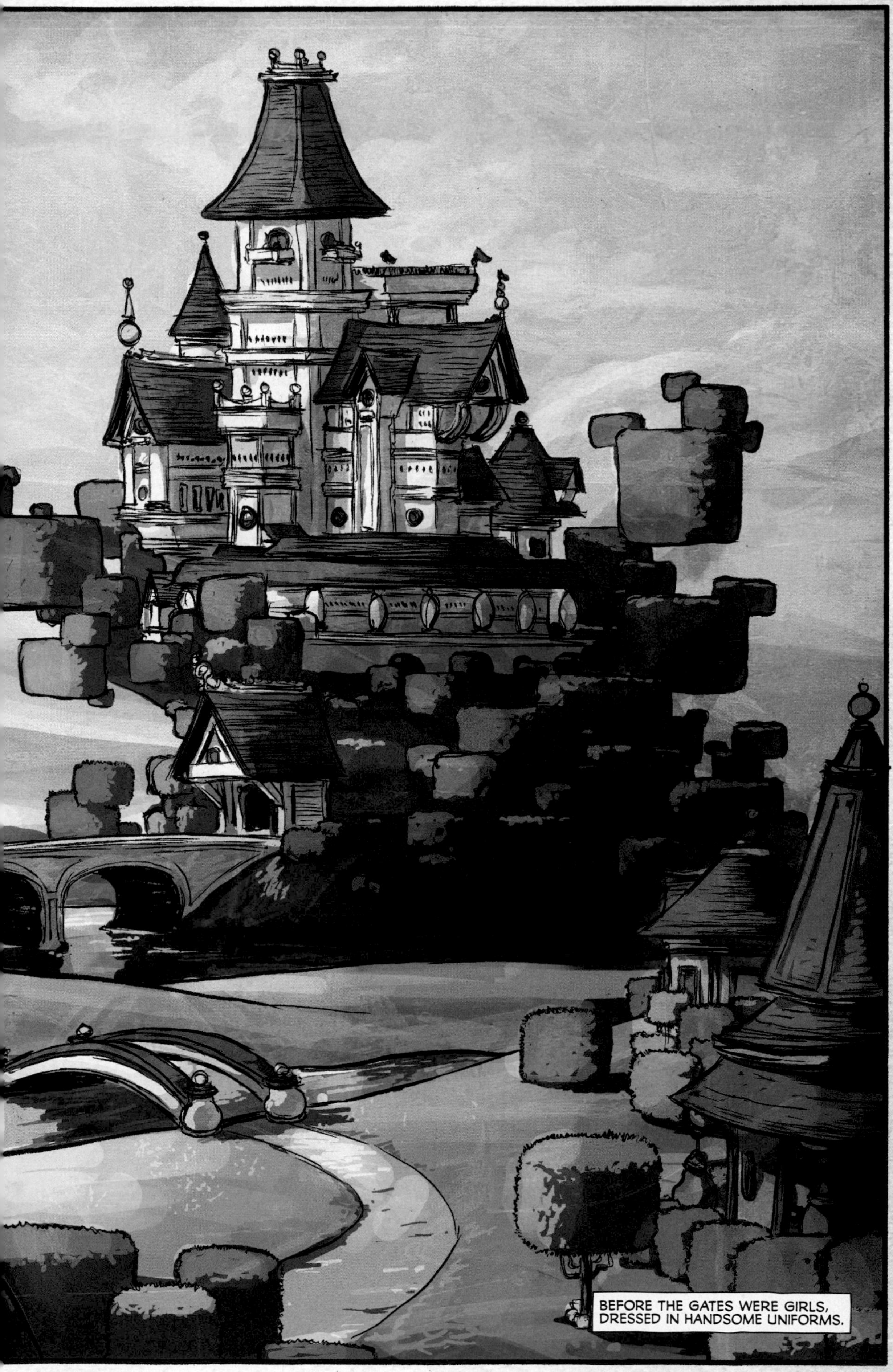
BEFORE THE GATES WERE GIRLS, DRESSED IN HANDSOME UNIFORMS.

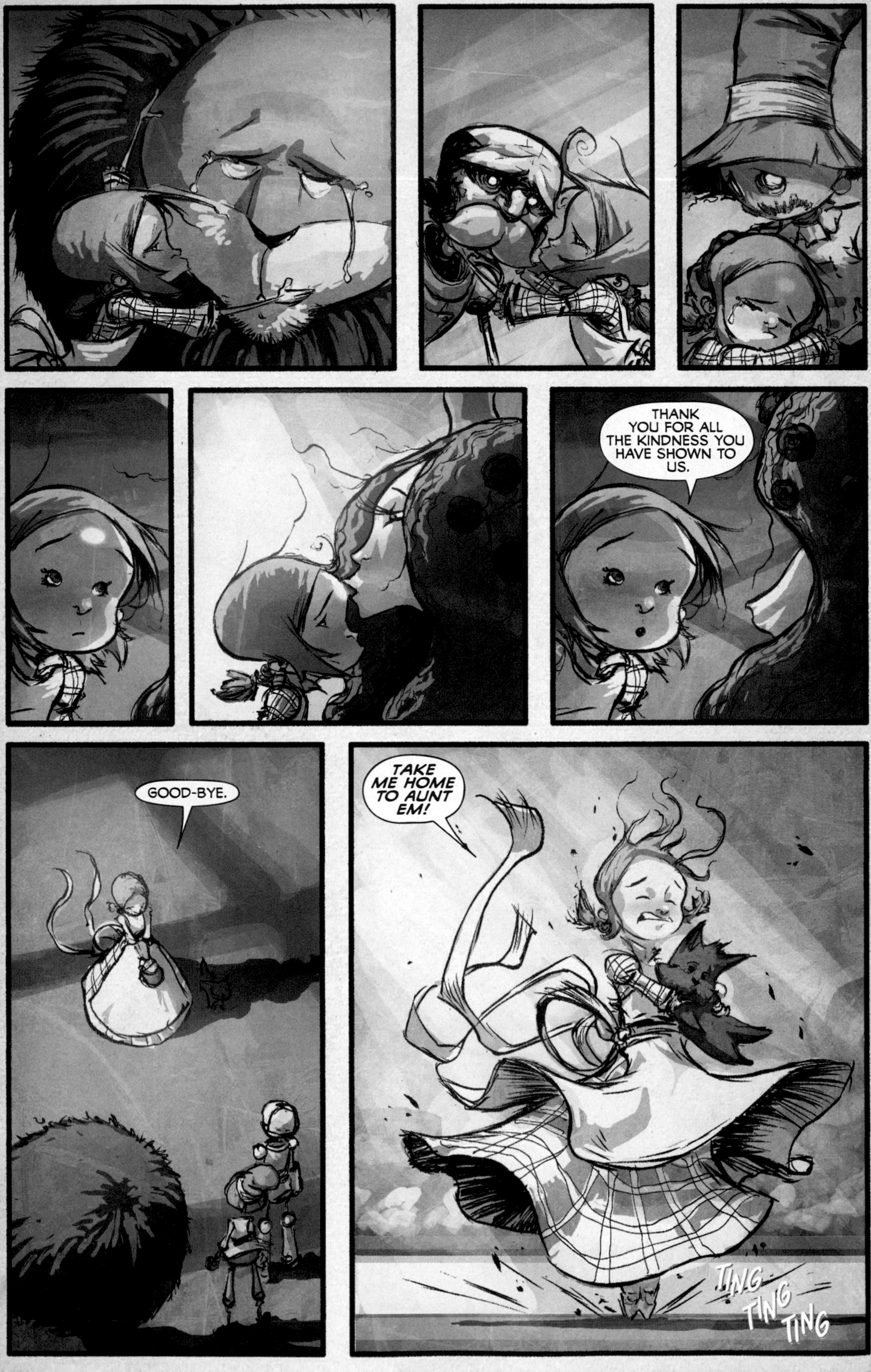
THANK YOU FOR ALL THE KINDNESS YOU HAVE SHOWN TO US.
GOOD-BYE.
TAKE ME HOME TO AUNT EM!
TING TING TING

ONE --

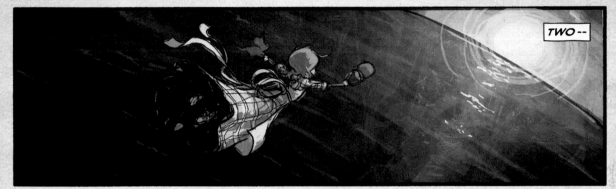

TWO --

THREE!

THE SILVER SHOES HAD FALLEN OFF IN HER FLIGHT, AND WERE LOST FOREVER.

Wuff

GOOD GRACIOUS!

THE STORY CONTINUES IN...

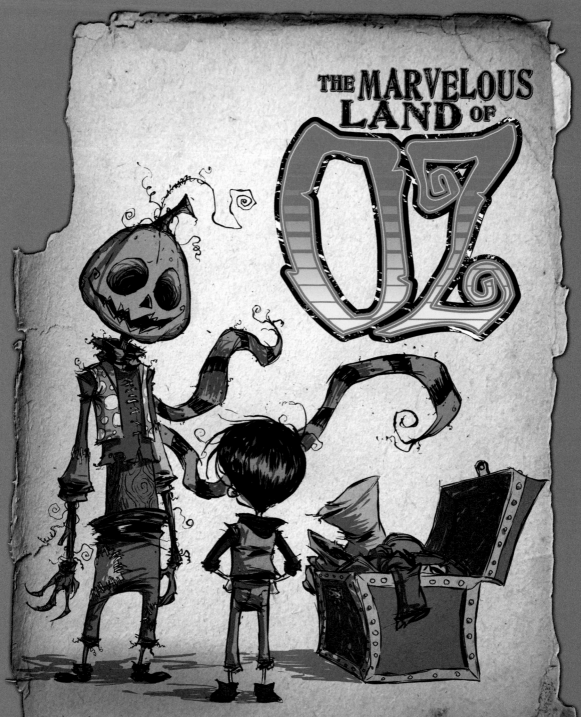

THE MARVELOUS LAND OF **OZ**

"So good a man as this must surely have a name. I believe.
I will name the fellow 'Jack Pumpkinhead!'"

ERIC SHANOWER & SKOTTIE YOUNG

ONE

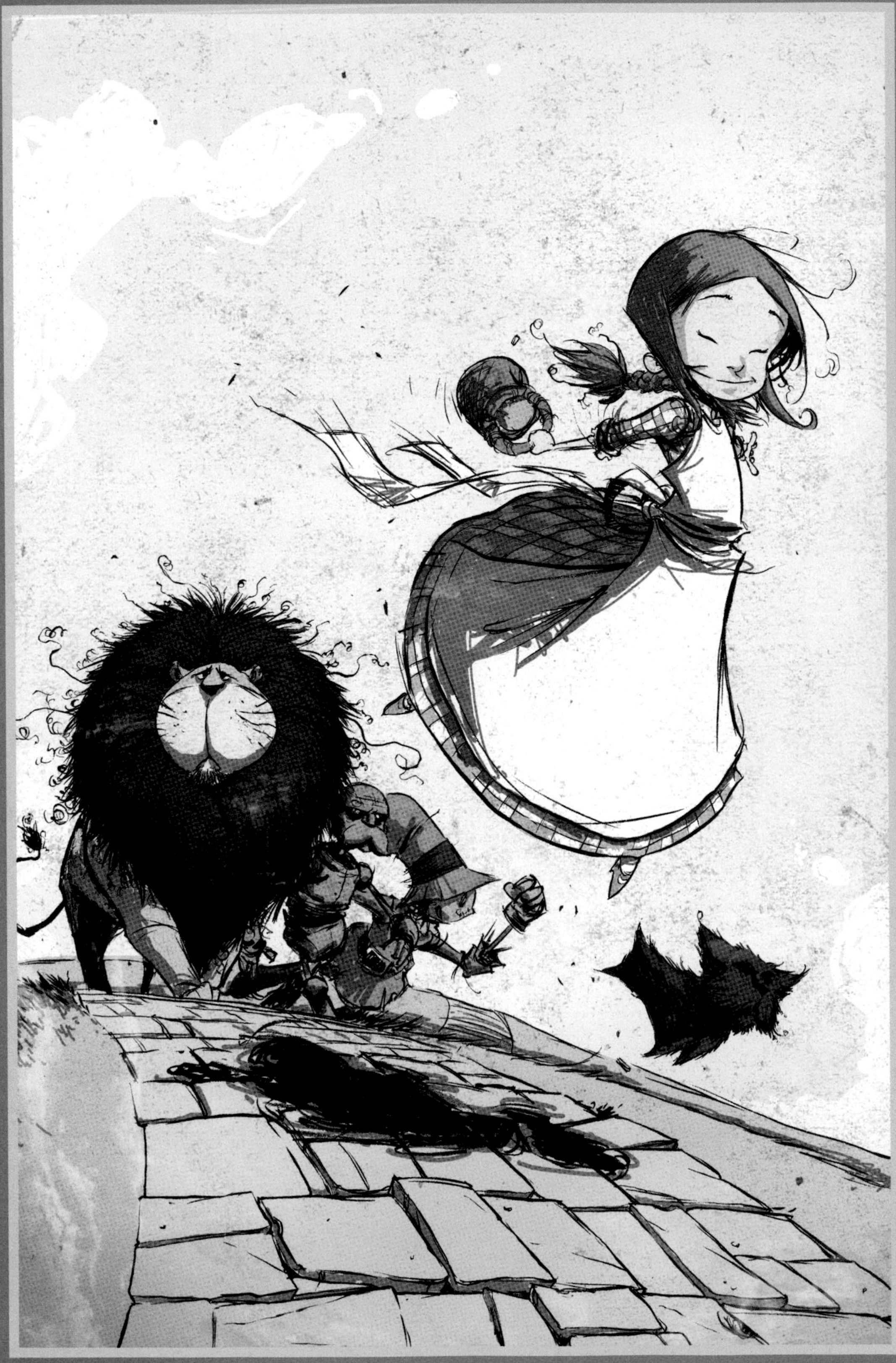

ONE

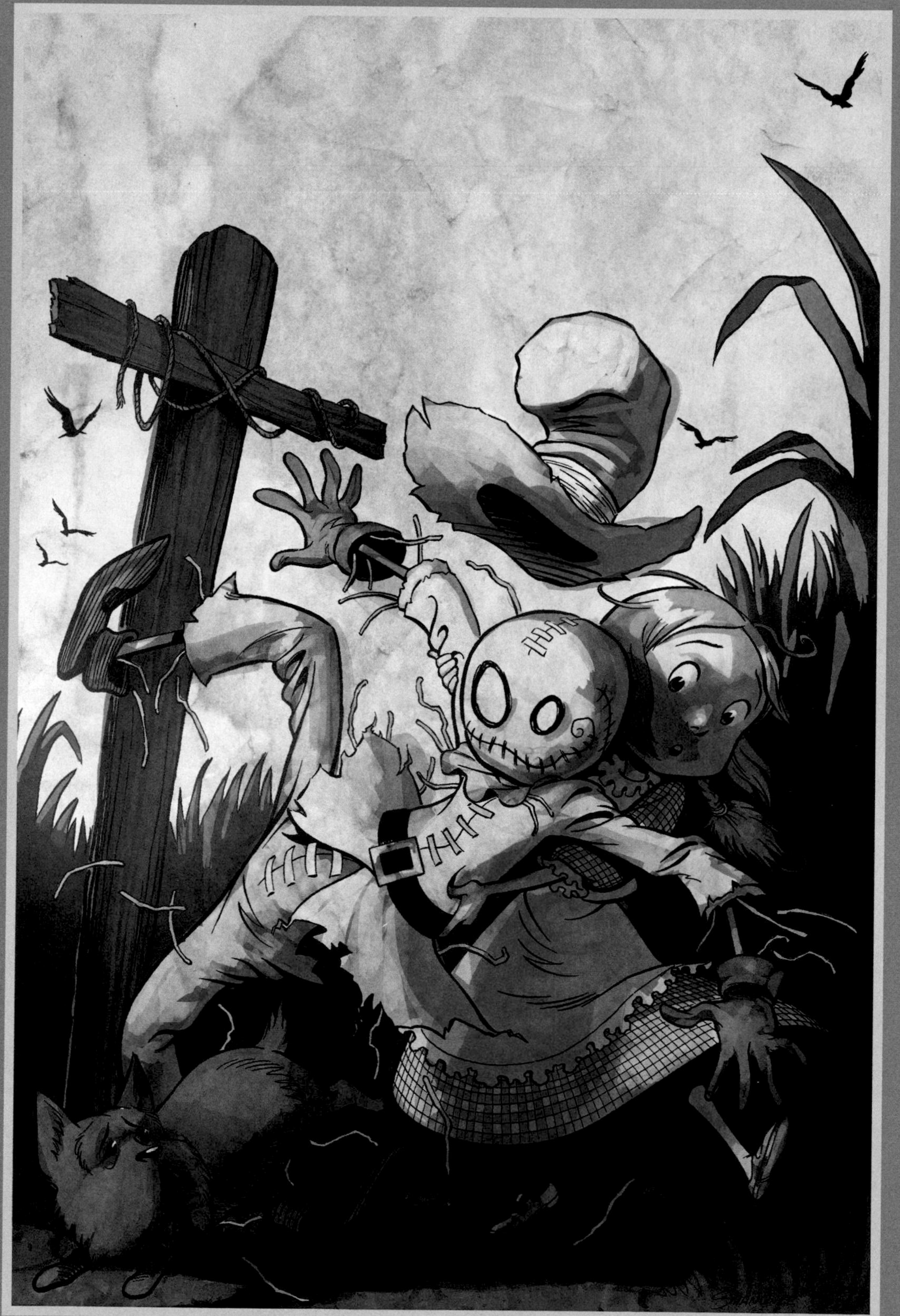

Variant Cover by Eric Shanower

ONE

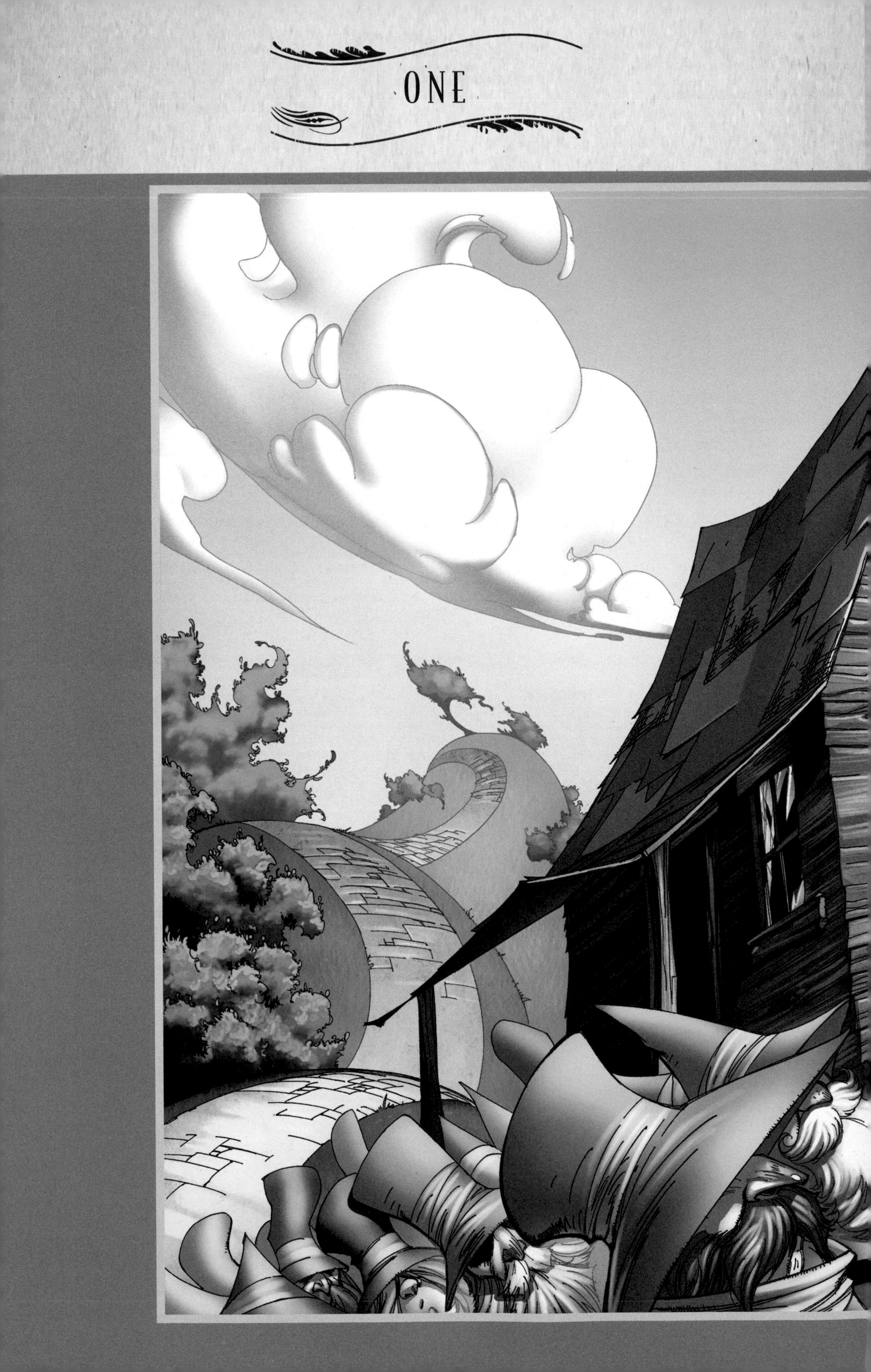

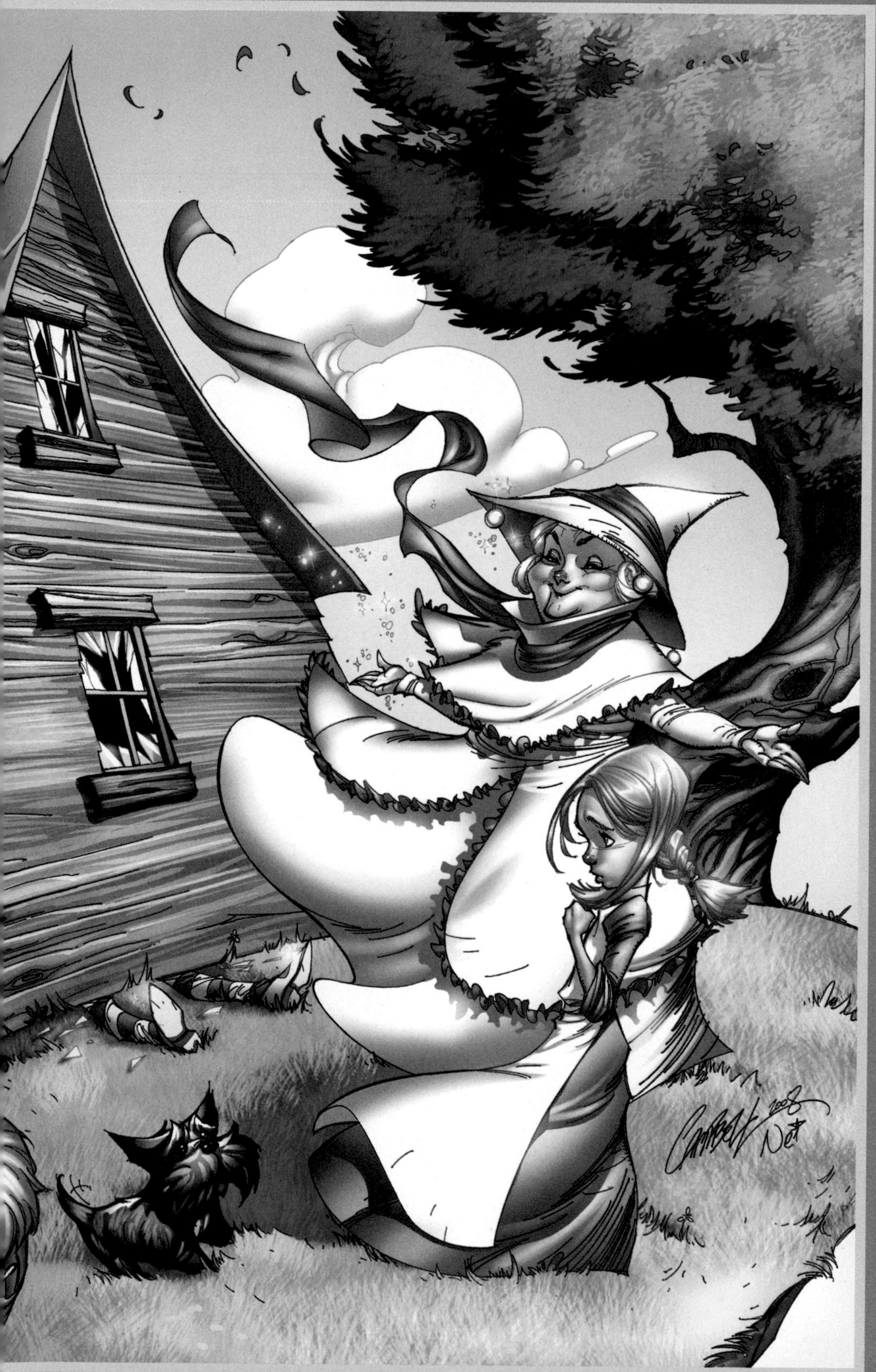
Campbell 2008

Variant Cover by J. Scott Campbell

TWO

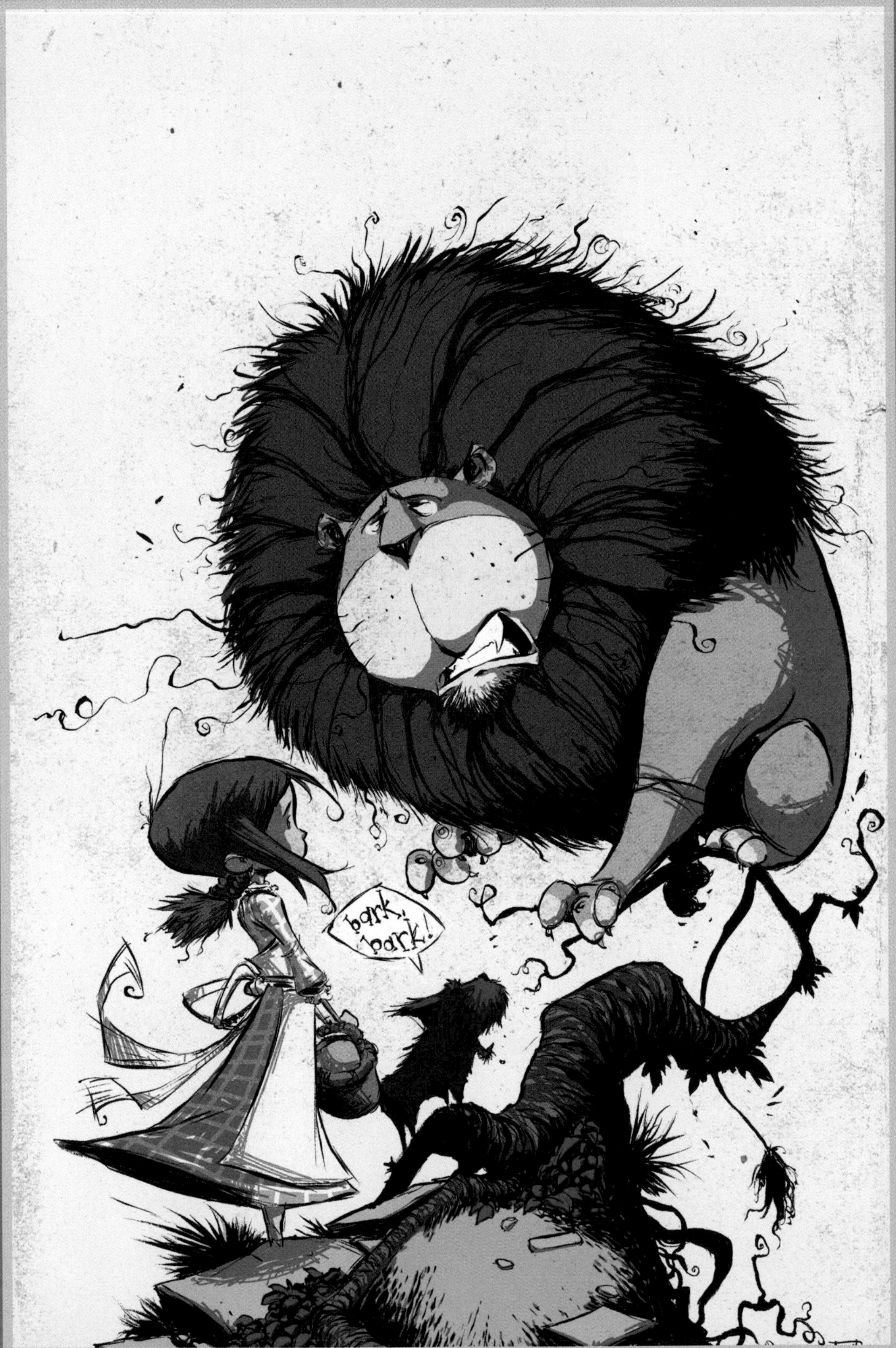
bark, bark!

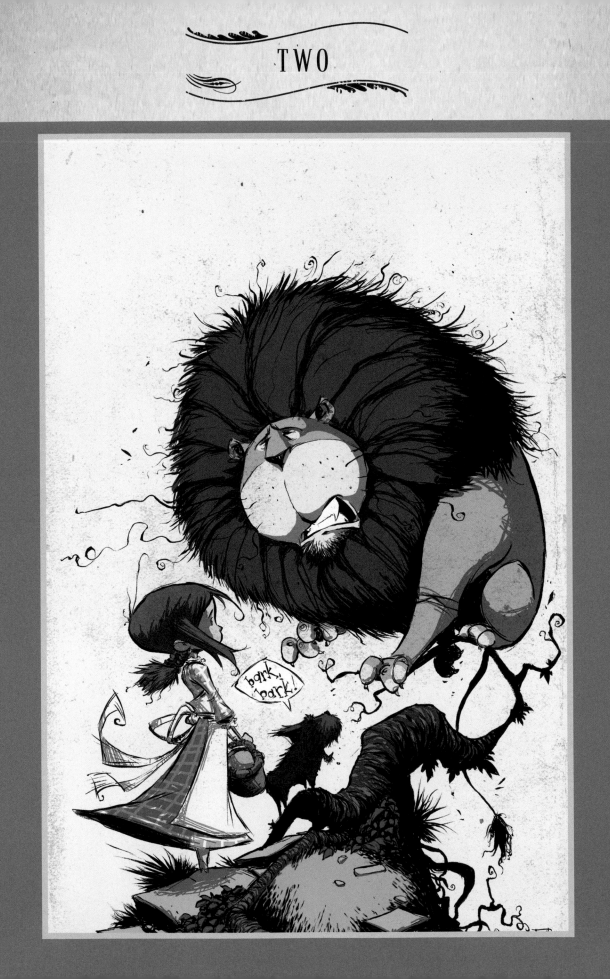

THREE

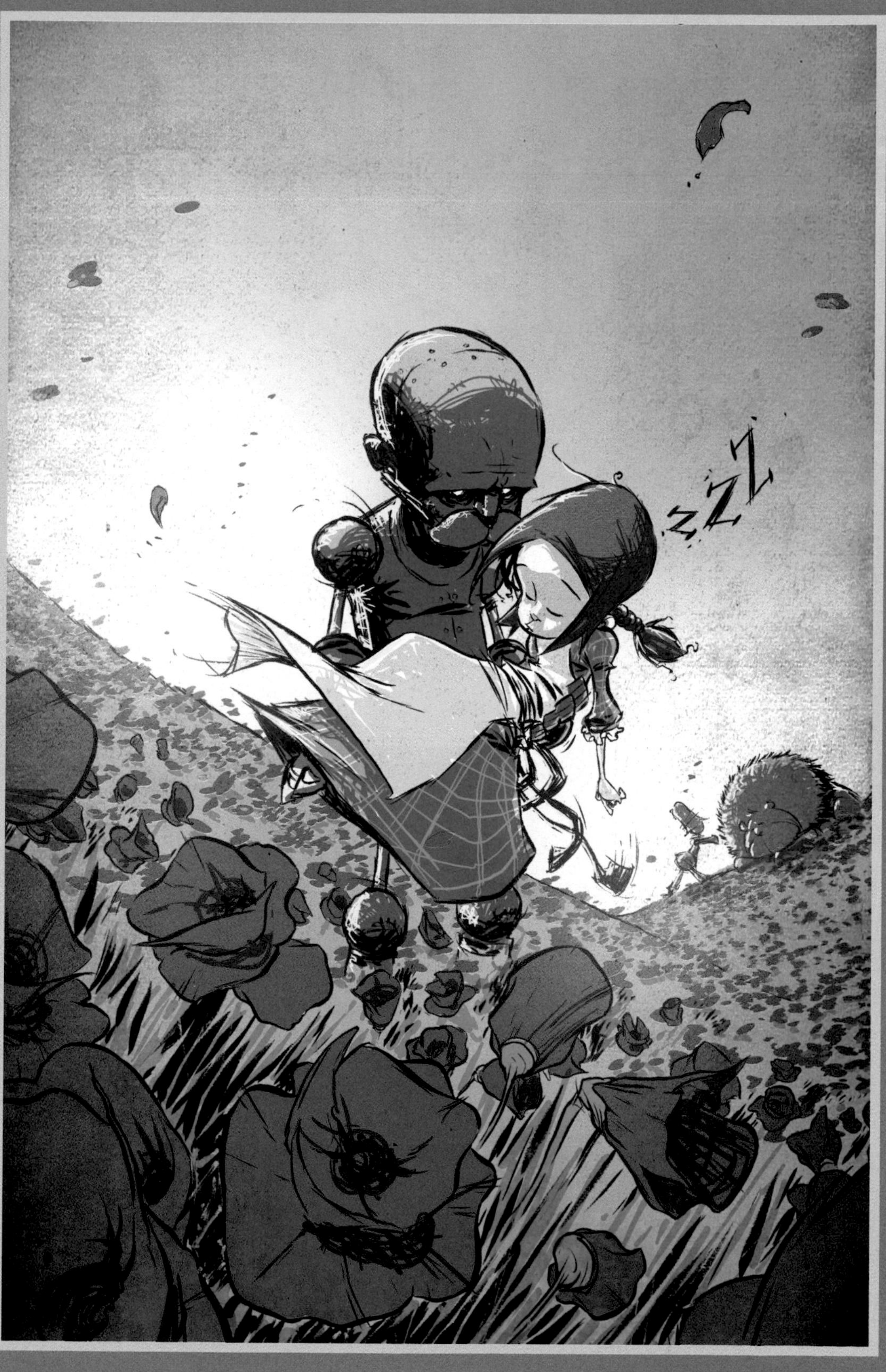
zZZ

FOUR

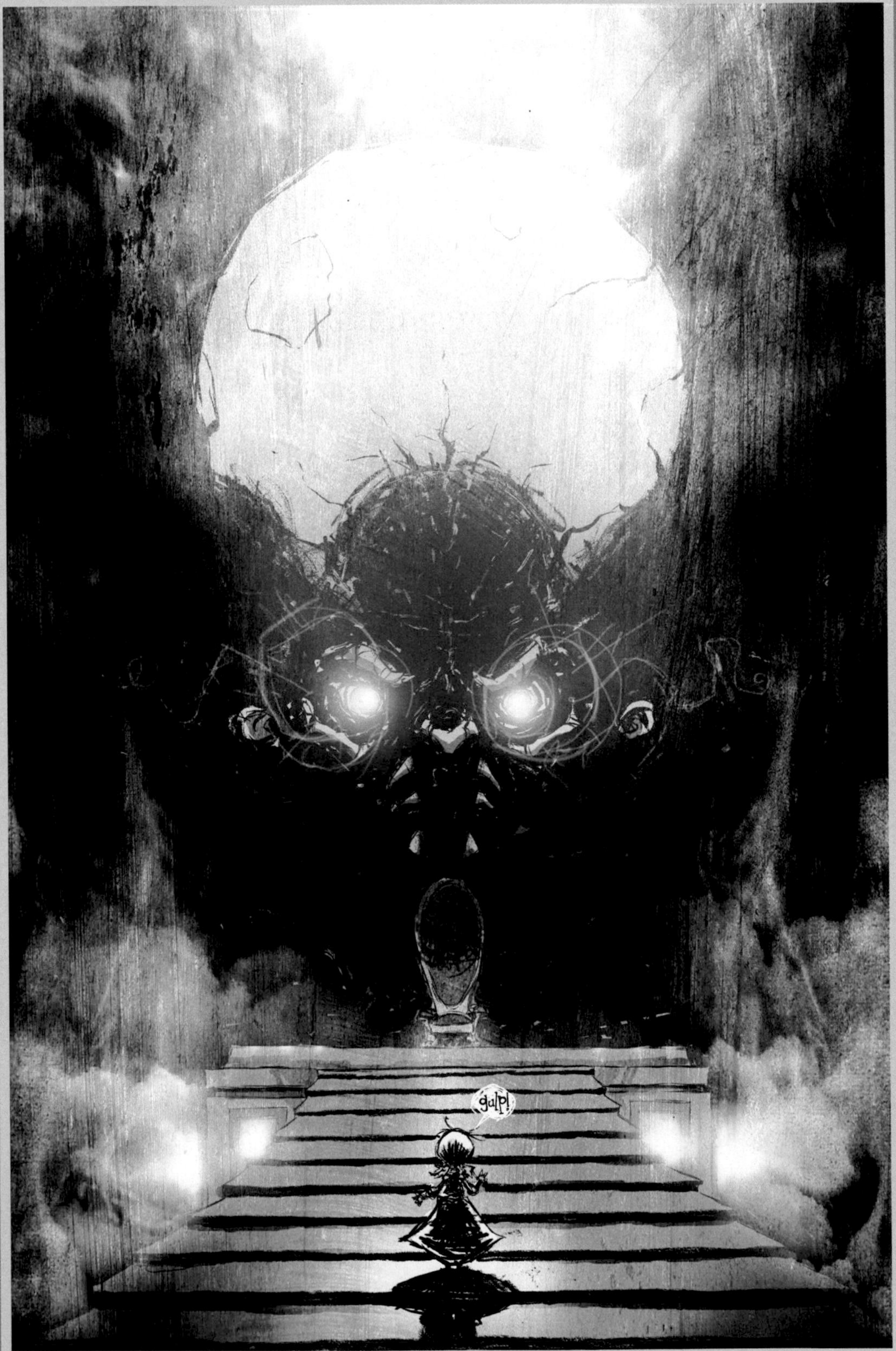
gulp!

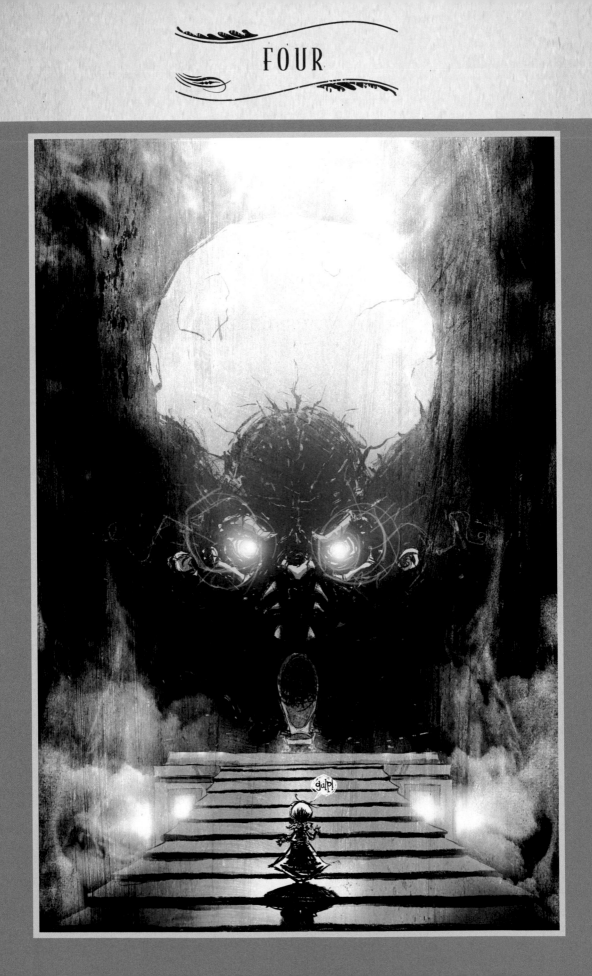

FIVE

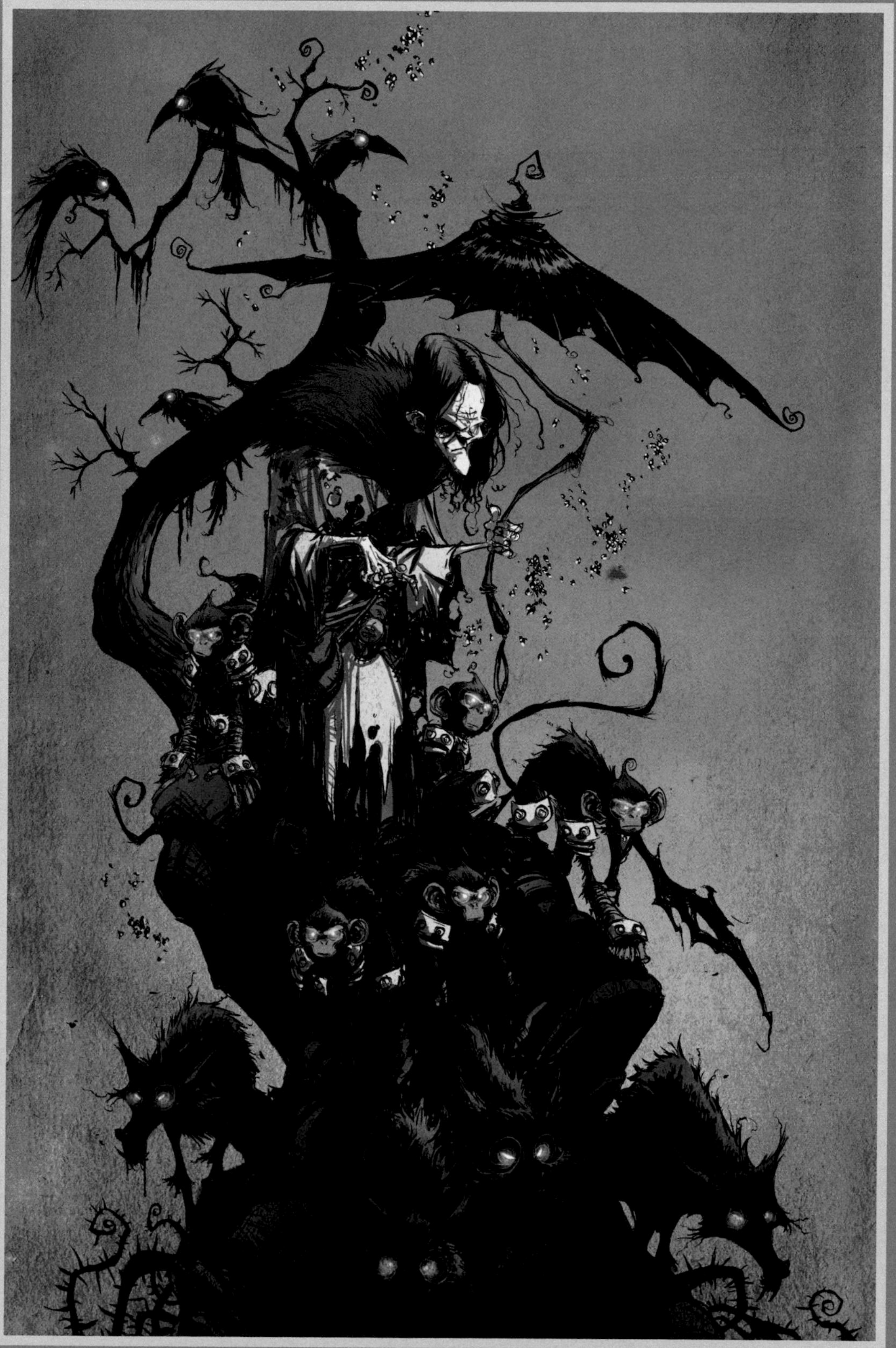

SIX

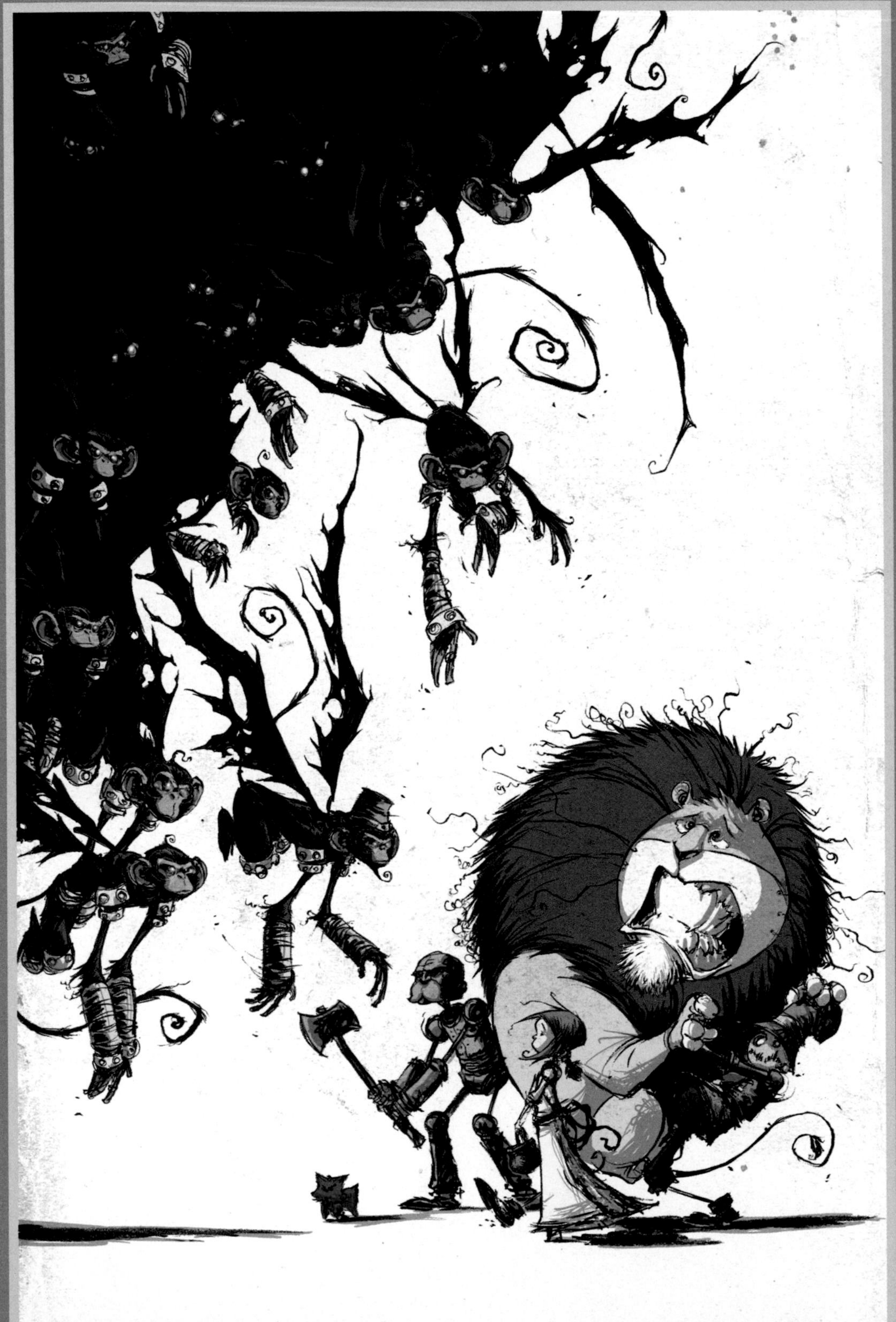

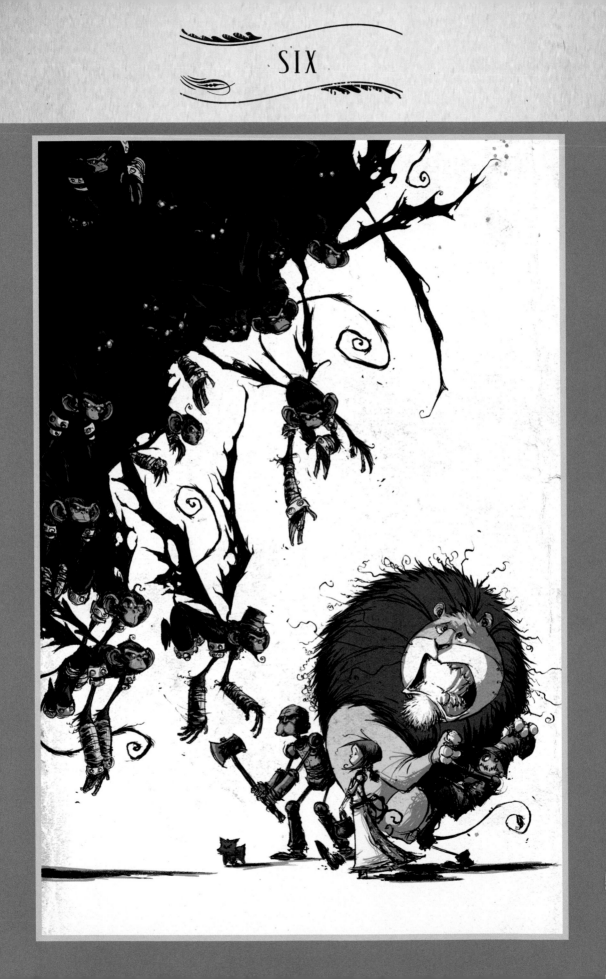

SEVEN

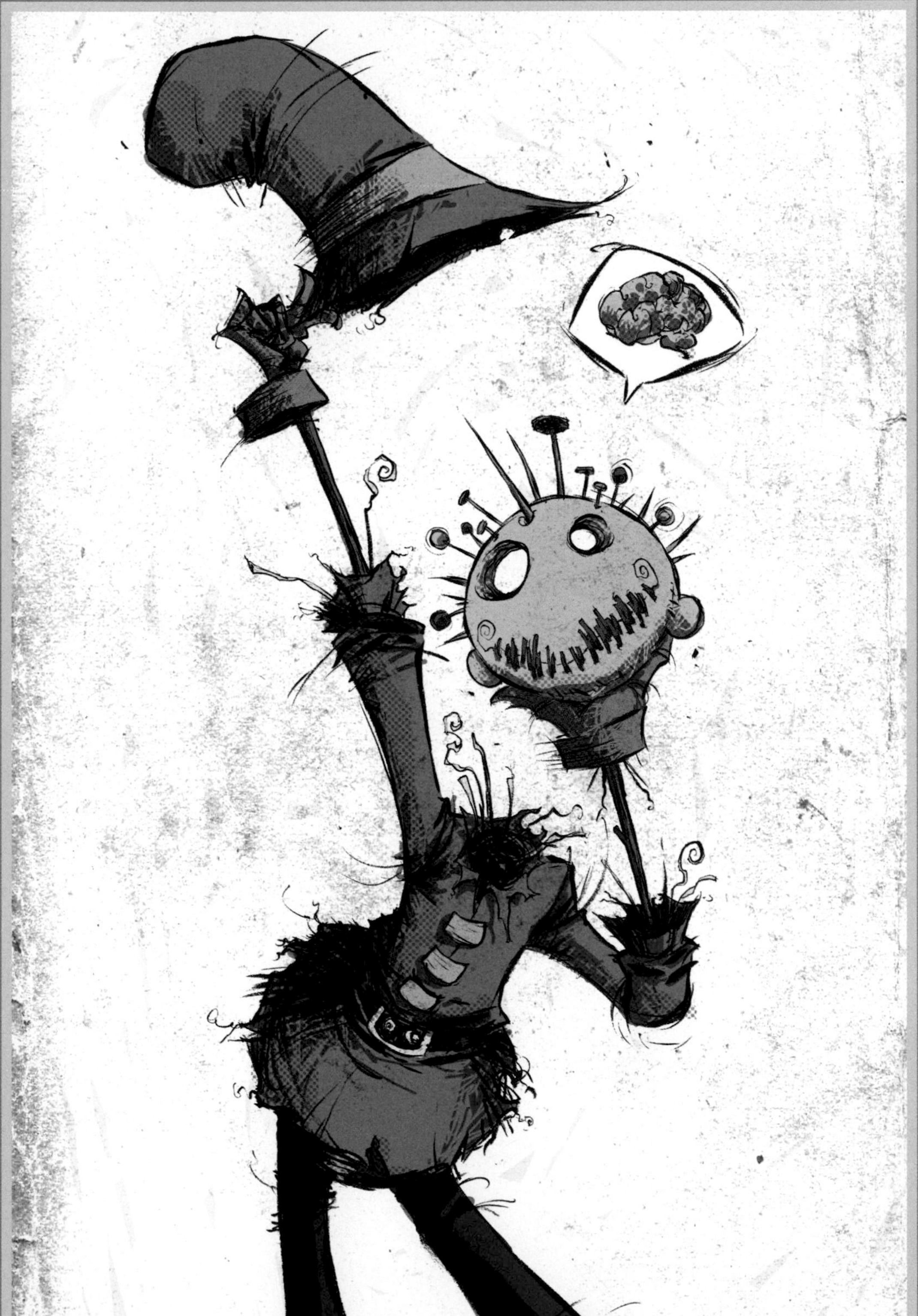

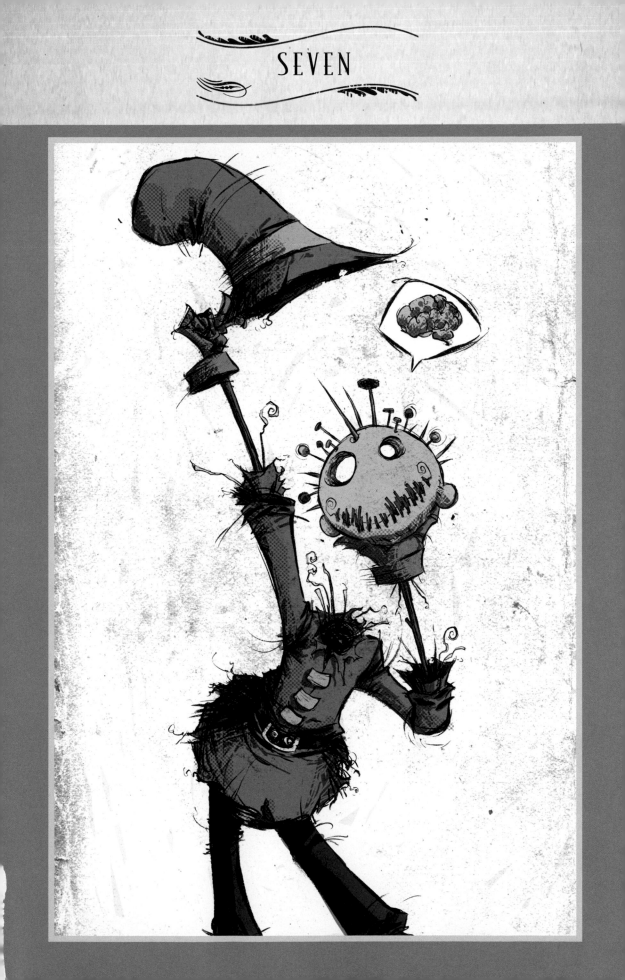

EIGHT

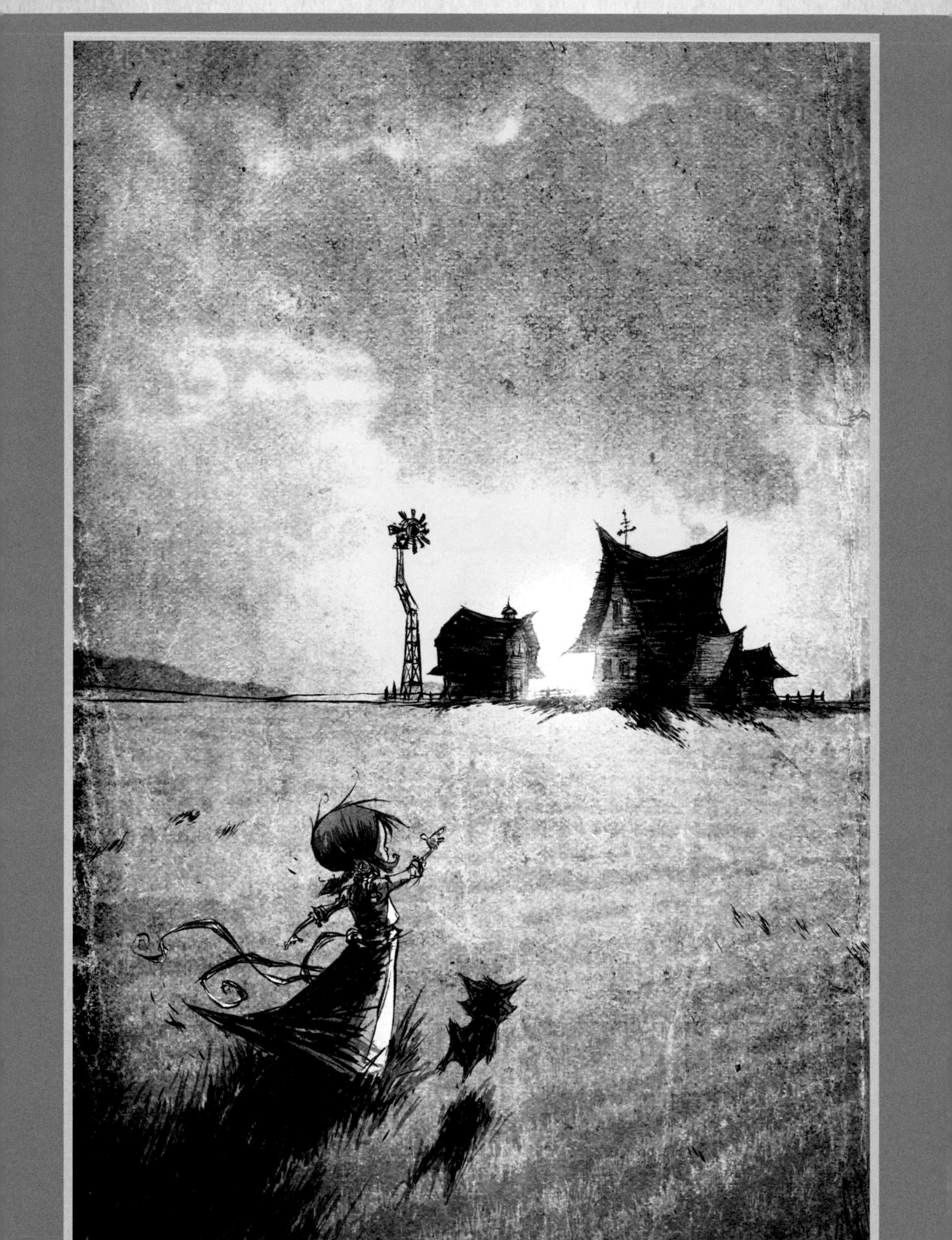

The Wonderful Wizard of Oz

by L. Frank Baum earned the status of bestseller almost immediately upon publication in 1900. Its lavish illustrations by W. W. Denslow raised the bar for excellence in book design. Baum's story, too, set a new standard. This wasn't the first time an American author had created a fantasy using American themes, setting aside elves, fairies, and the trappings of medieval Europe. But it was the first time an American fairy tale struck a lasting chord with readers and took its place on the shelves of great American literature.

Shortly after the book's publication, adaptations began. Baum took his story to Broadway, where *The Wizard of Oz* became the most popular show of 1903. This success prompted first a sequel to the book, then a whole series of Oz books, while more stage shows and films quickly followed. The book series proved so popular that it outlived Baum, officially continued by six writers through 1963 and unofficially continued by dozens of writers since.

The motion picture adaptation of *The Wizard of Oz* starring Judy Garland opened in 1939 and is now considered one of the most popular movies of all time. Since 1956, when the book entered the public domain, newly illustrated editions have proliferated worldwide. Russian children enjoy *The Wizard of the Emerald City,* the 1939 translation by Alexander Volkov, who spun off his own series of books, continued by others after Volkov's death.

Comic adaptations of Oz flourished alongside the other adaptations. Newspapers in 1904-05 carried two separate Oz series—one by author Baum, another by illustrator Denslow—featuring adventures of Oz characters in the USA. A daily newspaper comic strip by Walt Spouse adapted Baum's Oz books in the 1930s. In 1956 the first stand-alone comic book adaptation of *The Wizard of Oz* appeared, *Dell Junior Treasury* #5.

Since then Oz comics have flourished. Twenty-first century Oz comics are surprisingly varied. Dark overtones, steampunk backgrounds, team-ups with other children's book characters, Japanese manga, Korean manwha, French bande dessinée, web comics—it's all there. Now, Marvel is taking Oz back to its roots with a faithful comics adaptation of the book that began it all, *The Wonderful Wizard of Oz,* with a script by yours truly and glorious art by Skottie Young.

Young has set aside previous versions of Oz and reached inside himself for his own response to Baum's story. He's brought forth a brand new vision of Oz, firmly rooted in the original, yet with life bursting out all around. Young's Dorothy is unmistakably a Kansas farm girl, whisked away to a magical land. It's a journey we're glad to take with her because she is so obviously sensible, human, and down-to-earth. Young's solid designs of Dorothy's companions, the Scarecrow and the Tin Woodman, make these preposterous creatures easy to believe in. And Young's Cowardly Lion . . . well, Young's big, bashful fur ball is my favorite.

Just turn the page, take a look, and see if you don't agree.

—Eric Shanower

Dorothy

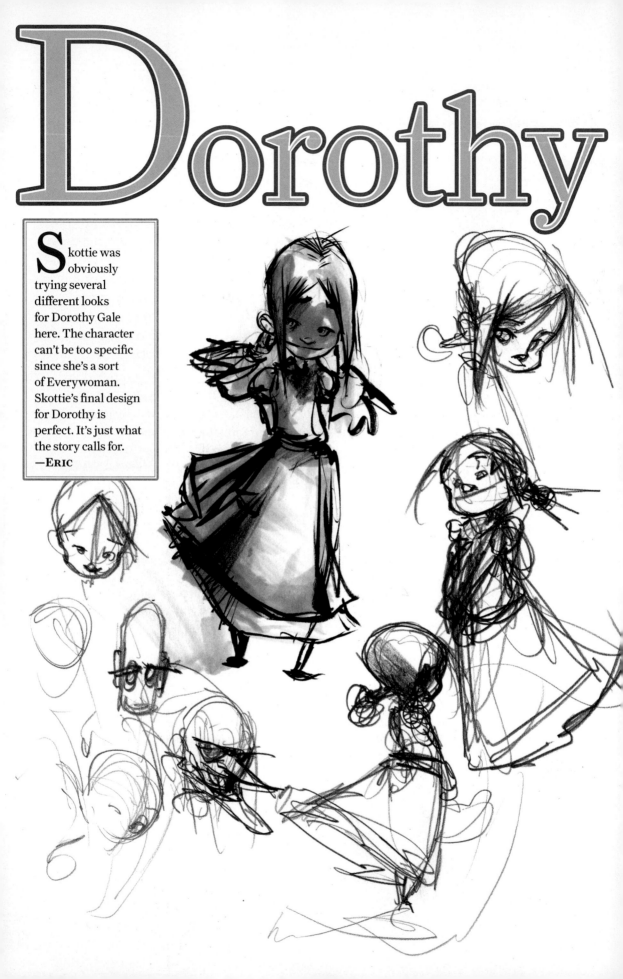

Skottie was obviously trying several different looks for Dorothy Gale here. The character can't be too specific since she's a sort of Everywoman. Skottie's final design for Dorothy is perfect. It's just what the story calls for.
—ERIC

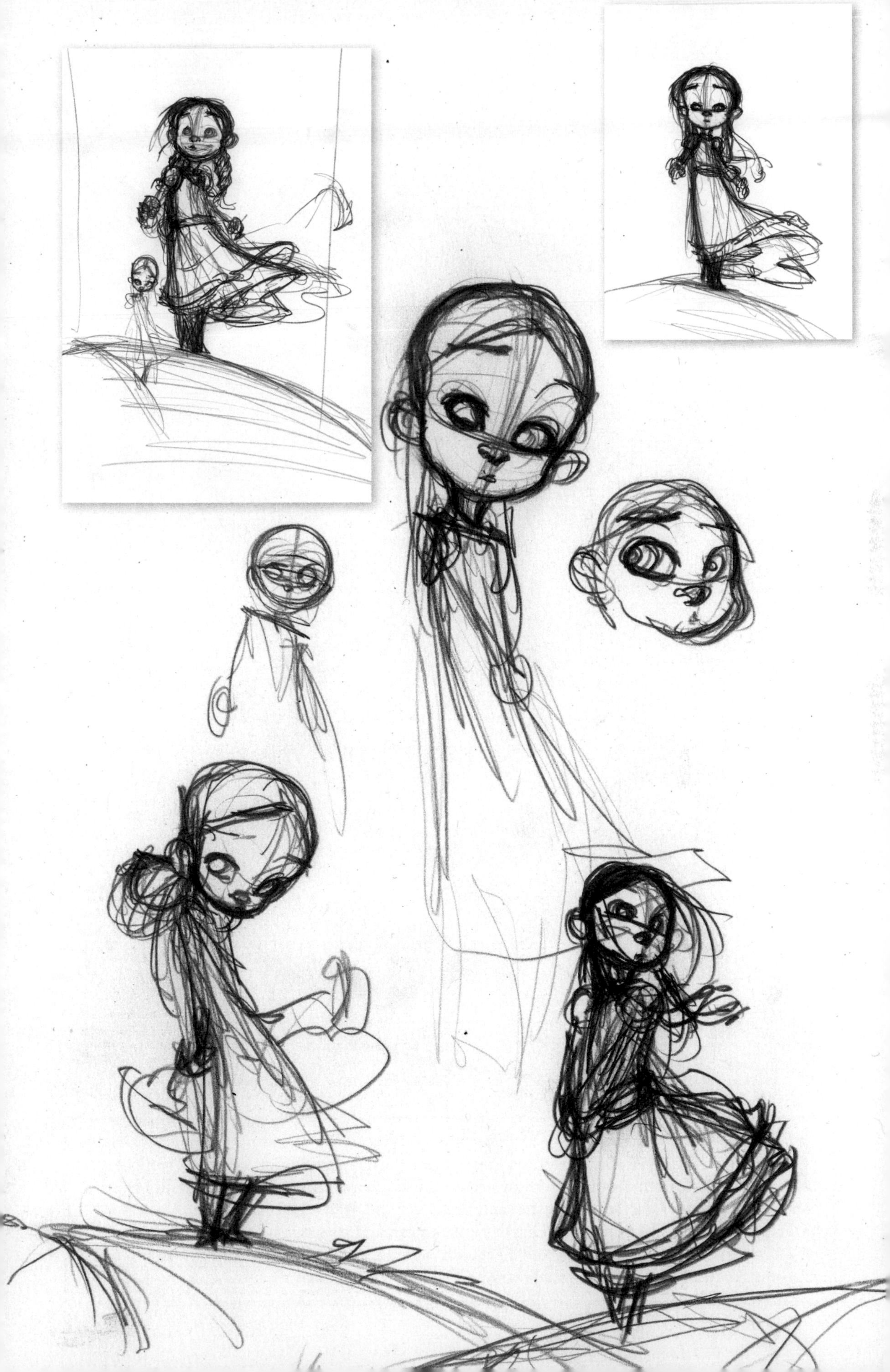

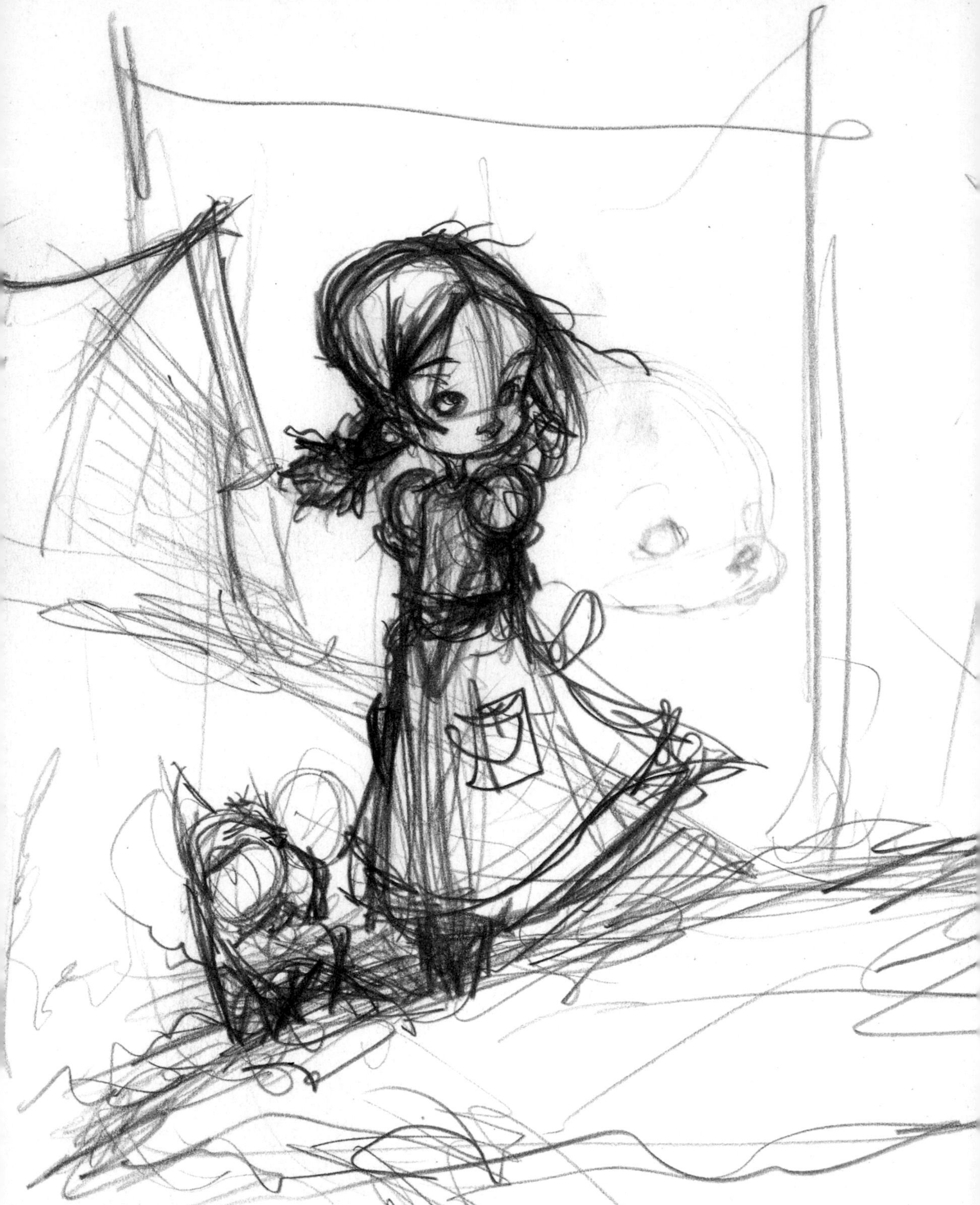

I may have drawn Dorothy's head 300 times. From the day I got the job while still working on X-Men, I started doodling Dorothy heads. It was always a very subtle change and to someone else it may look like I drew the same head over and over. I had a good idea of where I wanted her to go, but I tried every kind of eye, nose, ear, and strand of hair you could think of. Dorothy is the soul of this story and if I couldn't convince you to love her within two seconds of seeing her on the page, then I should take another job. —**Skottie**

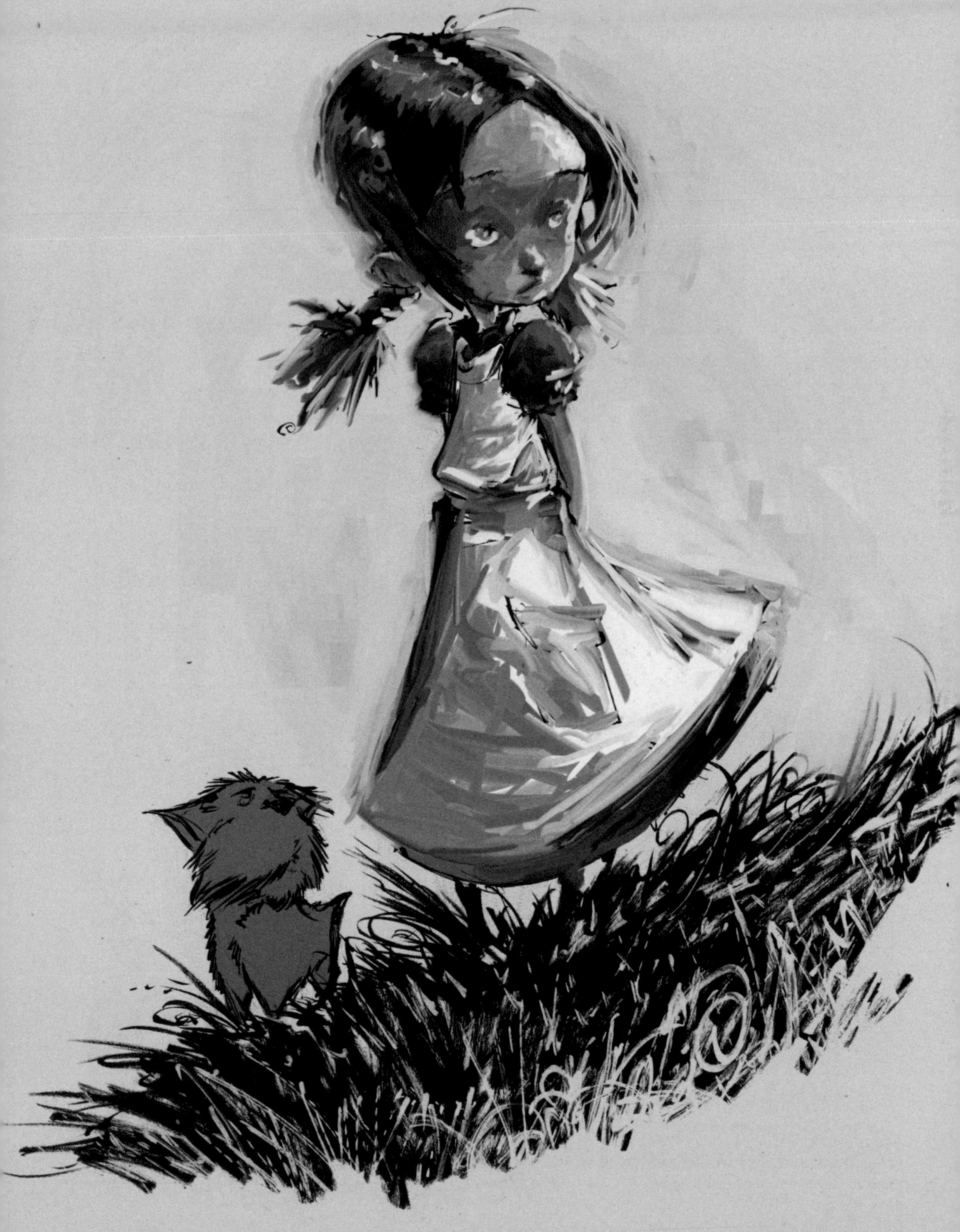

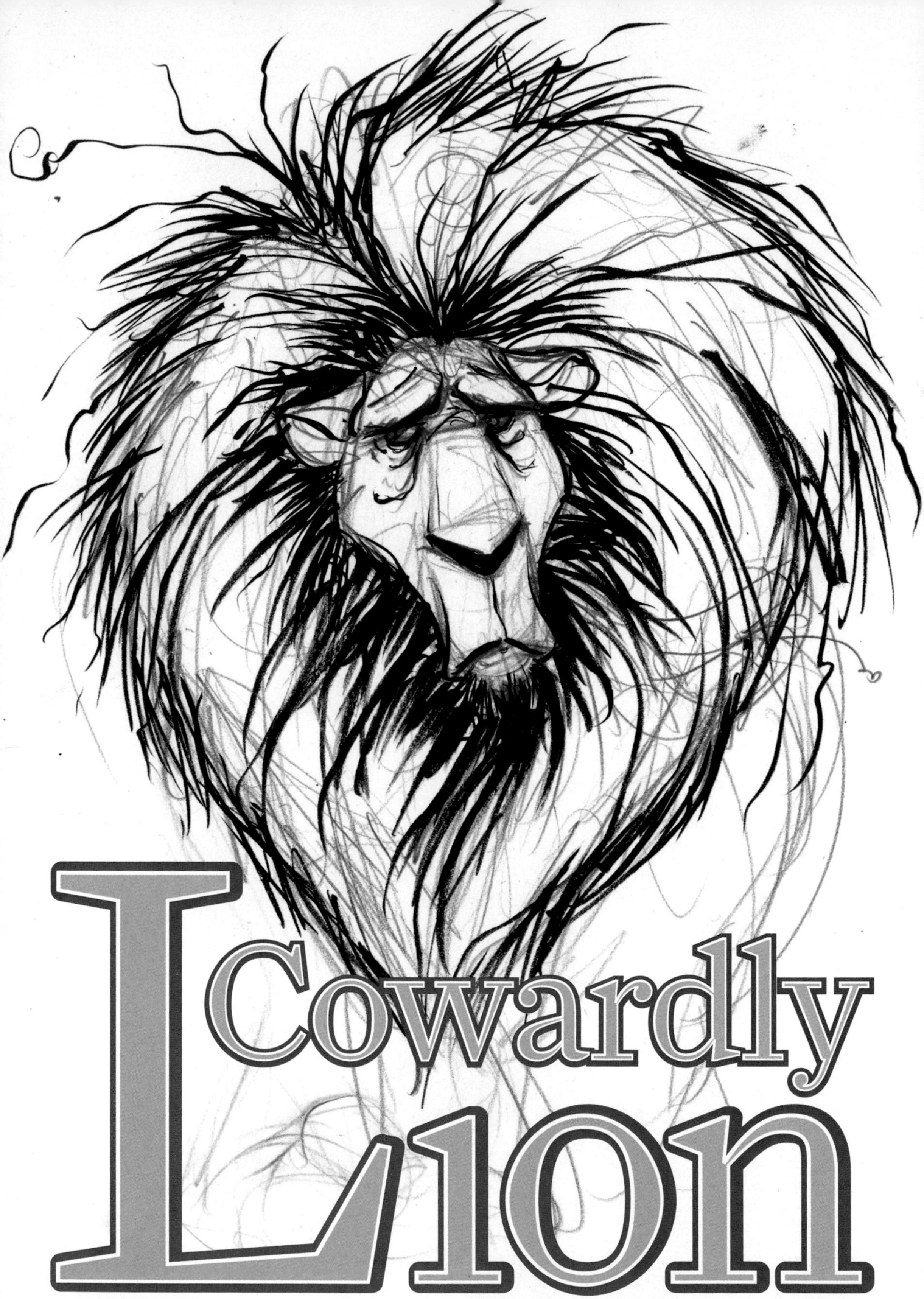

Cowardly Lion

The Cowardly Lion with a sophisticated look. Skottie's final Lion design captures the character more successfully. —**Eric**

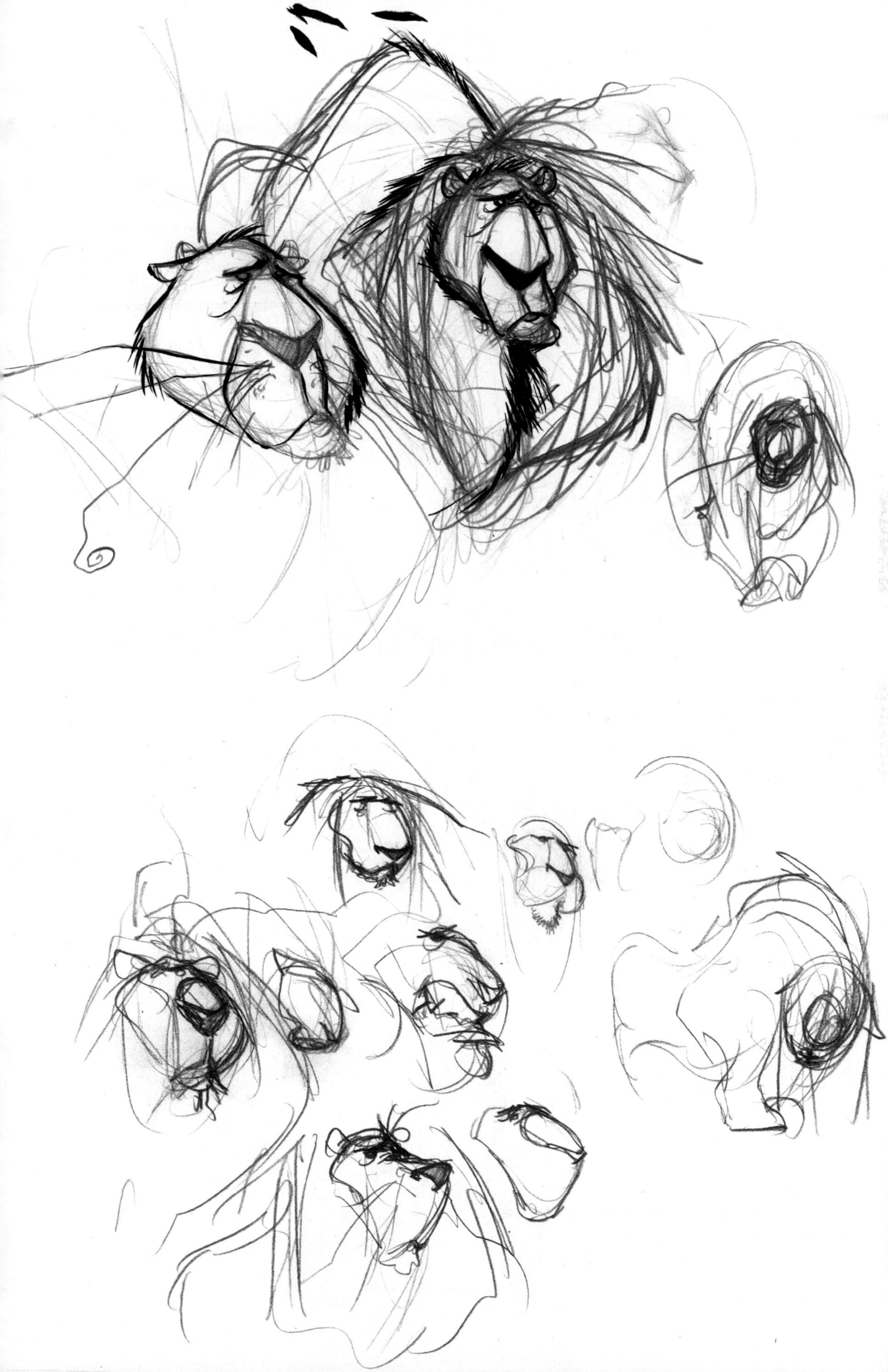

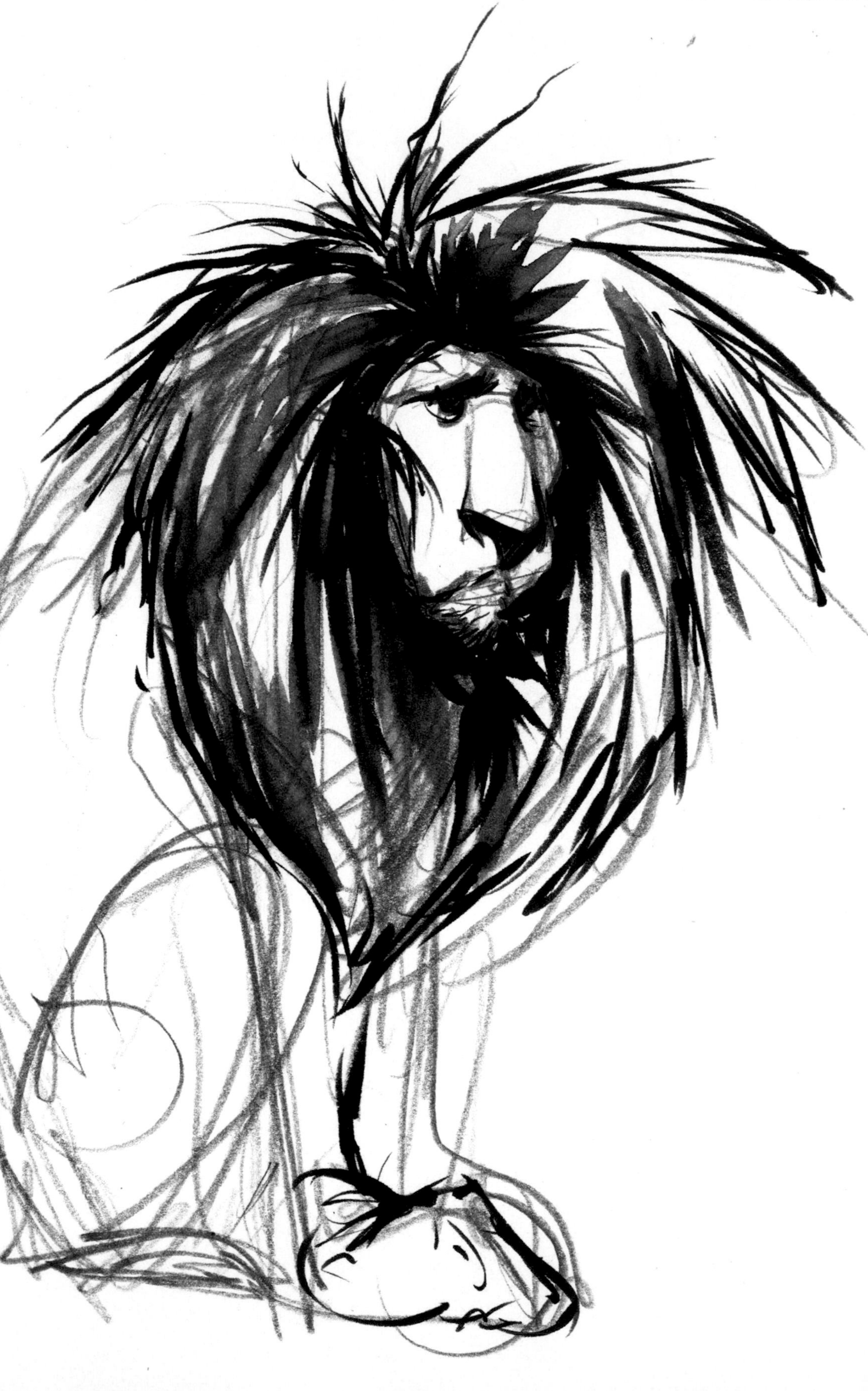

The lion was tough because when you think of lions you think of beautiful, majestic beasts. But we need you to think, "What a pussy cat." You can see that I first played with more traditional lion shapes but ended up somewhere very different. I needed to be soft and nothing says soft like big, round, puffy circles. I went with that for the face. Just a big circle with all the trappings of a lions face inside of it. Add a big frizzed-out mane of hair and we've got a lion out of a shape that you might not think screams lion. —**Skottie**

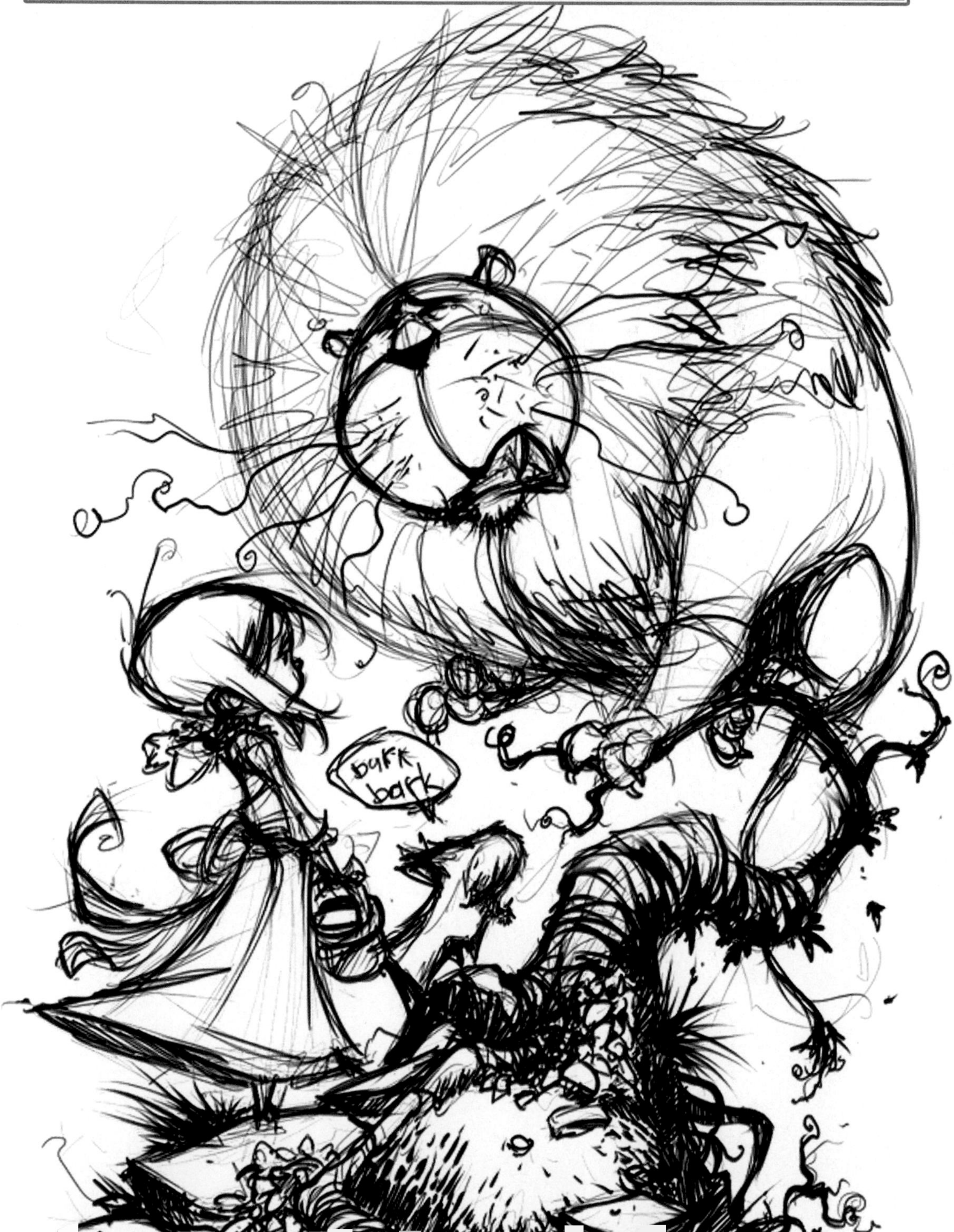
bark bark

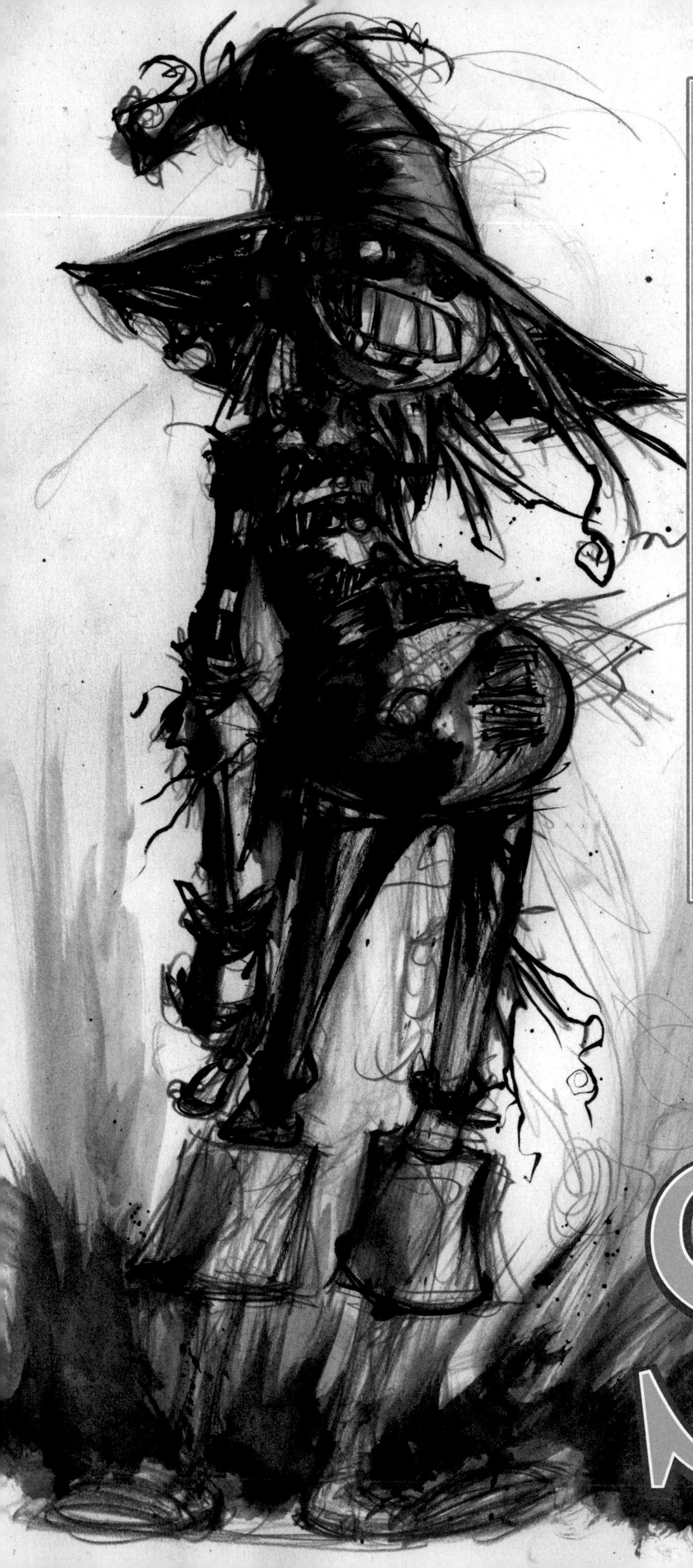

Get the Scarecrow to a dentist—quick!—**Eric**

As you'll notice, my first version of the Scarecrow was a tad over the top. I loved this version, but elements didn't illustrate Baum's vision very well. I gave him a fully functioning mouth, but he should really be more Scarecrow than person. Once I took him back to being more of a stuffed man, I tried to focus on the hat. After going through many versions of the traditional pointy hat, I landed on a bit more of a rounded one. I felt it gave him a great shape and matched the round theme I had going through his body.
—**Skottie**

Sc

Everyone's favorite straw man.
—ERIC

arecrow

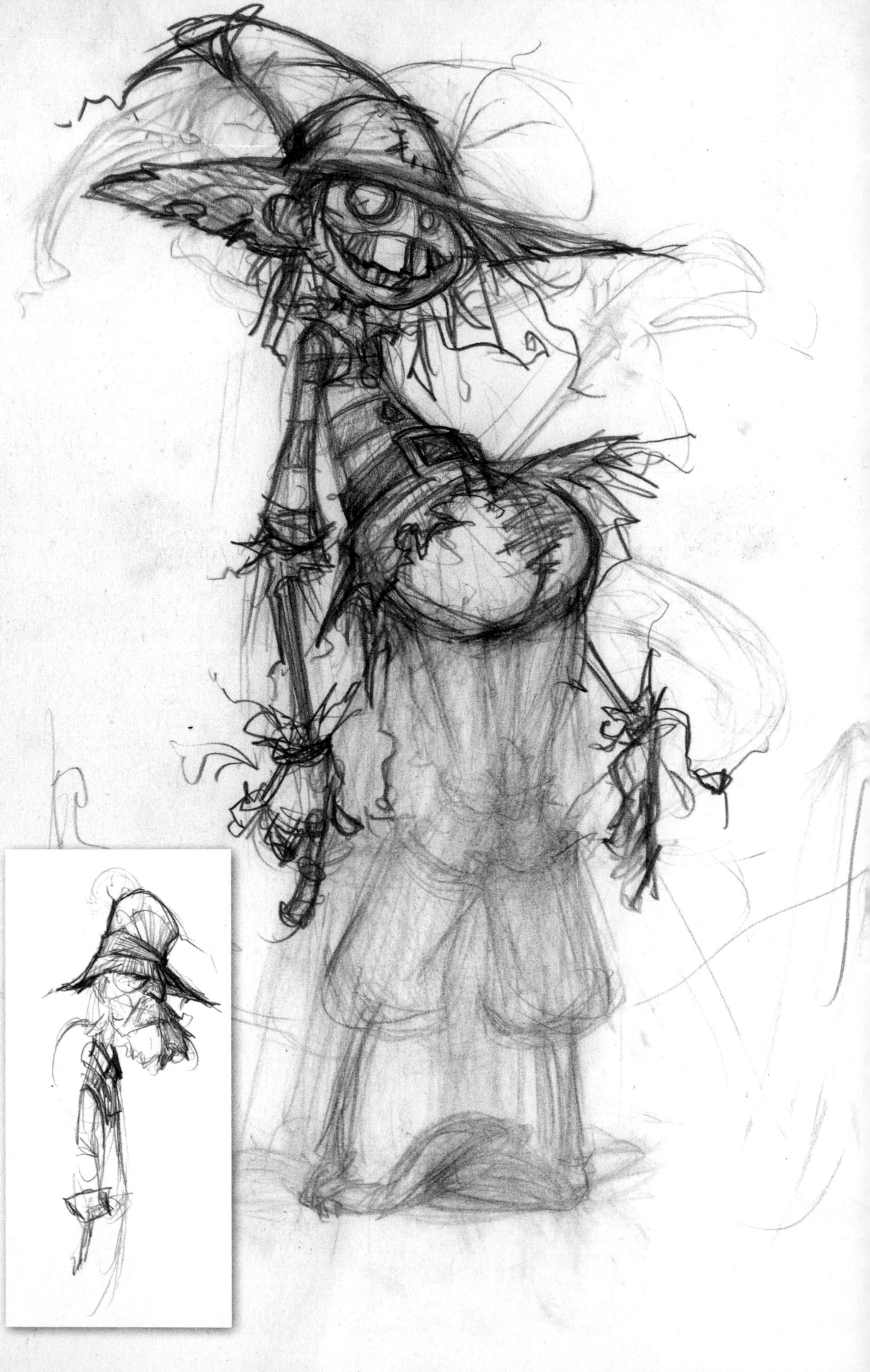

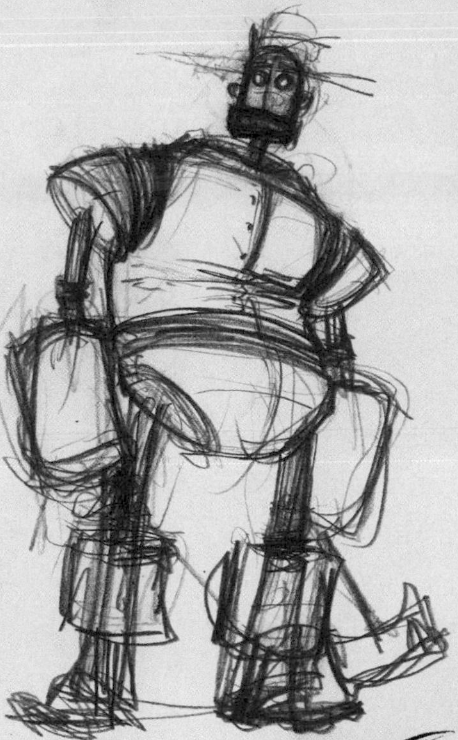

Tin Woodman

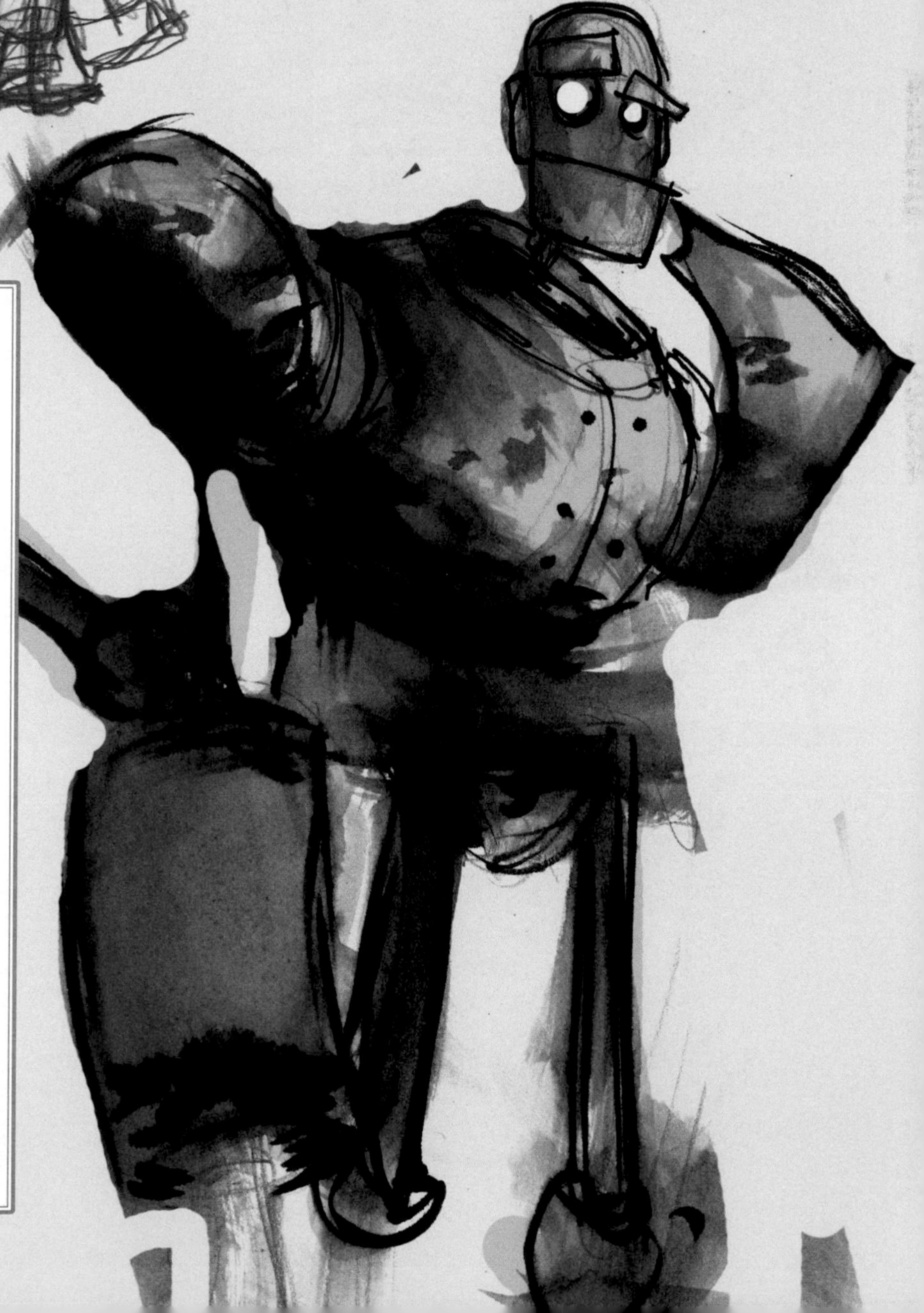

This Tin Woodman doesn't look like he'd need an axe to chop down trees.
—**Eric**

At first you can see that I was wanting to go super-big and more robotic. I wanted to show off how crazy I could make shapes. In the end I brought it back to the spirit of the character and who he is. I needed him to have a few features that could be pushed and pulled to lend some emotion that the "big cool robot" style just didn't give.
—**Skottie**

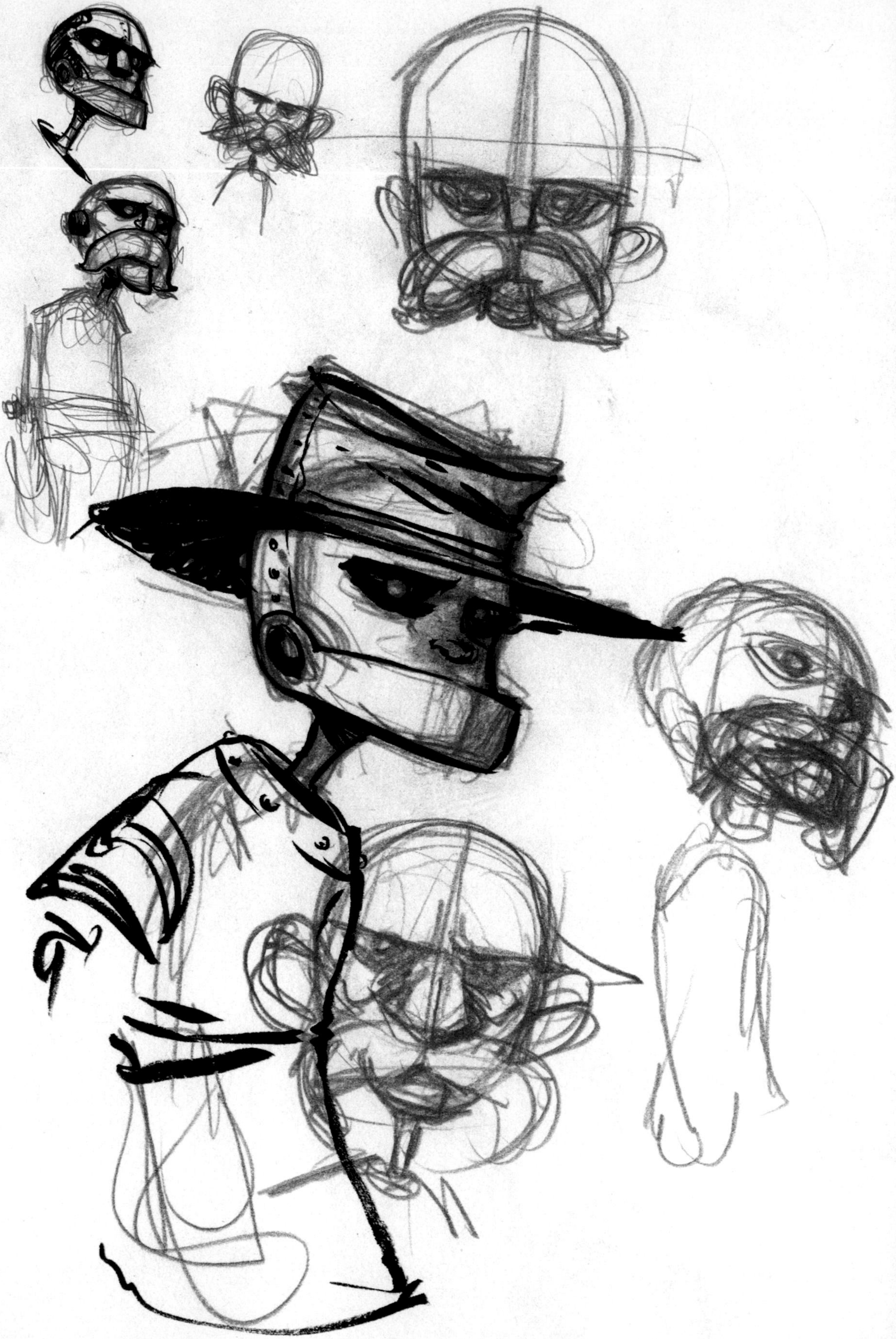

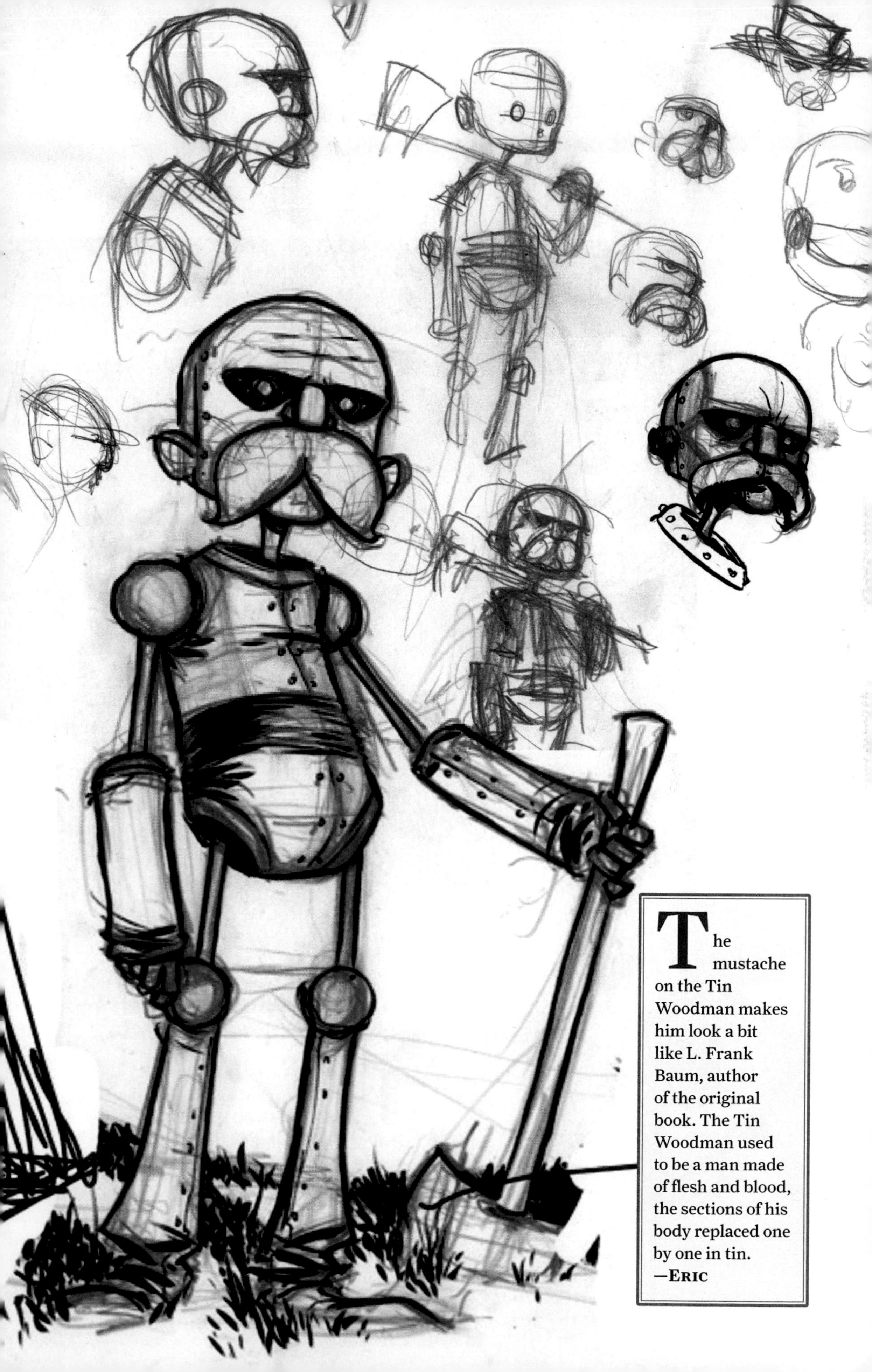

The mustache on the Tin Woodman makes him look a bit like L. Frank Baum, author of the original book. The Tin Woodman used to be a man made of flesh and blood, the sections of his body replaced one by one in tin.
—Eric

Good Witch of the North

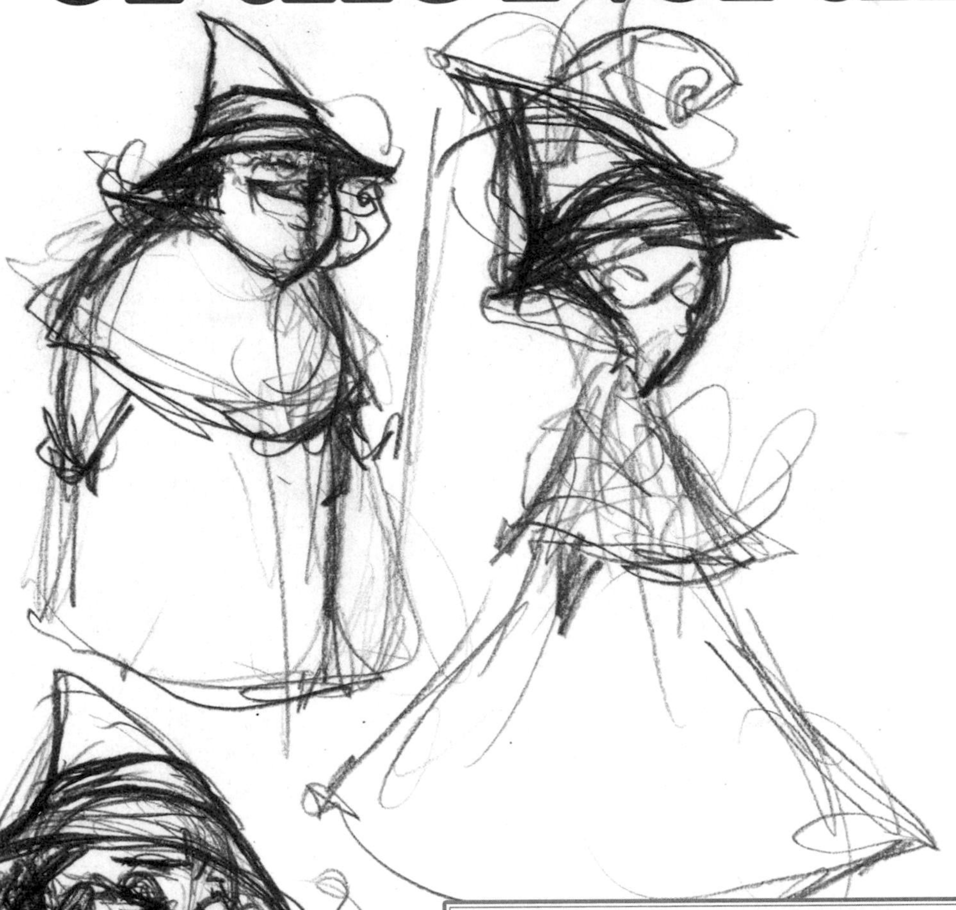

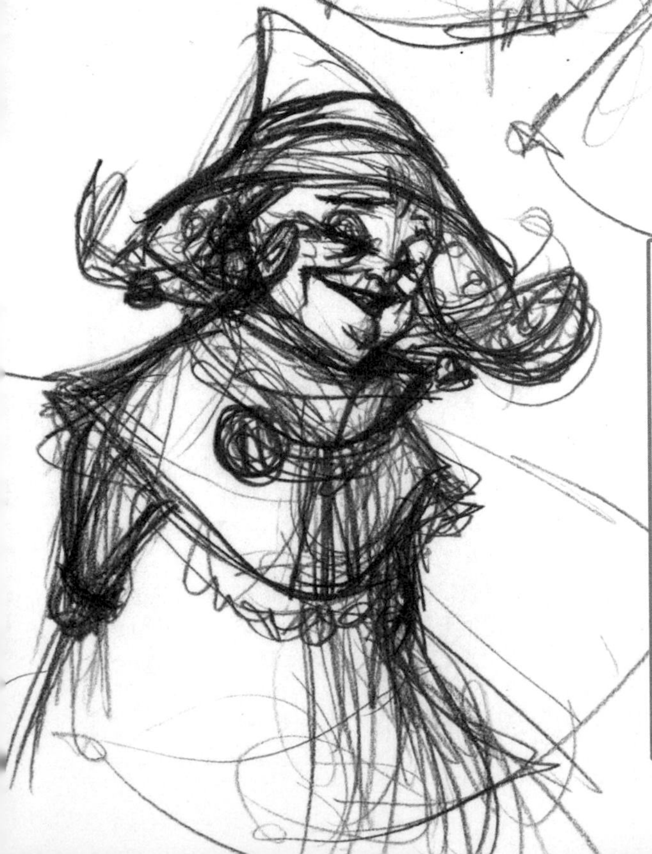

The Good Witch of the North is the first person to welcome Dorothy to the Land of Oz. —**Eric**

I was looking for a soft and calming shape to give to the Good Witch. I wanted her to look like a wonderful grandmother-type figure at first glance without having to say anything. I almost went a little too funny-looking. It's a fine line to walk while cartooning not to make things look silly. There needs to be real emotion behind the fantasy style lines. —**Skottie**

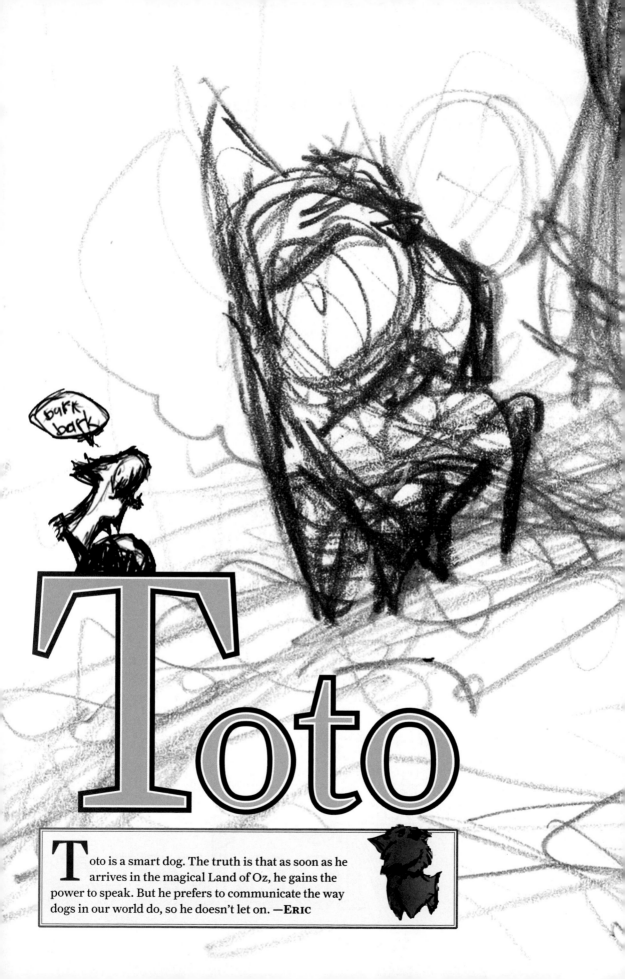

Toto

T oto is a smart dog. The truth is that as soon as he arrives in the magical Land of Oz, he gains the power to speak. But he prefers to communicate the way dogs in our world do, so he doesn't let on. —ERIC

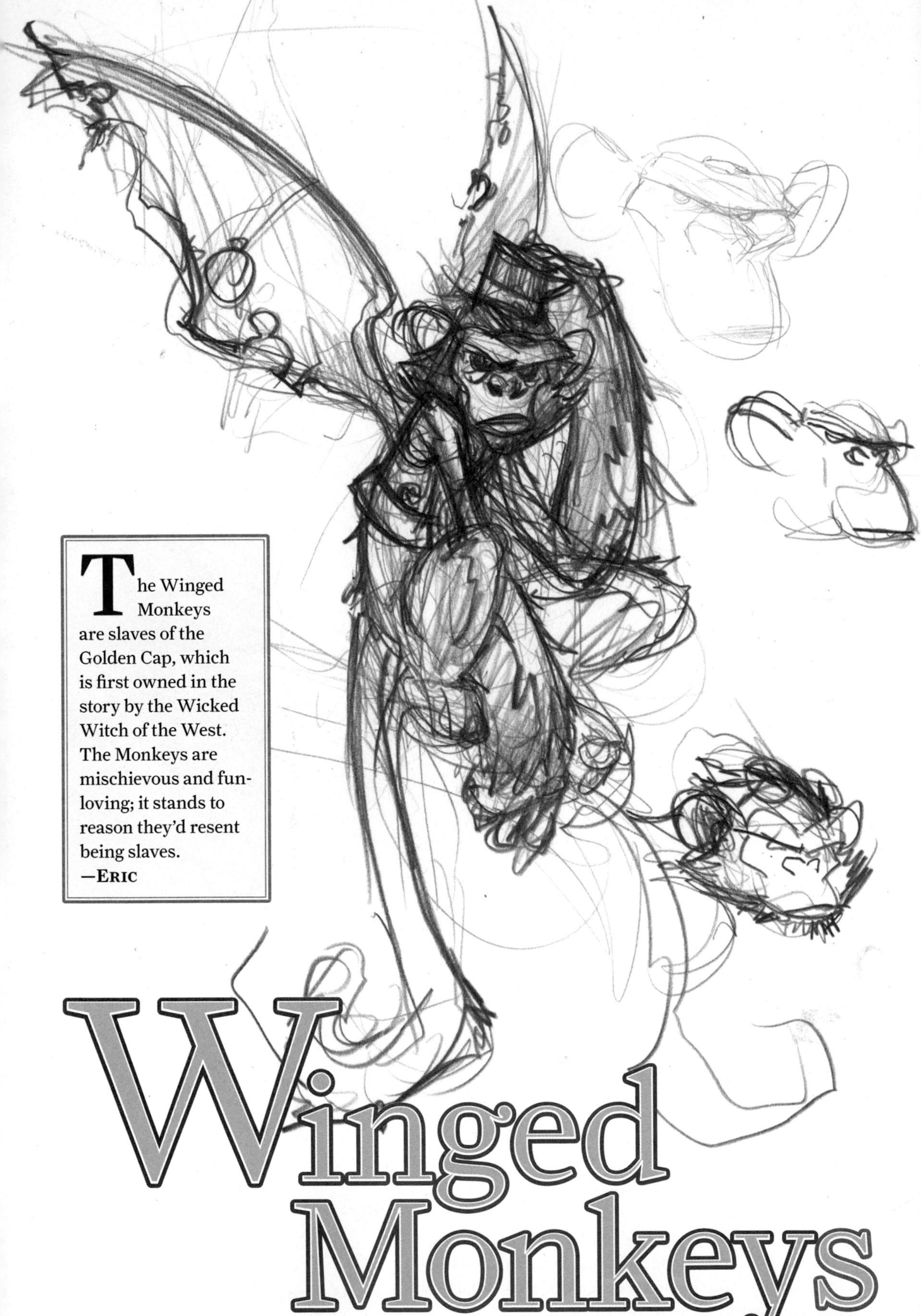

The Winged Monkeys are slaves of the Golden Cap, which is first owned in the story by the Wicked Witch of the West. The Monkeys are mischievous and fun-loving; it stands to reason they'd resent being slaves.
—**Eric**

Winged Monkeys

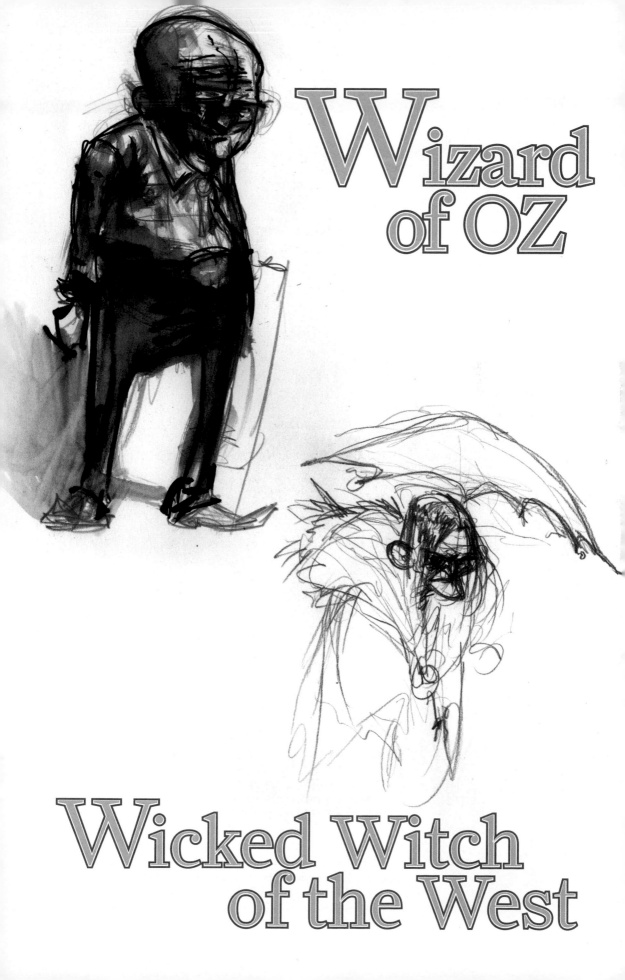

Wizard of OZ

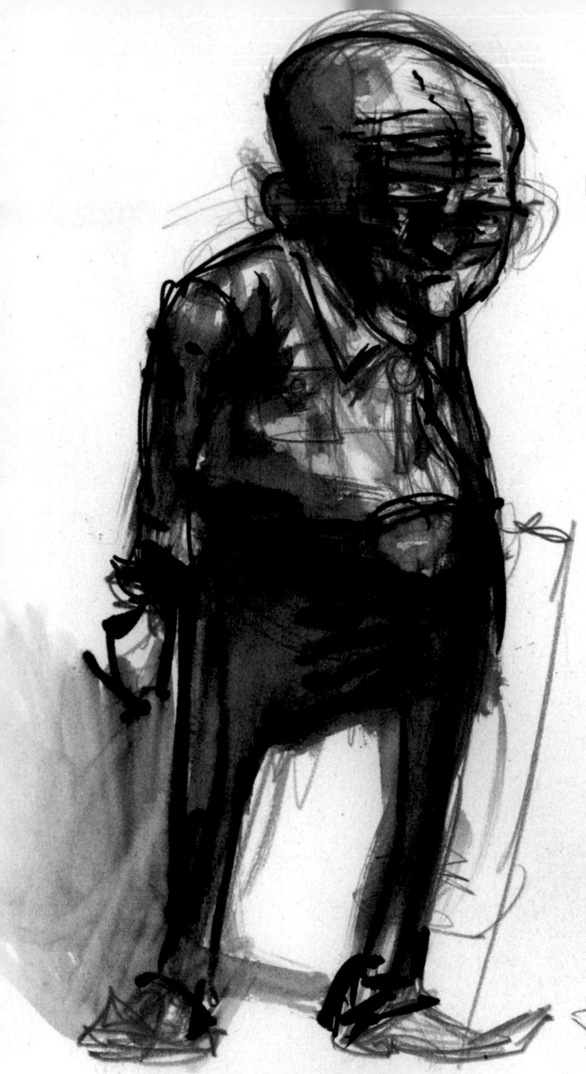

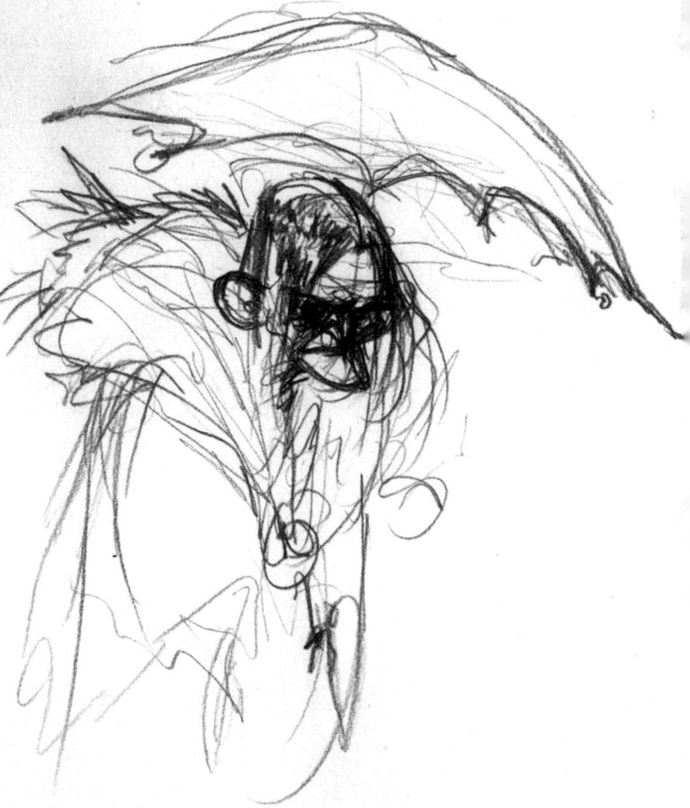

Wicked Witch of the West

Issue #1 Cover

A characteristic grouping. Here the Lion looks more like his roly-poly self. —ERIC

Designing the characters that fill up the pages of The Wonderful Wizard of Oz was probably the biggest challenge I've had. Besides the original illustrations in the novels, there have been countless versions of these characters out in the world. Trying to figure how to give them my visual twist while staying true to the text was a difficult challenge. In the end, it always comes down to shapes. All the bells and whistles will never make up for what shape can do for the character. Each character having a unique shape helps remind you of what kind of person (or not so...um...person) they are. Bringing these characters to life was a true adventure! —SKOTTIE

I chose one of them, *The Road to Oz*, and my fate was sealed. I wanted to read *all* the Oz books and decided that when I grew up, I'd write and illustrate new Oz books for the world to read. But why wait till I grew up? I began to write Oz stories and draw Oz illustrations. I constructed Oz pop-ups, directed and acted in Oz plays with my sister and neighborhood friends, and joined The International Wizard of Oz Club (www.ozclub.org).

I finally did grow up—more or less—and began to publish my own Oz books. Only these books weren't quite the same sort I'd envisioned as a child. They were comics. For many years I'd loved comics as much as I loved Oz. And now I was joining these two passions of my life.

But it didn't stop with comics. I've continued with other Oz projects, writing and illustrating more traditional Oz books, co-founding a publishing house—Hungry Tiger Press—devoted to Oz and the works of L. Frank Baum, writing reviews and articles, attending Oz conventions, even choreographing and performing in an Oz ballet. The impact of Oz on my life—the people I've met, the places I've gone, the things I've learned and seen and read and absorbed—is impossible to detail.

Needless to state, not everyone is influenced by Oz so strongly. But Oz pervades American culture to such an extent that few people don't recognize some version of Dorothy, the Scarecrow, the Wicked Witch of the West, and the story's other prominent characters. And beyond America, *The Wizard of Oz* is translated into many languages, inspiring further variations—including a completely different series of books in Russia, which has gone on to spawn its own movies, comics, and more.

If Toto hadn't scrambled under the bed to escape the cyclone, there's no telling how huge a gap would have been left—not only in Dorothy's life, not only in L. Frank Baum's life, not only in my life, but in the life of the entire world.

The fact that Marvel Comics chose to publish this version of *The Wonderful Wizard of Oz* as one of their comics adaptations of classic literature is yet another indication of the story's import. Baum's book is now a classic. That this comics adaptation goes back to that book as its source is one of the aspects that drew me to this project. *The Wonderful Wizard of Oz* has been told again and again in so many different versions and permutations that many of the original's details have been obscured or forgotten. But they haven't been lost. Here they are again, those wonderful Baum touches—the green spectacles, the Good Witch of the North's kiss, and—one of my favorites—the way the Soldier with the Green Whiskers makes Dorothy and her friends wipe their feet before they enter the Wizard's palace. It's all here, brought to life anew by the lively art of Skottie Young and the vibrant color of Jean-François Beaulieu.

I hope you enjoy it. It was created, as Baum himself said in his introduction to the original book, "to pleasure the children of today"—whether those children are actually young or simply young-at-heart.

And if you do enjoy it, you might take a moment to murmur a word of thanks to Toto.

Eric Shanower
San Diego, July 2009

Folklore, legends, myths and fairy tales have followed childhood through the ages, for every healthy youngster has a wholesome and instinctive love for stories fantastic, marvelous and manifestly unreal.

The story of "The Wonderful Wizard of Oz" was written solely to please children of today. It aspires to being a modernized fairy tale, in which the wonderment and joy are retained and the heartaches and nightmares are left out.

L. FRANK BAUM CHICAGO, APRIL, 1900.

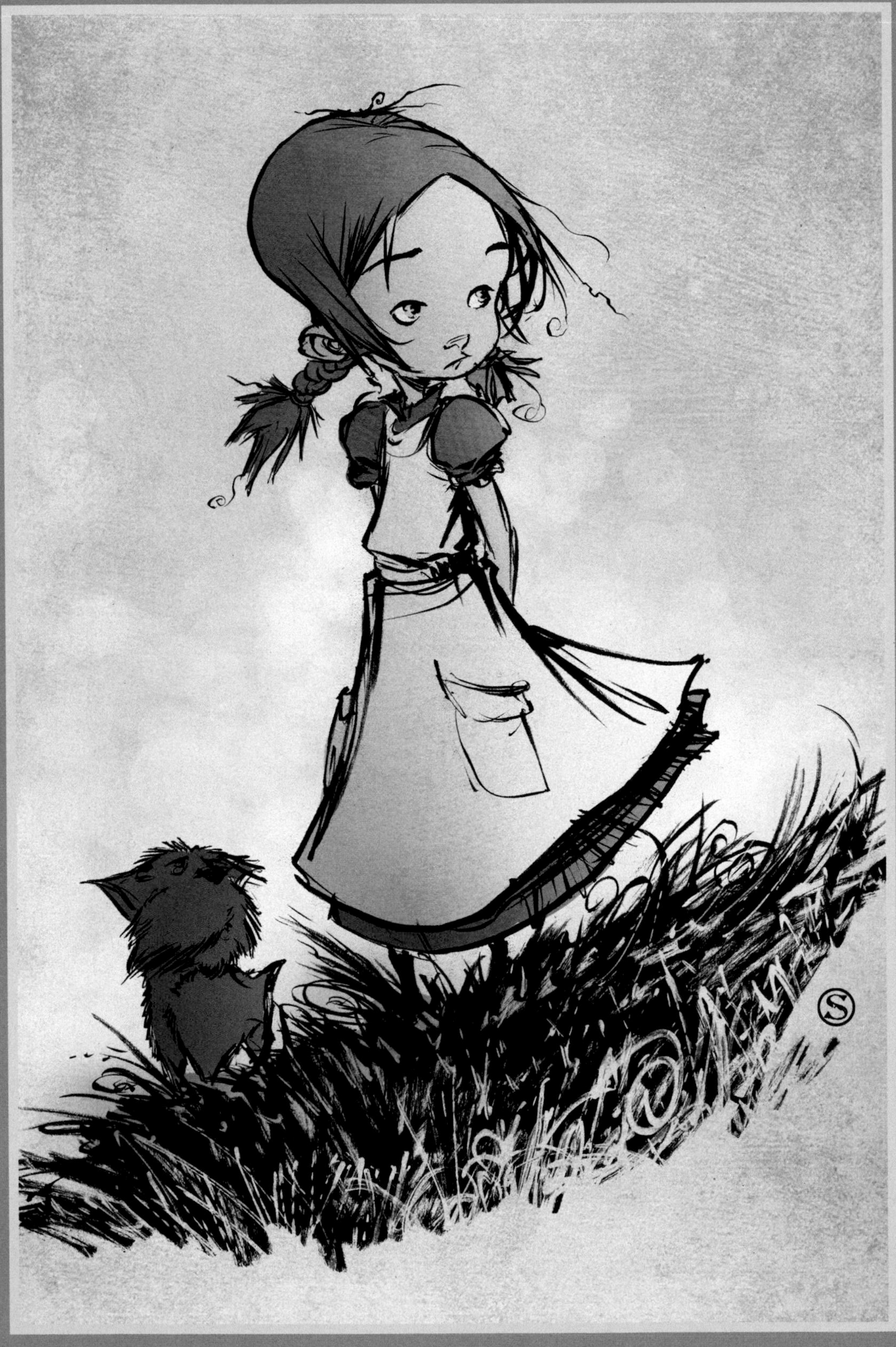

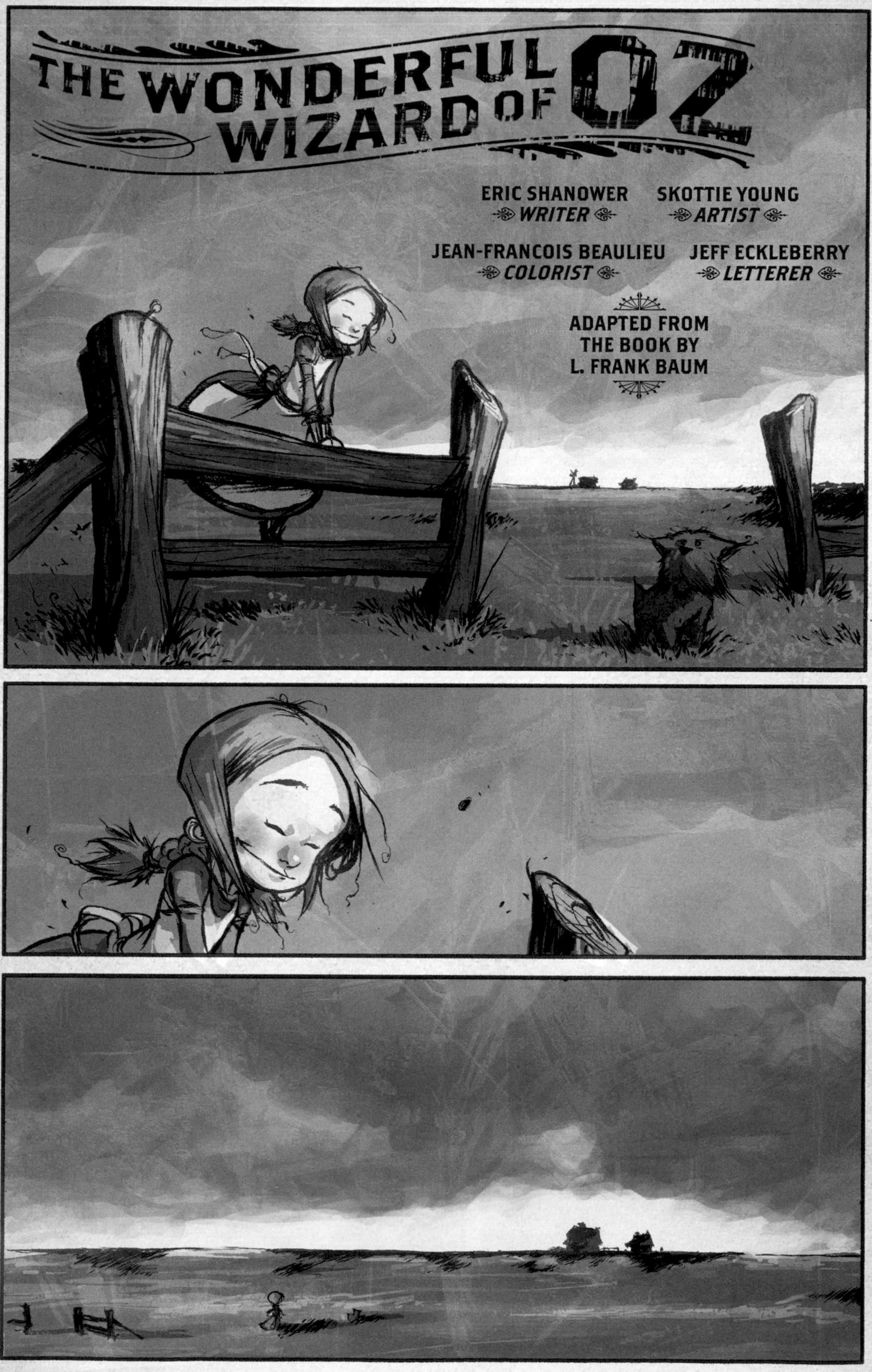
THE WONDERFUL WIZARD OF OZ
ERIC SHANOWER
WRITER
SKOTTIE YOUNG
ARTIST
JEAN-FRANCOIS BEAULIEU
COLORIST
JEFF ECKLEBERRY
LETTERER
ADAPTED FROM THE BOOK BY L. FRANK BAUM

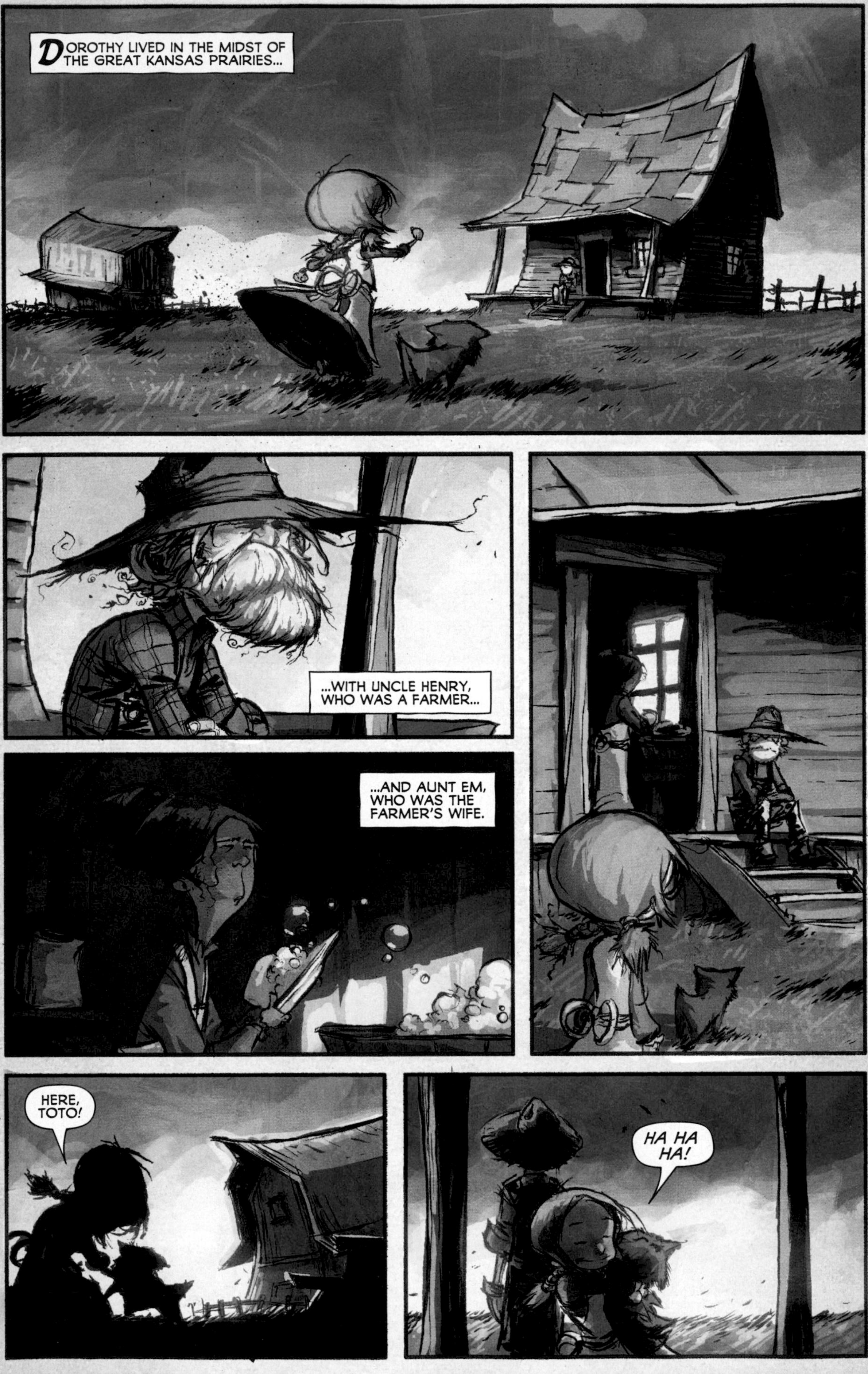
DOROTHY LIVED IN THE MIDST OF THE GREAT KANSAS PRAIRIES...
...WITH UNCLE HENRY, WHO WAS A FARMER...
...AND AUNT EM, WHO WAS THE FARMER'S WIFE.
HERE, TOTO!
HA HA HA!

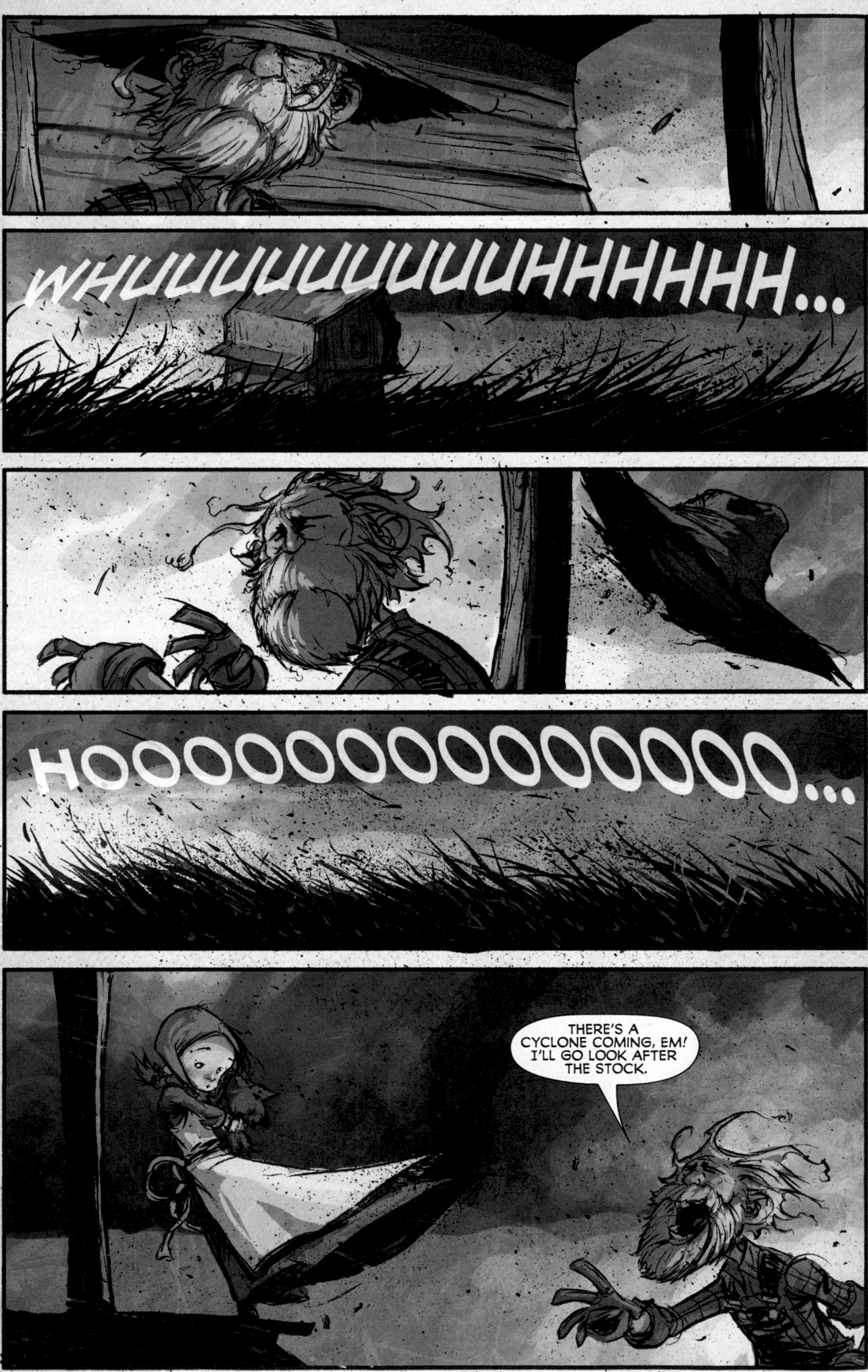
WHUUUUUUUUUUHHHHHH...
HOOOOOOOOOOOOOOO...
THERE'S A CYCLONE COMING, EM! I'LL GO LOOK AFTER THE STOCK.

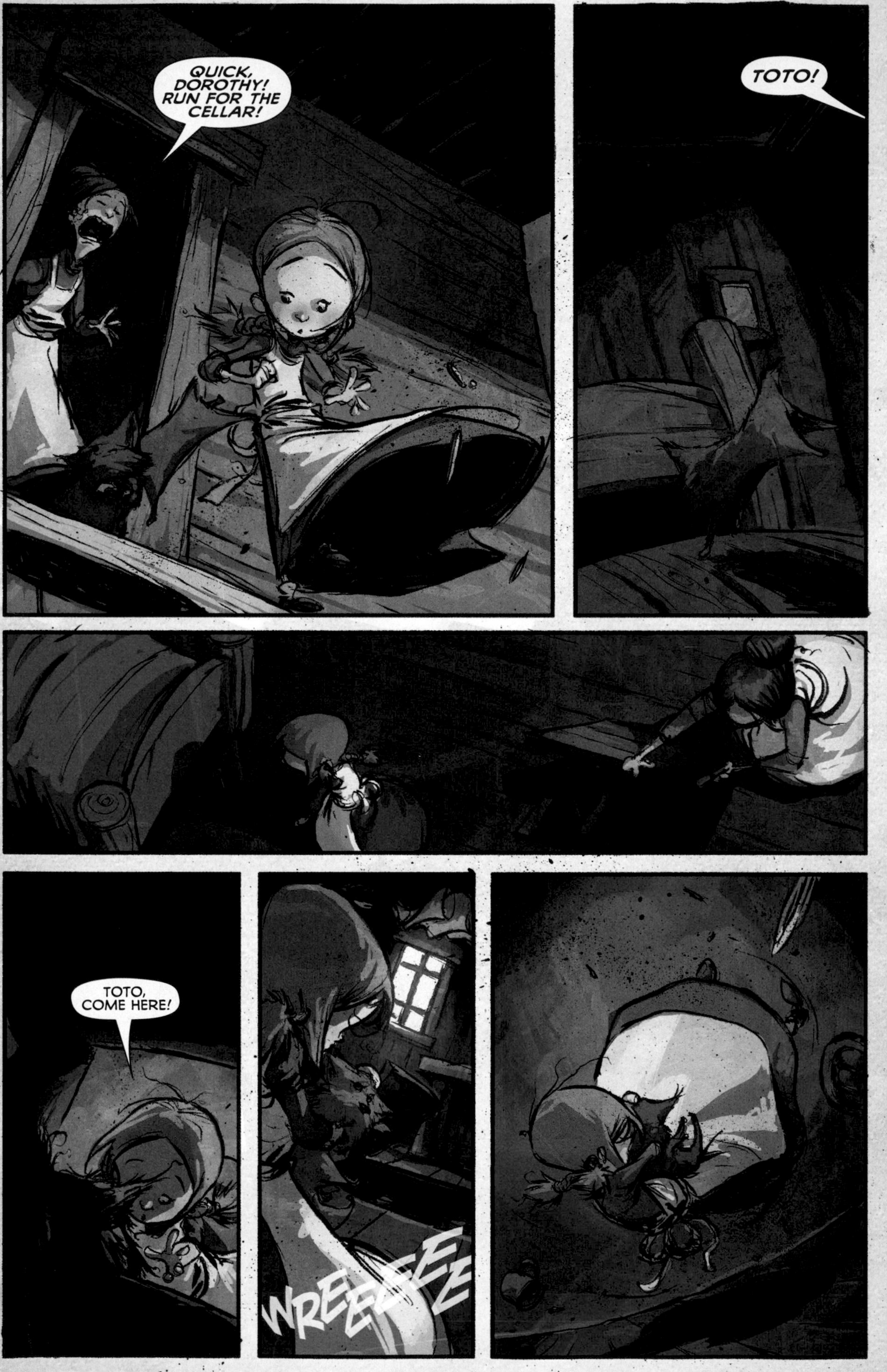
QUICK, DOROTHY! RUN FOR THE CELLAR!
TOTO!
TOTO, COME HERE!
WREEEEEE

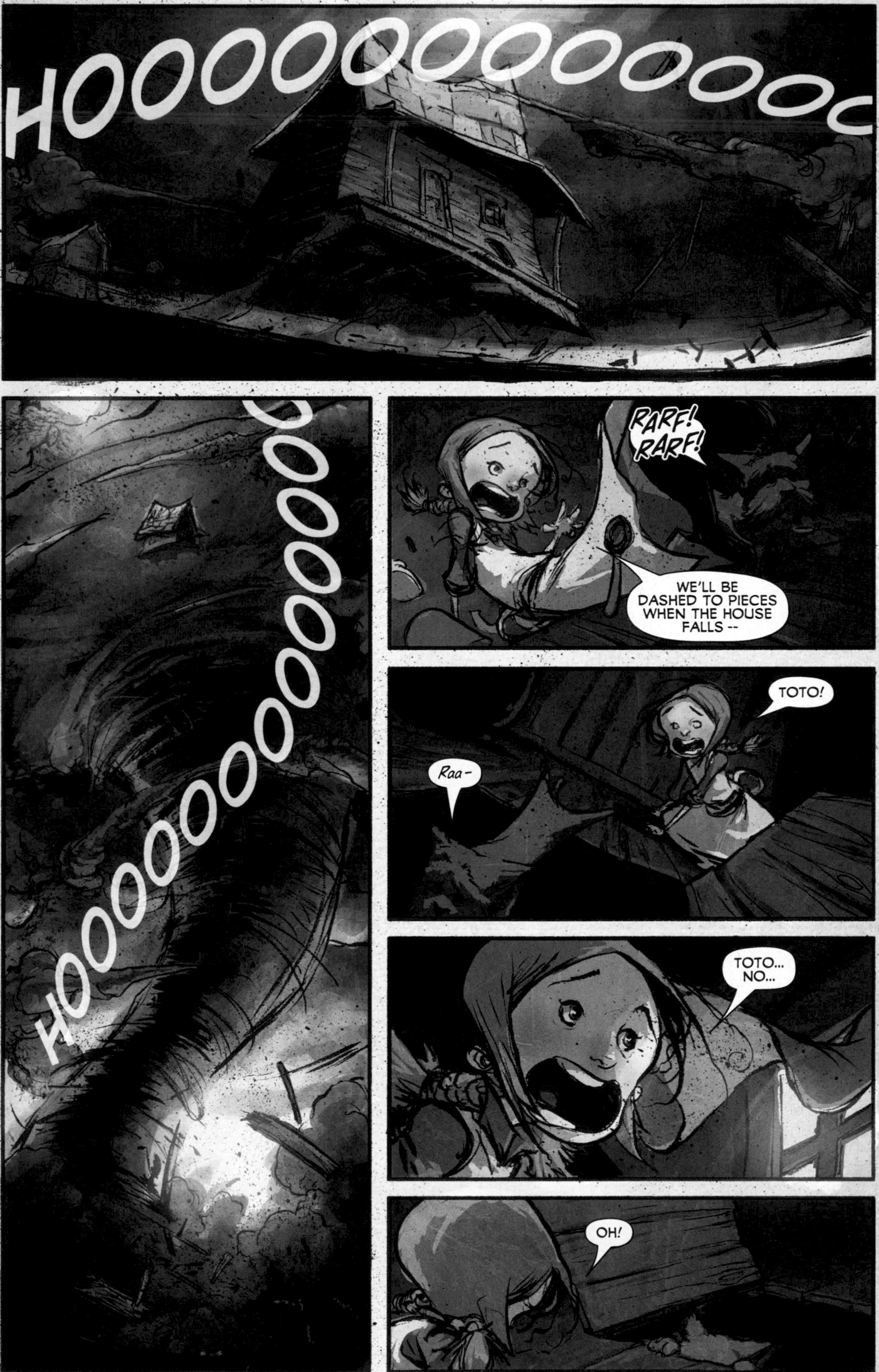
HOOOOOOOOOOOOC
OOOOOOOOOOOOOO
HOOOOOOOOOOOOOO
RARF! RARF!
WE'LL BE DASHED TO PIECES WHEN THE HOUSE FALLS --
TOTO!
Raa-
TOTO... NO...
OH!

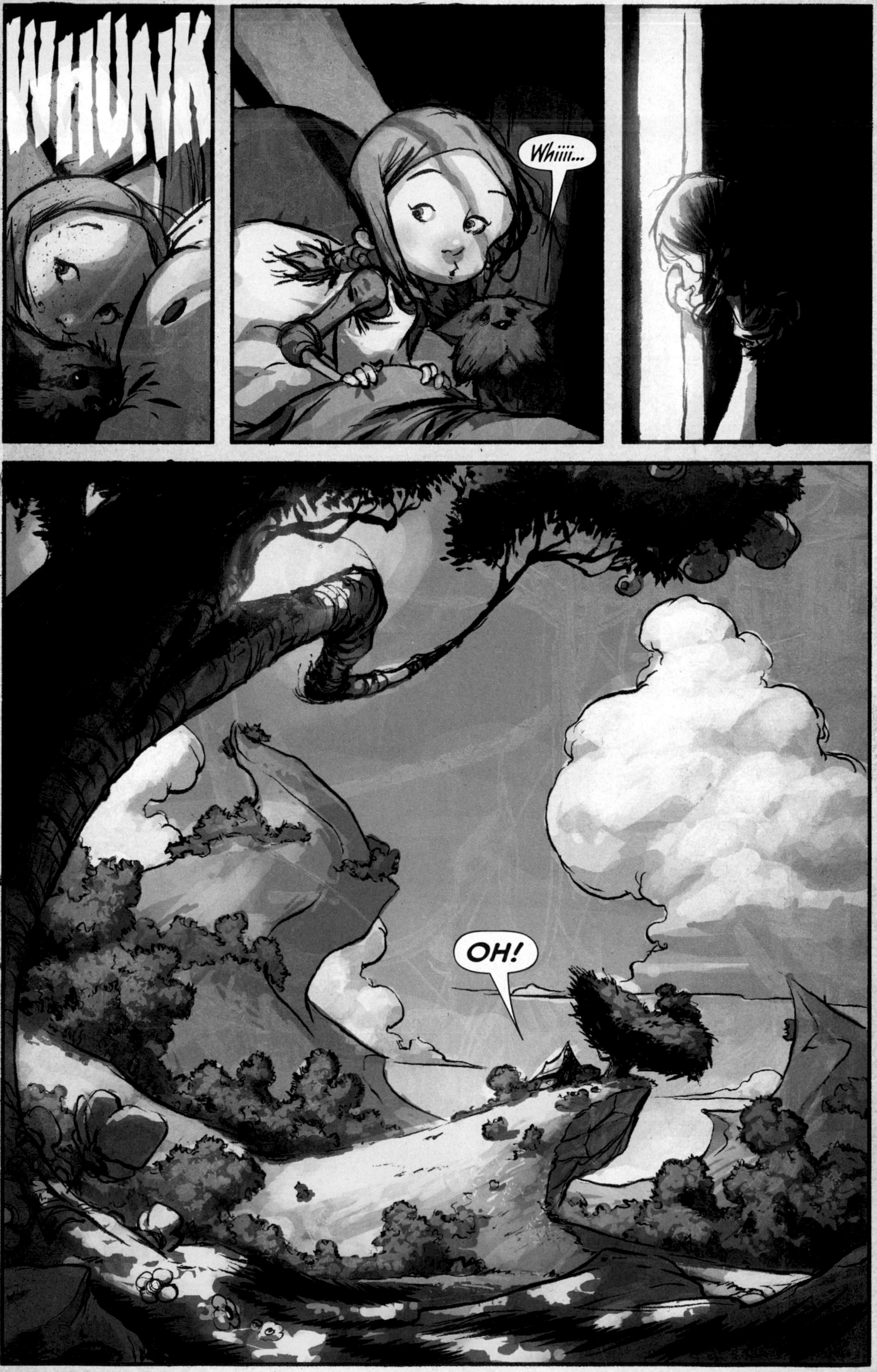
WHUNK
Whiiii...
OH!

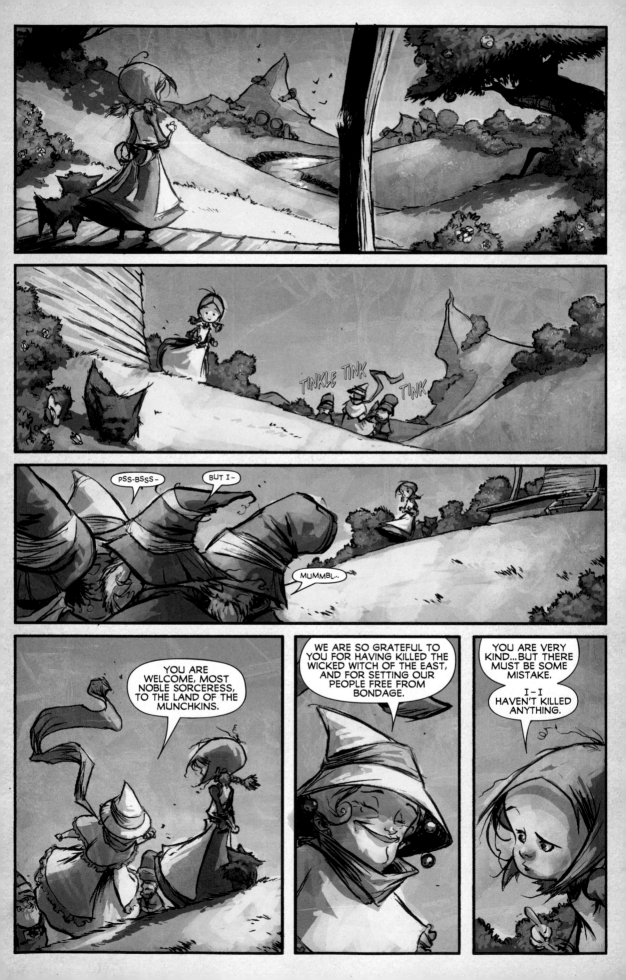

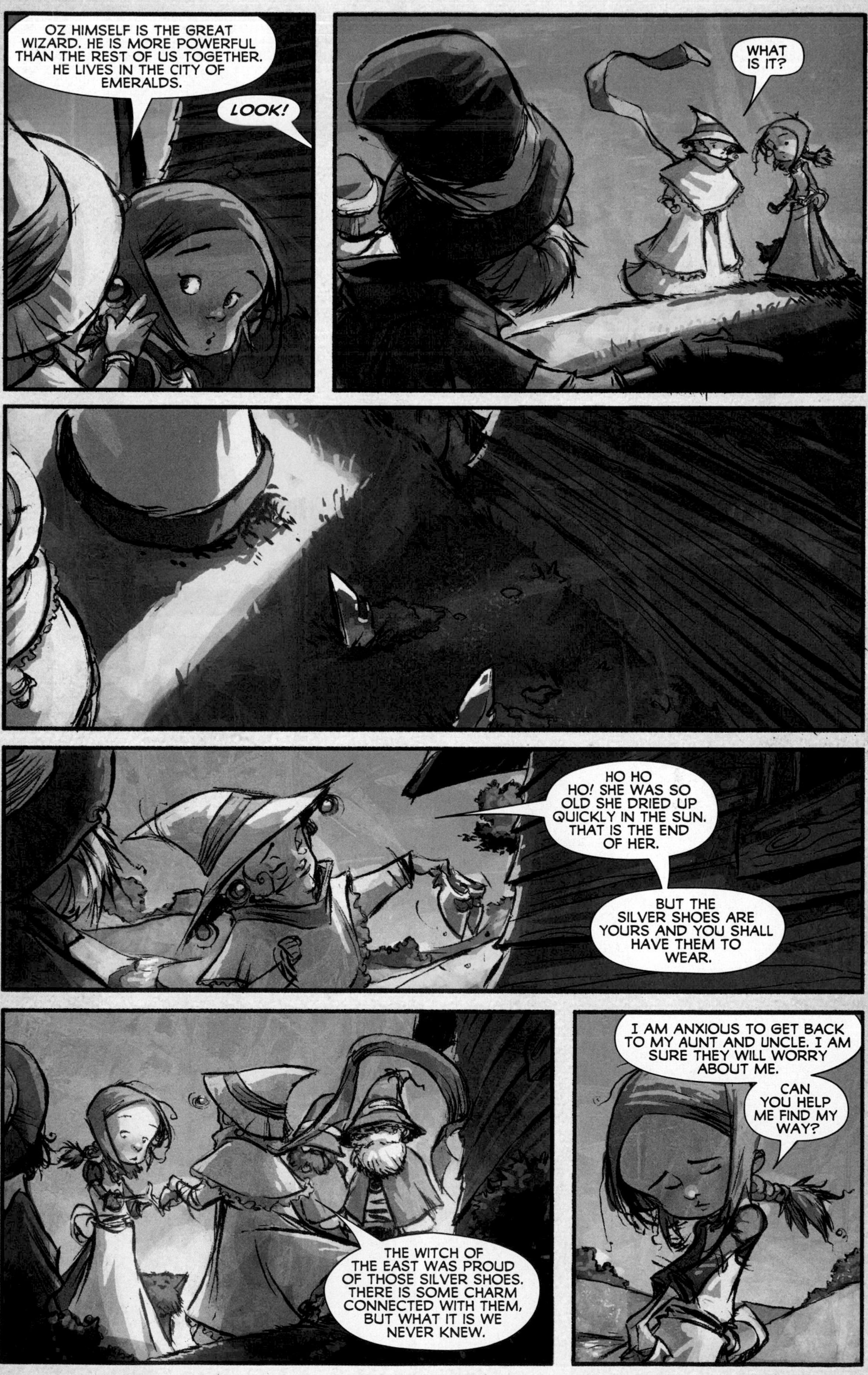
OZ HIMSELF IS THE GREAT WIZARD. HE IS MORE POWERFUL THAN THE REST OF US TOGETHER. HE LIVES IN THE CITY OF EMERALDS.
LOOK!
WHAT IS IT?
HO HO HO! SHE WAS SO OLD SHE DRIED UP QUICKLY IN THE SUN. THAT IS THE END OF HER.
BUT THE SILVER SHOES ARE YOURS AND YOU SHALL HAVE THEM TO WEAR.
THE WITCH OF THE EAST WAS PROUD OF THOSE SILVER SHOES. THERE IS SOME CHARM CONNECTED WITH THEM, BUT WHAT IT IS WE NEVER KNEW.
I AM ANXIOUS TO GET BACK TO MY AUNT AND UNCLE. I AM SURE THEY WILL WORRY ABOUT ME.
CAN YOU HELP ME FIND MY WAY?

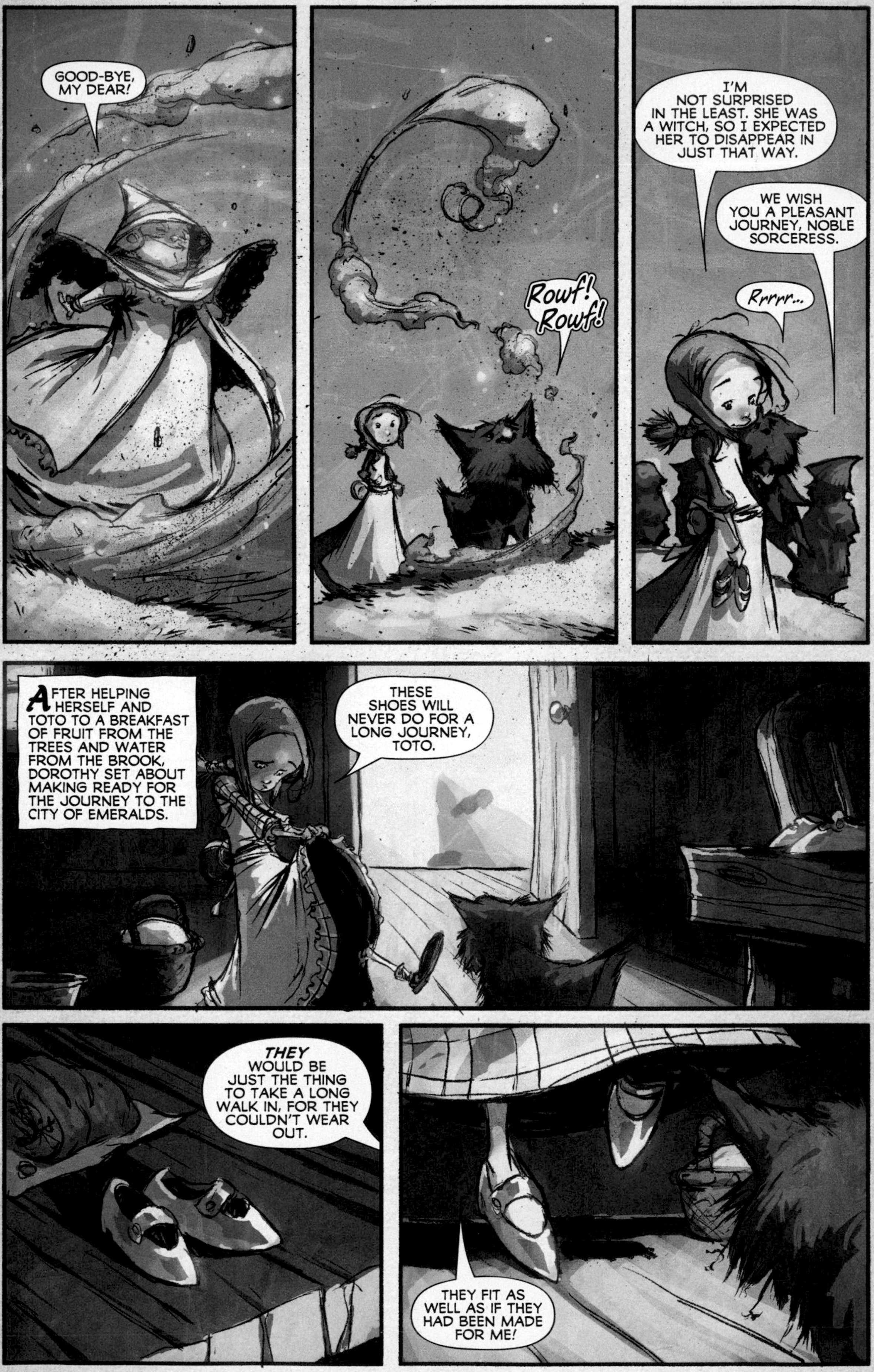
GOOD-BYE, MY DEAR!
Rowf! Rowf!
I'M NOT SURPRISED IN THE LEAST. SHE WAS A WITCH, SO I EXPECTED HER TO DISAPPEAR IN JUST THAT WAY.
WE WISH YOU A PLEASANT JOURNEY, NOBLE SORCERESS.
Rrrrr...
AFTER HELPING HERSELF AND TOTO TO A BREAKFAST OF FRUIT FROM THE TREES AND WATER FROM THE BROOK, DOROTHY SET ABOUT MAKING READY FOR THE JOURNEY TO THE CITY OF EMERALDS.
THESE SHOES WILL NEVER DO FOR A LONG JOURNEY, TOTO.
THEY WOULD BE JUST THE THING TO TAKE A LONG WALK IN, FOR THEY COULDN'T WEAR OUT.
THEY FIT AS WELL AS IF THEY HAD BEEN MADE FOR ME!

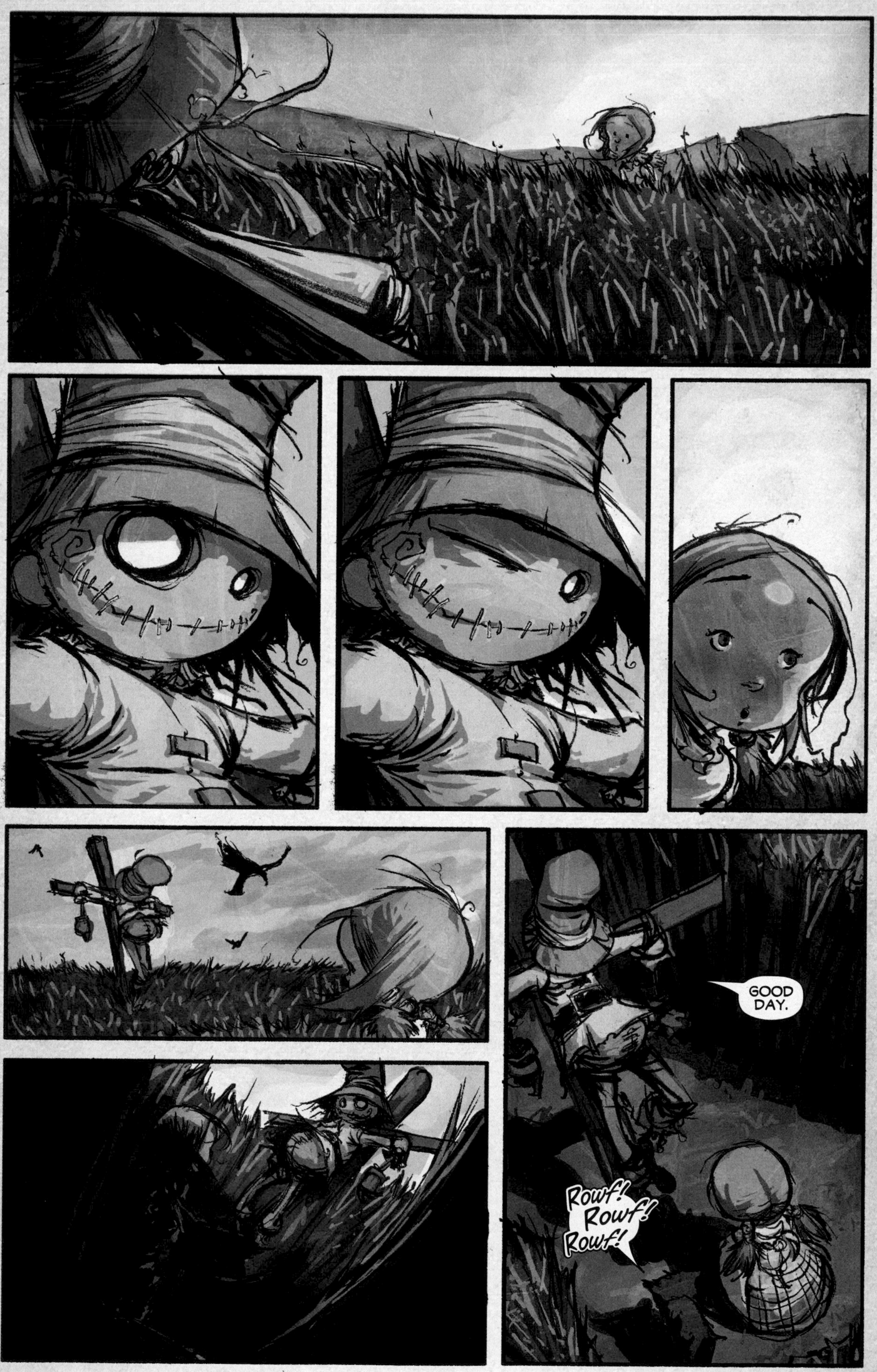
GOOD DAY.
Rowf! Rowf! Rowf!

THE FARTHER THEY WENT, THE MORE DISMAL AND LONESOME THE COUNTRY BECAME.

OH!

HAVING NO BRAINS I WALK STRAIGHT AHEAD, AND SO I STEP INTO THE HOLES.

IT NEVER HURTS ME, HOWEVER.

SHUFF

AT NOON THEY SAT DOWN BY THE ROADSIDE AND DOROTHY OPENED HER BASKET.

I'M NEVER HUNGRY AND IT'S A LUCKY THING I'M NOT.

MY MOUTH IS ONLY PAINTED, AND IF I SHOULD CUT A HOLE IN IT SO I COULD EAT, THE STRAW I'M STUFFED WITH WOULD COME OUT, AND THAT WOULD SPOIL THE SHAPE OF MY HEAD.

TELL ME SOMETHING ABOUT YOURSELF AND THE COUNTRY YOU CAME FROM.

SO SHE TOLD HIM ALL ABOUT KANSAS, AND HOW GRAY EVERYTHING WAS THERE.

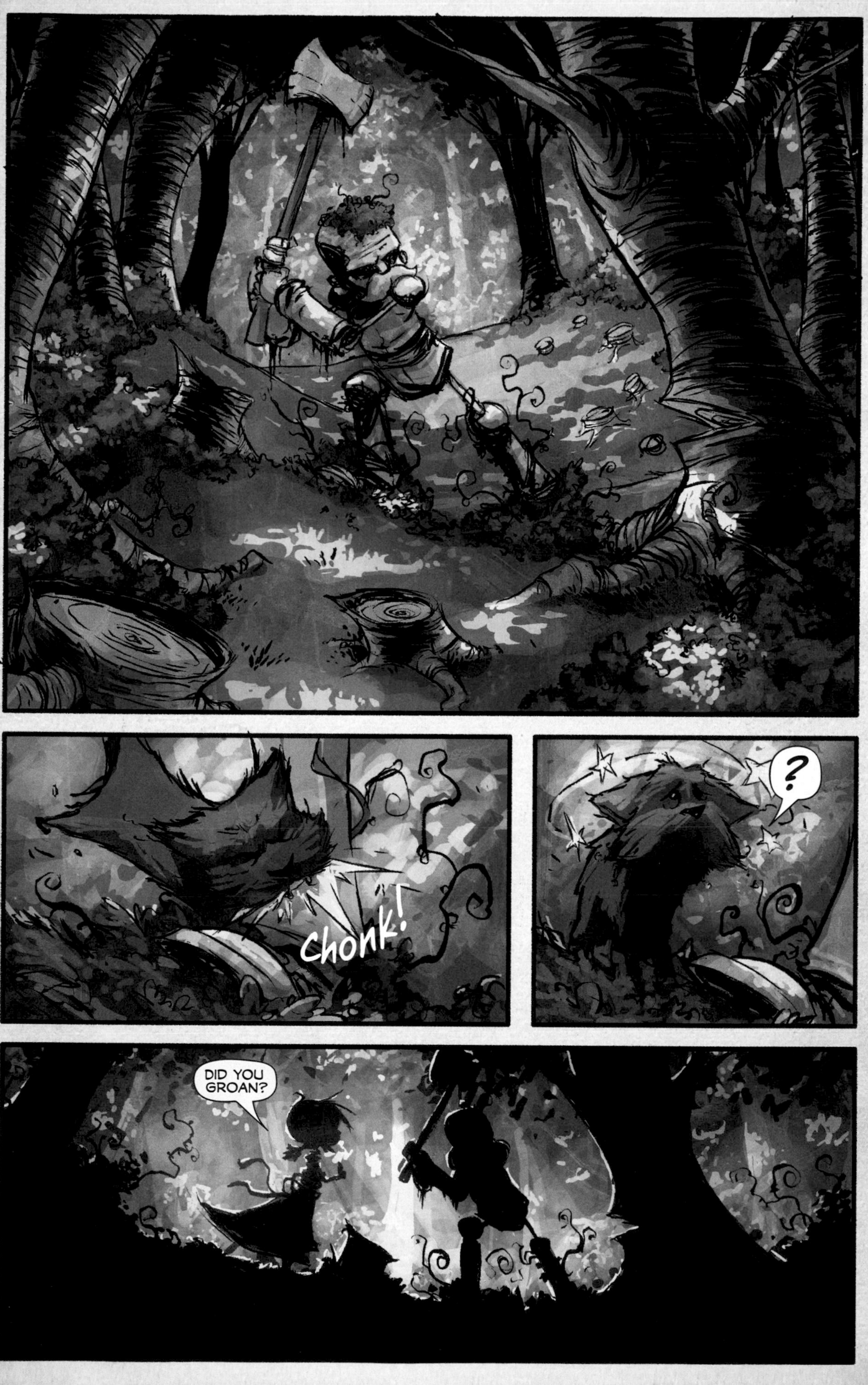

Chonk!
?
DID YOU GROAN?

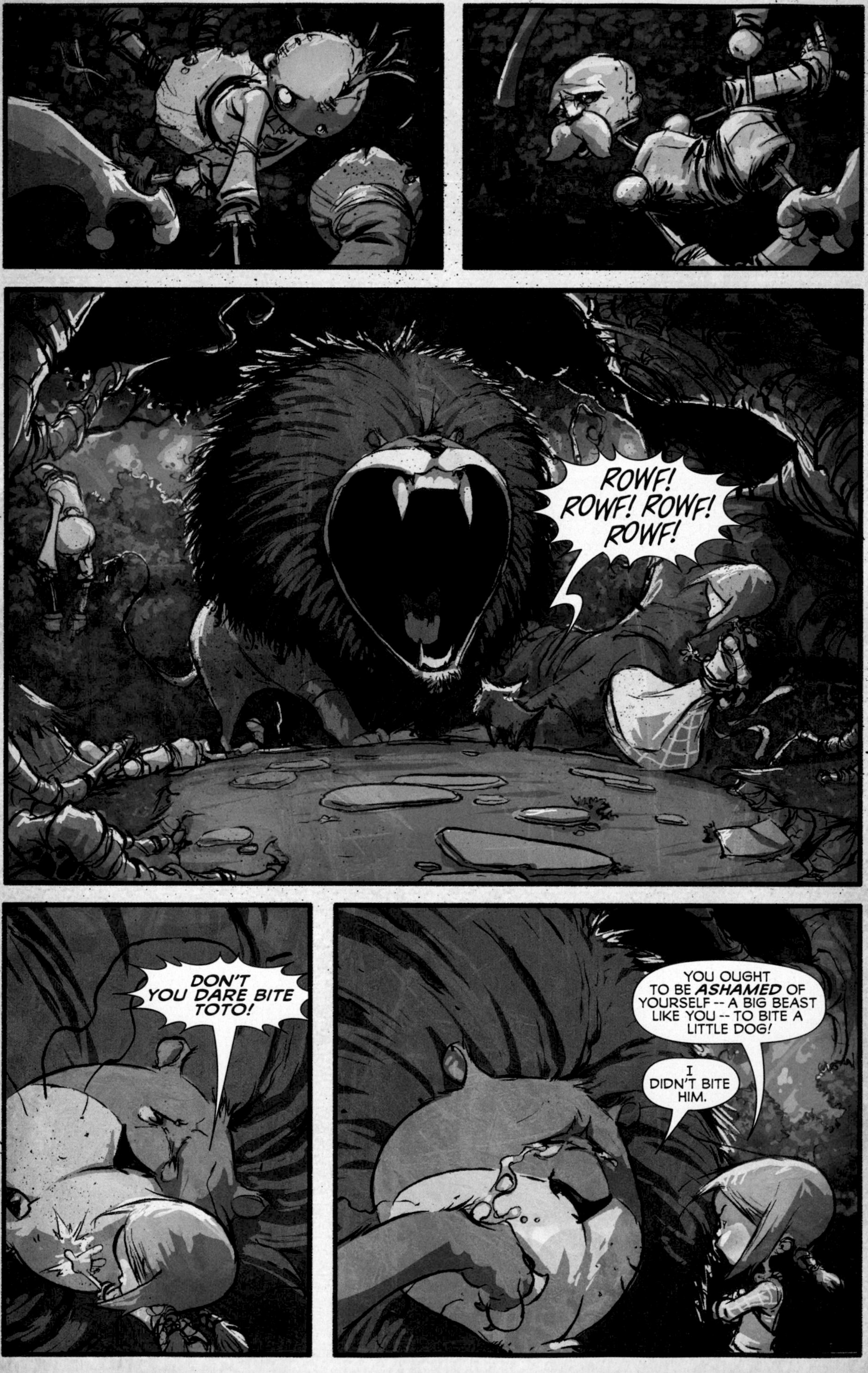
ROWF! ROWF! ROWF! ROWF!
DON'T YOU DARE BITE TOTO!
YOU OUGHT TO BE ASHAMED OF YOURSELF -- A BIG BEAST LIKE YOU -- TO BITE A LITTLE DOG!
I DIDN'T BITE HIM.

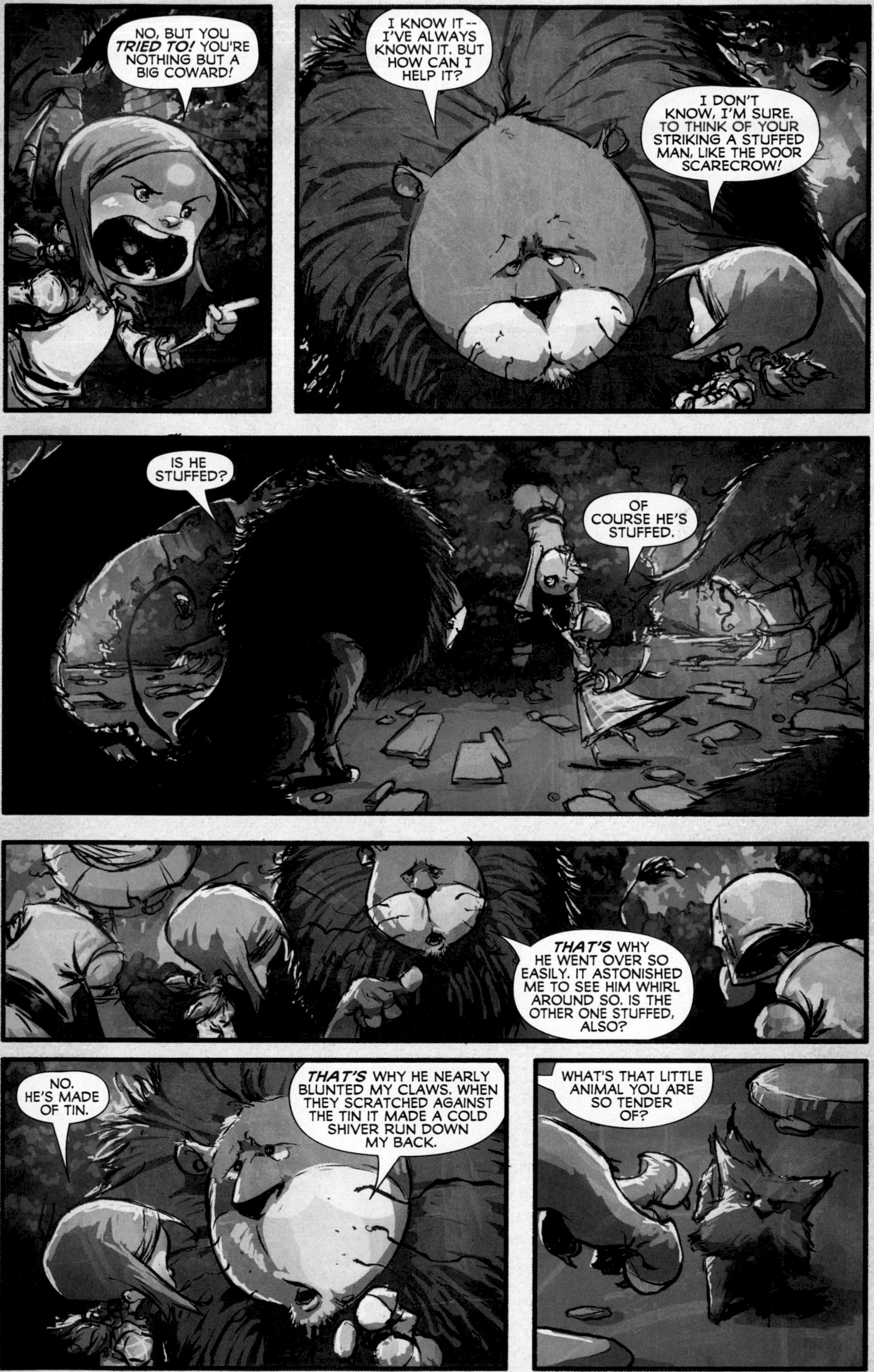
NO, BUT YOU TRIED TO! YOU'RE NOTHING BUT A BIG COWARD!
I KNOW IT -- I'VE ALWAYS KNOWN IT. BUT HOW CAN I HELP IT?
I DON'T KNOW, I'M SURE. TO THINK OF YOUR STRIKING A STUFFED MAN, LIKE THE POOR SCARECROW!
IS HE STUFFED?
OF COURSE HE'S STUFFED.
THAT'S WHY HE WENT OVER SO EASILY. IT ASTONISHED ME TO SEE HIM WHIRL AROUND SO. IS THE OTHER ONE STUFFED, ALSO?
NO. HE'S MADE OF TIN.
THAT'S WHY HE NEARLY BLUNTED MY CLAWS. WHEN THEY SCRATCHED AGAINST THE TIN IT MADE A COLD SHIVER RUN DOWN MY BACK.
WHAT'S THAT LITTLE ANIMAL YOU ARE SO TENDER OF?

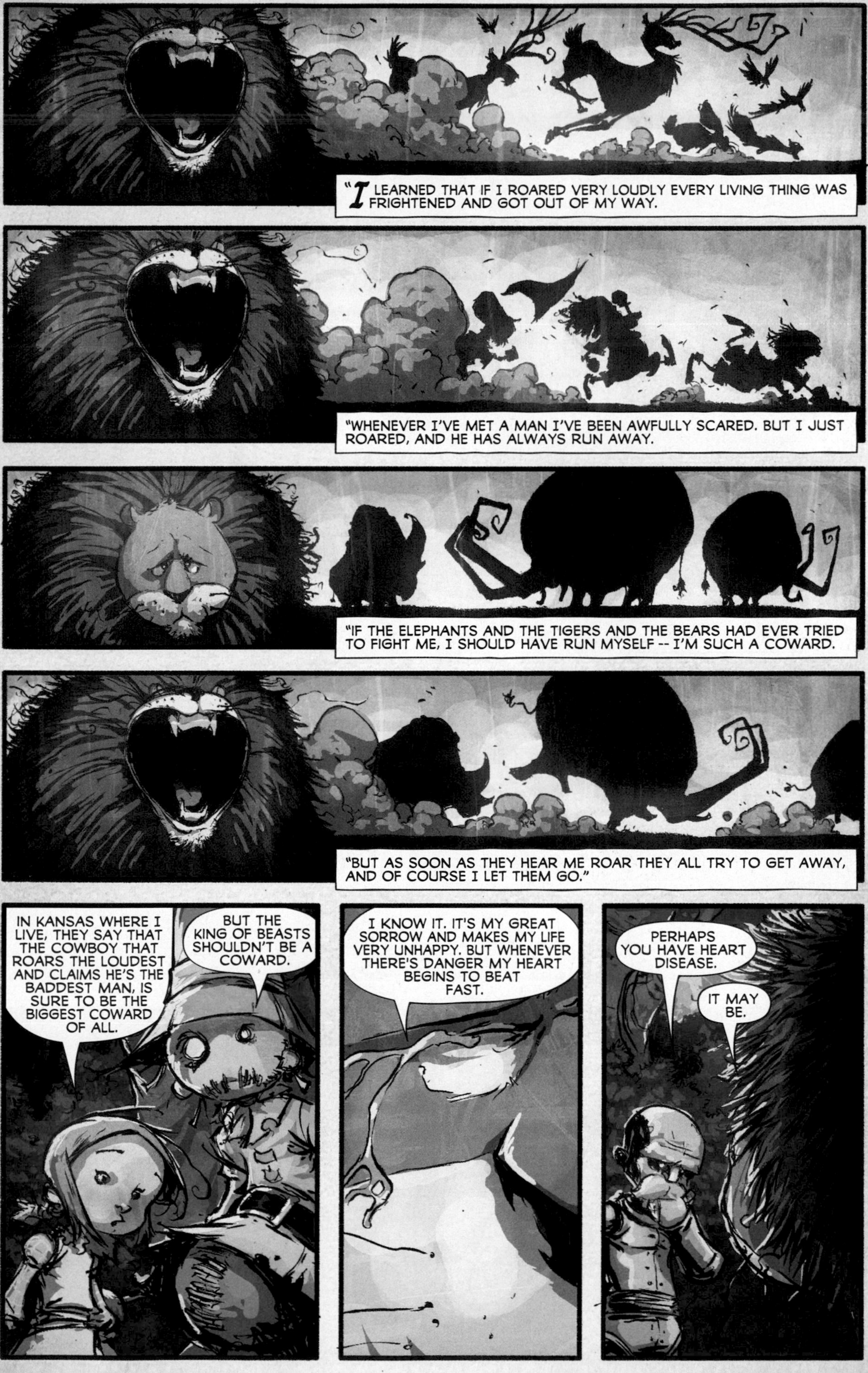
"I LEARNED THAT IF I ROARED VERY LOUDLY EVERY LIVING THING WAS FRIGHTENED AND GOT OUT OF MY WAY.
"WHENEVER I'VE MET A MAN I'VE BEEN AWFULLY SCARED. BUT I JUST ROARED, AND HE HAS ALWAYS RUN AWAY.
"IF THE ELEPHANTS AND THE TIGERS AND THE BEARS HAD EVER TRIED TO FIGHT ME, I SHOULD HAVE RUN MYSELF -- I'M SUCH A COWARD.
"BUT AS SOON AS THEY HEAR ME ROAR THEY ALL TRY TO GET AWAY, AND OF COURSE I LET THEM GO."
IN KANSAS WHERE I LIVE, THEY SAY THAT THE COWBOY THAT ROARS THE LOUDEST AND CLAIMS HE'S THE BADDEST MAN, IS SURE TO BE THE BIGGEST COWARD OF ALL.
BUT THE KING OF BEASTS SHOULDN'T BE A COWARD.
I KNOW IT. IT'S MY GREAT SORROW AND MAKES MY LIFE VERY UNHAPPY. BUT WHENEVER THERE'S DANGER MY HEART BEGINS TO BEAT FAST.
PERHAPS YOU HAVE HEART DISEASE.
IT MAY BE.

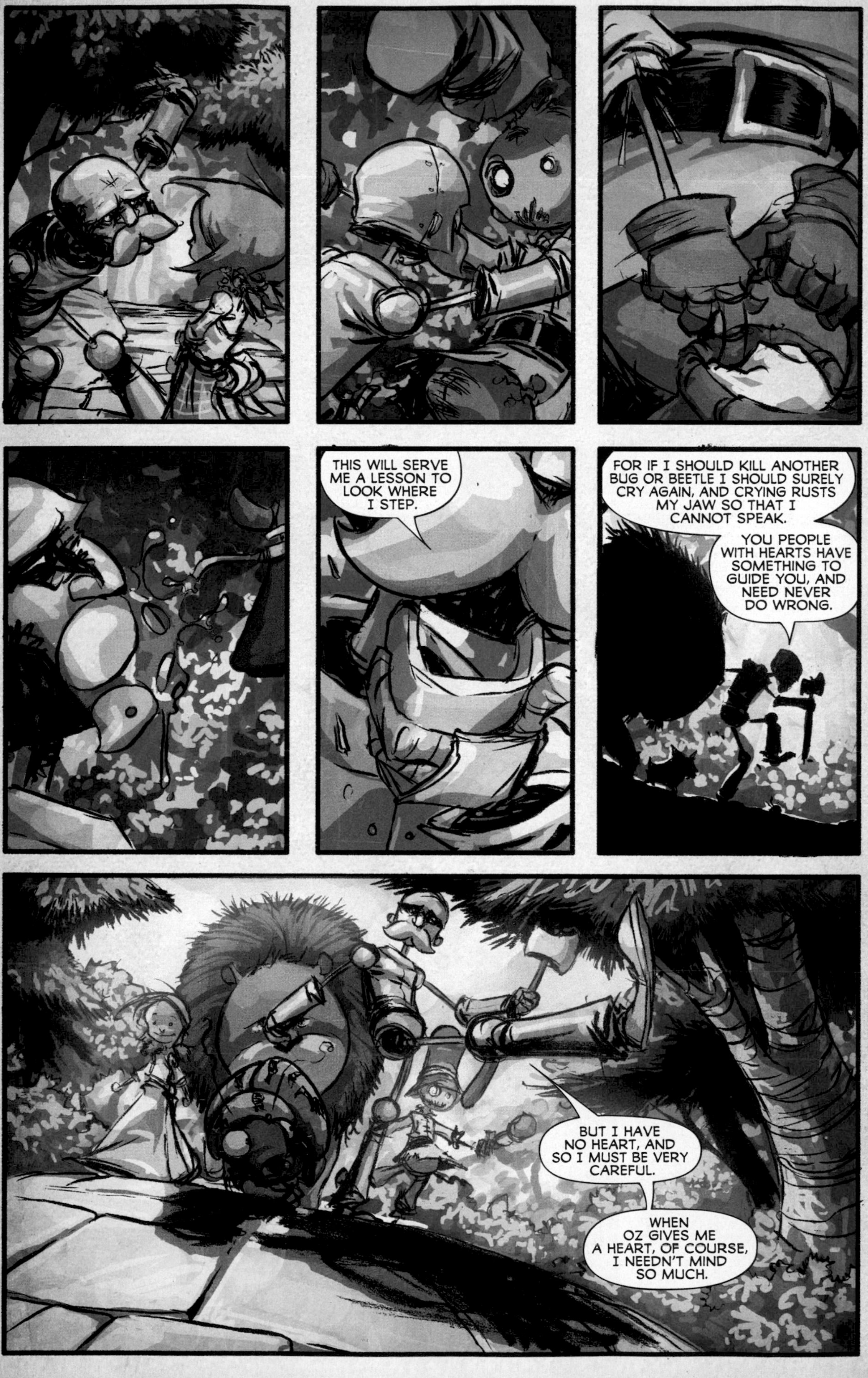
THIS WILL SERVE ME A LESSON TO LOOK WHERE I STEP.
FOR IF I SHOULD KILL ANOTHER BUG OR BEETLE I SHOULD SURELY CRY AGAIN, AND CRYING RUSTS MY JAW SO THAT I CANNOT SPEAK.
YOU PEOPLE WITH HEARTS HAVE SOMETHING TO GUIDE YOU, AND NEED NEVER DO WRONG.
BUT I HAVE NO HEART, AND SO I MUST BE VERY CAREFUL.
WHEN OZ GIVES ME A HEART, OF COURSE, I NEEDN'T MIND SO MUCH.

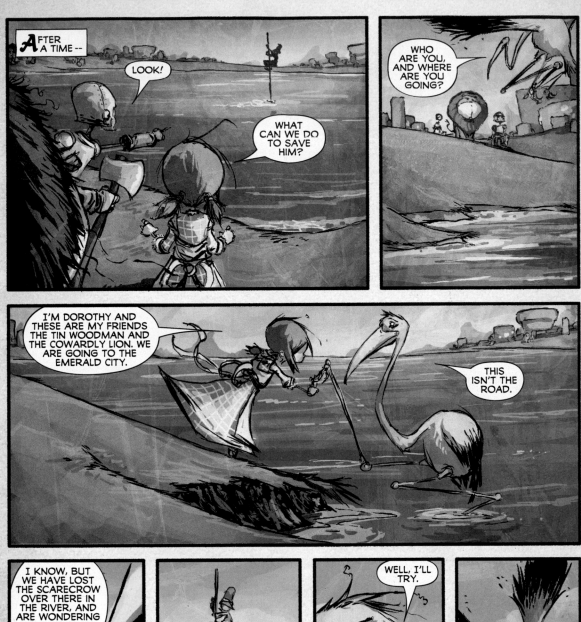

AFTER A TIME --

LOOK!

WHAT CAN WE DO TO SAVE HIM?

WHO ARE YOU, AND WHERE ARE YOU GOING?

I'M DOROTHY AND THESE ARE MY FRIENDS THE TIN WOODMAN AND THE COWARDLY LION. WE ARE GOING TO THE EMERALD CITY.

THIS ISN'T THE ROAD.

I KNOW, BUT WE HAVE LOST THE SCARECROW OVER THERE IN THE RIVER, AND ARE WONDERING HOW WE SHALL GET HIM AGAIN.

IF HE WASN'T SO BIG AND HEAVY I WOULD GET HIM FOR YOU.

HE ISN'T HEAVY A BIT, FOR HE IS STUFFED WITH STRAW. IF YOU'LL BRING HIM BACK, WE'LL THANK YOU EVER AND EVER SO MUCH.

WELL, I'LL TRY.

BUT IF I FIND HE IS TOO HEAVY TO CARRY I SHALL HAVE TO DROP HIM IN THE RIVER AGAIN.

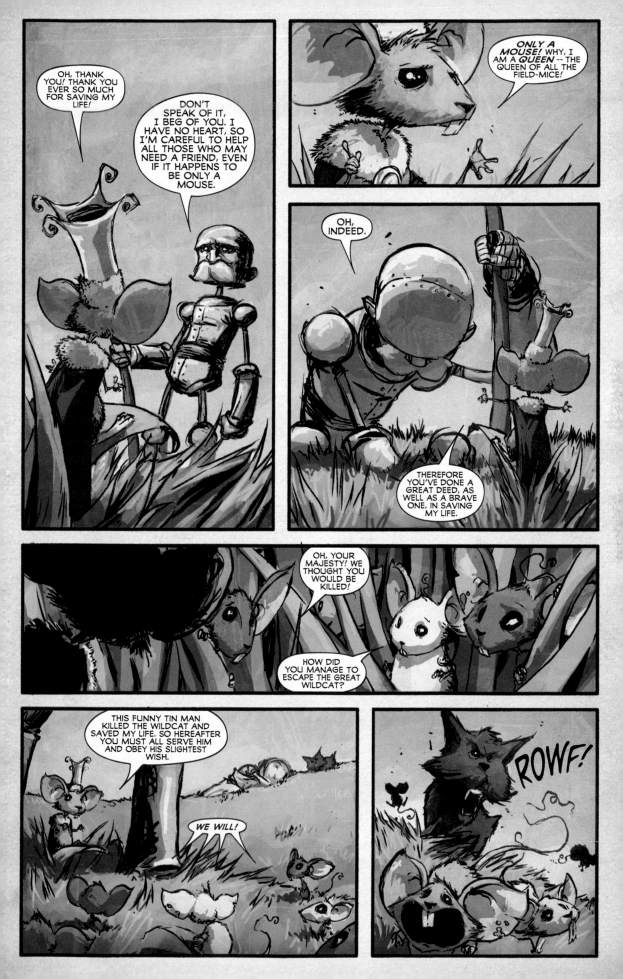

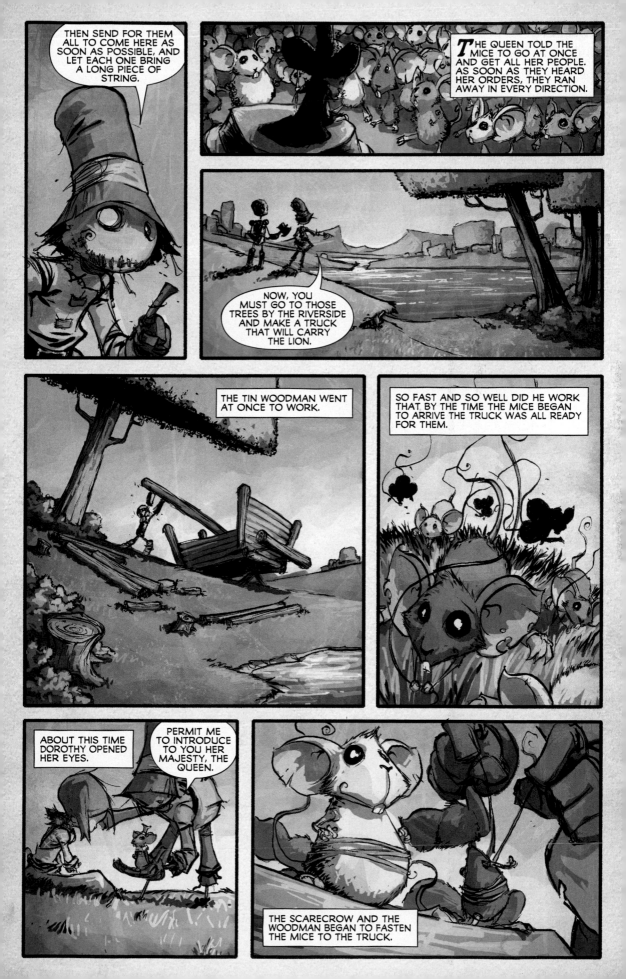

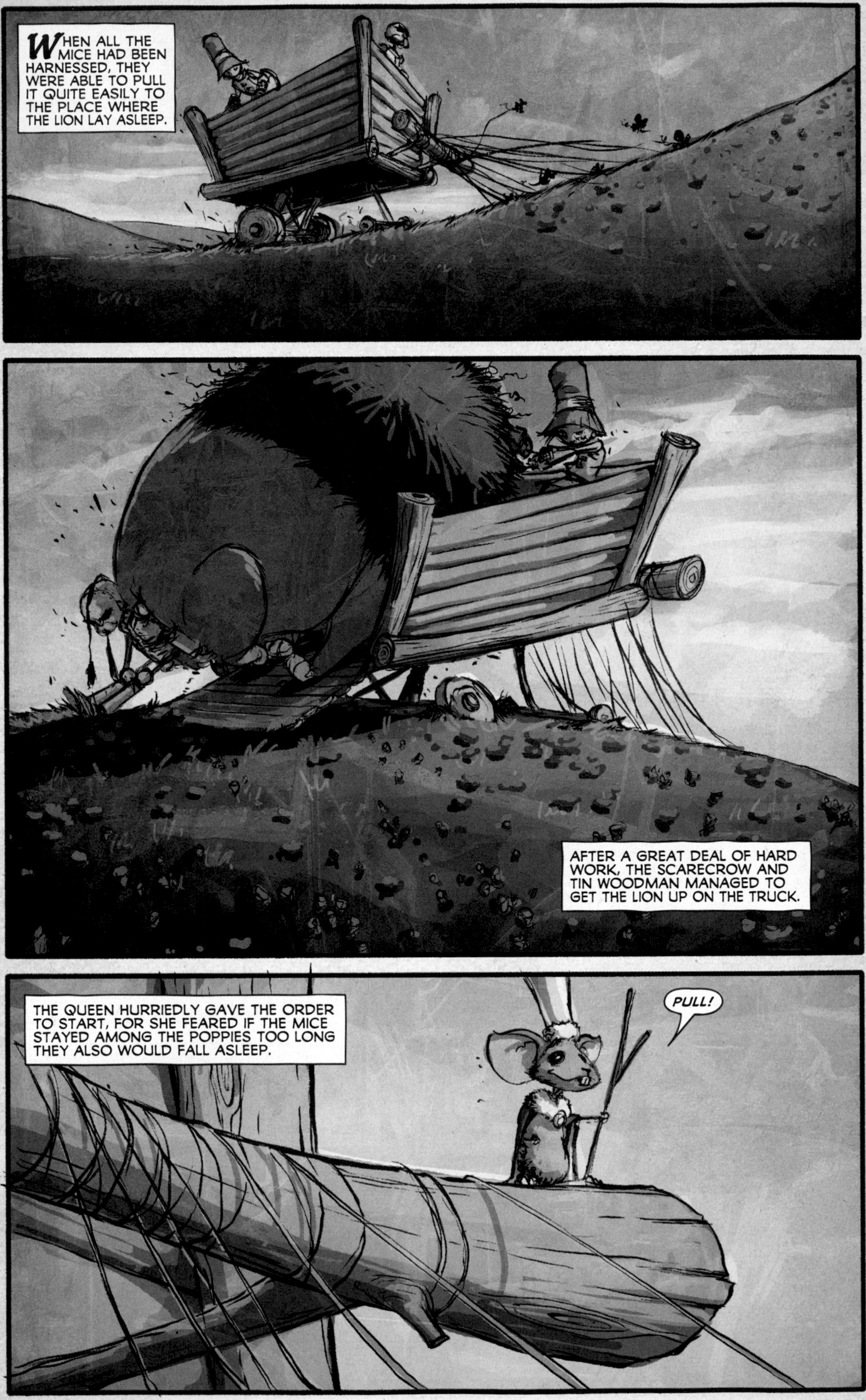
WHEN ALL THE MICE HAD BEEN HARNESSED, THEY WERE ABLE TO PULL IT QUITE EASILY TO THE PLACE WHERE THE LION LAY ASLEEP.
AFTER A GREAT DEAL OF HARD WORK, THE SCARECROW AND TIN WOODMAN MANAGED TO GET THE LION UP ON THE TRUCK.
THE QUEEN HURRIEDLY GAVE THE ORDER TO START, FOR SHE FEARED IF THE MICE STAYED AMONG THE POPPIES TOO LONG THEY ALSO WOULD FALL ASLEEP.
PULL!

THANK YOU! THANK YOU FOR SAVING HIM!

*T*HEN THE MICE WERE UNHARNESSED FROM THE TRUCK AND SCAMPERED AWAY TO THEIR HOMES.

IF YOU EVER NEED US AGAIN, COME OUT INTO THE FIELD AND BLOW THIS WHISTLE, AND WE SHALL HEAR YOU AND COME TO YOUR ASSISTANCE.

GOOD-BYE!

GOOD-BYE!

THEY SAT DOWN BESIDE THE LION...

...UNTIL HE SHOULD AWAKEN.

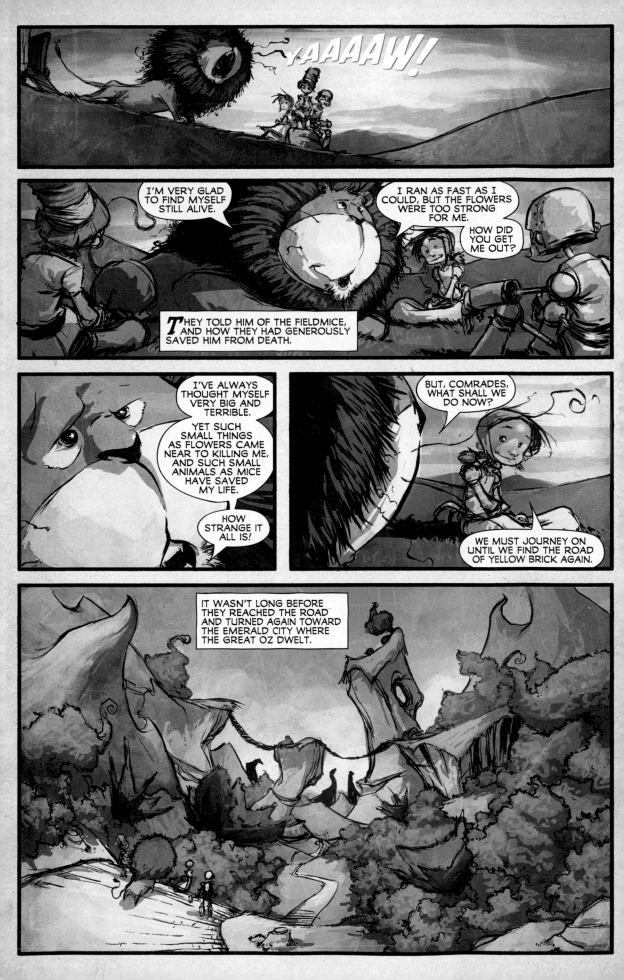

THEY PASSED BY SEVERAL HOUSES DURING THE AFTERNOON, BUT NO ONE CAME NEAR THEM BECAUSE OF THE GREAT LION.

THIS MUST BE THE LAND OF OZ, AND WE'RE SURELY GETTING NEAR THE EMERALD CITY.

THE PEOPLE DON'T SEEM TO BE AS FRIENDLY AS THE MUNCHKINS, AND I'M AFRAID WE SHALL BE UNABLE TO FIND A PLACE TO PASS THE NIGHT.

I SHOULD LIKE SOMETHING TO EAT BESIDES FRUIT, AND I'M SURE TOTO IS NEARLY STARVED.

LET'S STOP AT THE NEXT HOUSE AND TALK TO THE PEOPLE.

SO, WHEN THEY CAME TO A GOOD-SIZED FARM-HOUSE, DOROTHY WALKED BOLDLY UP TO THE DOOR AND KNOCKED.

WHAT DO YOU WANT, CHILD, AND WHY IS THAT GREAT LION WITH YOU?

WE WISH TO PASS THE NIGHT WITH YOU, IF YOU'LL ALLOW US.

THE LION IS MY FRIEND AND COMRADE, AND WOULDN'T HURT YOU FOR THE WORLD.

IS HE TAME?

OH, YES, AND HE'S A GREAT COWARD TOO. HE'LL BE MORE AFRAID OF YOU THAN YOU ARE OF HIM.

WELL...

IF THAT'S THE CASE, I'LL GIVE YOU SOME SUPPER AND A PLACE TO SLEEP.

SO THEY ALL ENTERED.

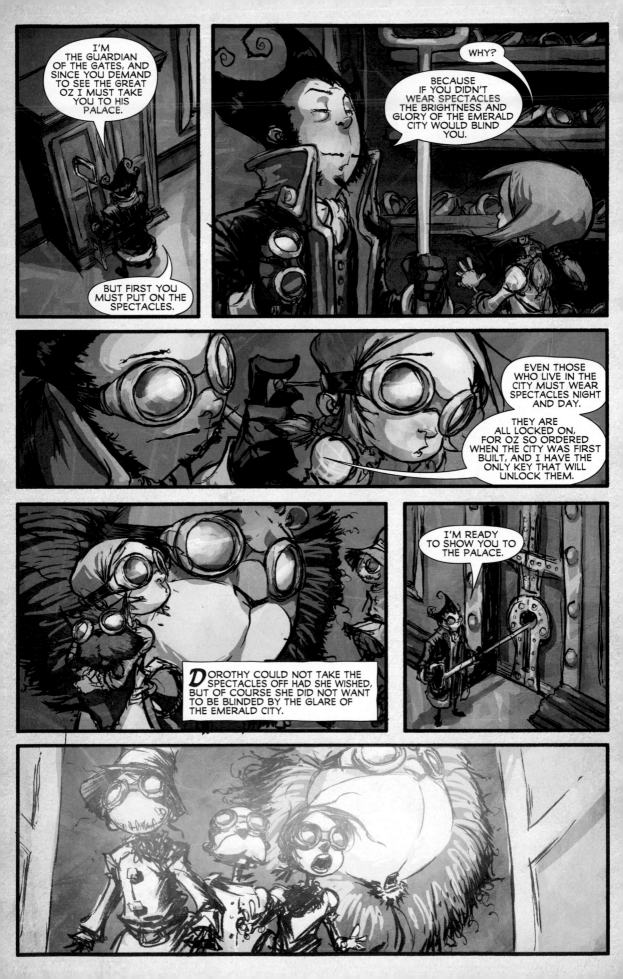

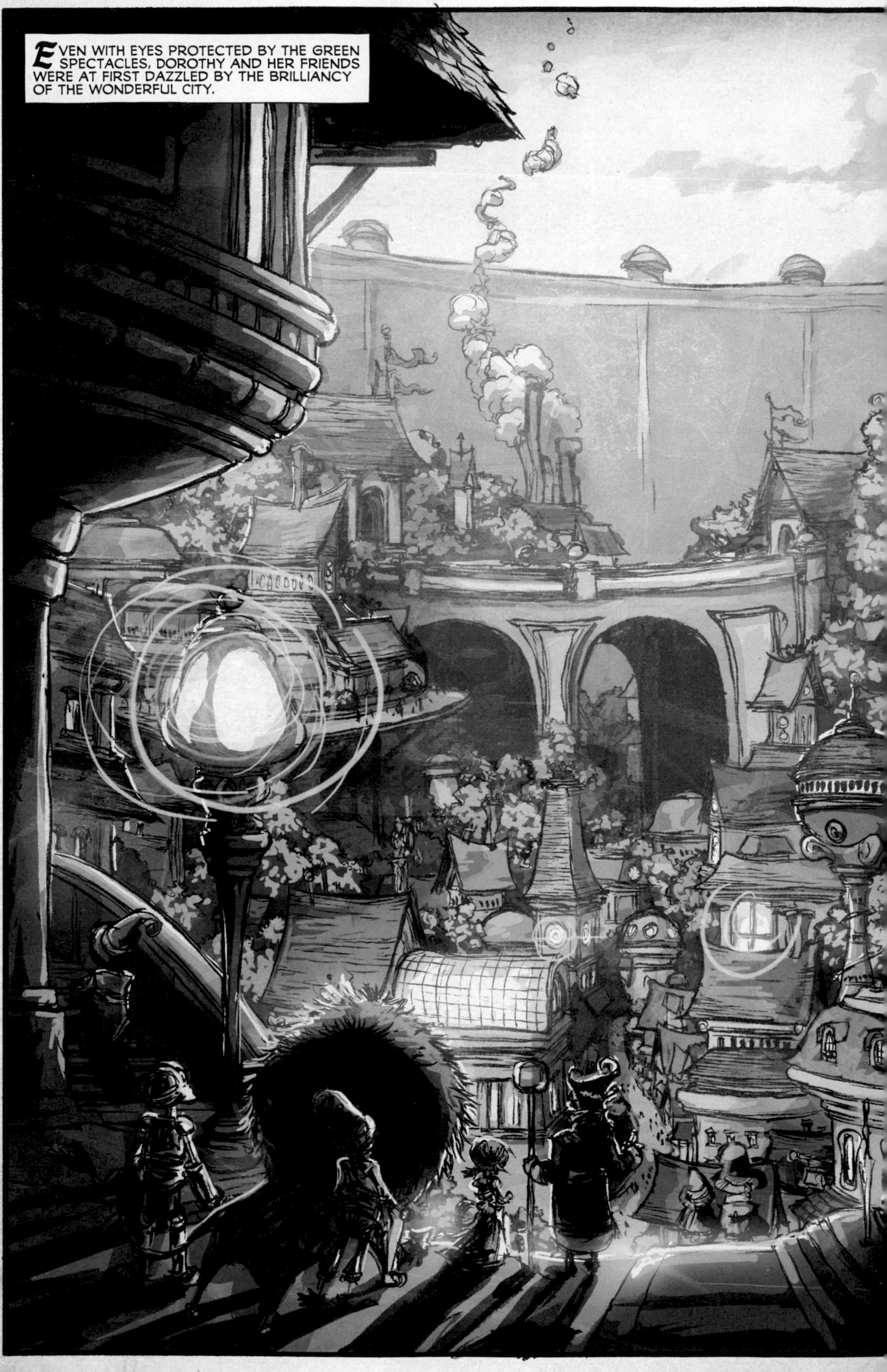
EVEN WITH EYES PROTECTED BY THE GREEN SPECTACLES, DOROTHY AND HER FRIENDS WERE AT FIRST DAZZLED BY THE BRILLIANCY OF THE WONDERFUL CITY.